A POOR MAN'S HOUSE

STEPHEN REYNOLDS was born at Devizes in 1881. He was educated at Bloxham and later gained a degree in chemistry at Manchester University. After quarrelling fiercely with his overbearing father, he turned his back on middle-class society and struggled at making a reputation and a living as a writer. Briefly he lived in Paris but, after illness, he visited Sidmouth in Devon in 1903 and met Bob Woolley, a local fisherman. From 1906 he made his home with Bob Woolley and his family and wrote several books about fishing life, including the autobiographical *A Poor Man's House* (1908) and *Alongshore* (1910). The portrayal of 'Uncle Jake', Sam Woolley, is a memorable aspect of both these books. The impact of *A Poor Man's House* led to the serialization of his only novel, *The Holy Mountain* (1909), in Ford Madox Hueffer's *English Review*. At this period Reynolds also met and corresponded with Joseph Conrad. Following the advice of Edward Garnett to 'feel the working man's life and interpret it back', he collaborated with Bob and Tom Woolley to write *Seems So! A Working-Class View of Politics* (1911). After *How 'Twas* (1912) and his outspoken views on naval reform, *The Lower Deck* (1912), he was taken up mostly with fisheries administration until his death in 1919. Throughout this time he maintained his friendship with the Woolleys and, after moving from the 'poor man's house', lived with them at Hope Cottage, Sidmouth, from 1916.

ROY HATTERSLEY was born in 1932 and educated at Sheffield City Grammar School and Hull University. In 1964 he became Member of Parliament for Birmingham Sparkbrook. He has held senior posts both in Government and in Opposition and is currently Principal Opposition Spokesman on Home Affairs. He is the author of *Nelson* (1974) and *Goodbye to Yorkshire* (1976) and contributes a weekly column to the *Listener* and to *Punch*.

STEPHEN REYNOLDS

A Poor Man's House

With an Introduction by
ROY HATTERSLEY

Oxford New York Toronto Melbourne
OXFORD UNIVERSITY PRESS
1982

Oxford University Press, Walton Street, Oxford OX2 6DP

London Glasgow New York Toronto
Delhi Bombay Calcutta Madras Karachi
Kuala Lumpur Singapore Hong Kong Tokyo
Nairobi Dar es Salaam Cape Town
Melbourne Auckland
and associate companies in
Beirut Berlin Ibadan Mexico City

Introduction © Roy Hattersley 1982
Biographical note on Reynolds © J. D. Osborne 1982

First Published 1908 by John Lane
First issued as an Oxford University Press paperback 1982

British Library Cataloguing in Publication Data

Reynolds, Stephen
A poor man's house.—(Oxford paperbacks)
1. Reynolds, Stephen 2. Fishermen—Sidmouth, Devon—Biography
I. Title
639'.2'09423570924   HD8039.66E1
ISBN 0–19–281326–9

Library of Congress Cataloging in Publication Data
Reynolds, Stephen Sydney, 1881–1919.
A poor man's house.
(Oxford paperbacks)
Originally published: London: J. Lane, 1908.
1. Reynolds, Stephen Sydney, 1881–1919 – Biography.
2. Authors, English – 20th century – Biography.
I. Title.
PR6035.E8Z47 1982   823'.912 [B]   81-18740
ISBN 0–19–281326–9 (pbk.)   AACR2

Set by Western Printing Services Ltd
Printed in Great Britain by
Richard Clay (The Chaucer Press) Ltd.
Bungay, Suffolk

To Bob and to Edward Garnett

INTRODUCTION
by Roy Hattersley

HAPPY is the novel that has no adjective. Add anything to the simple single noun and the quality is put in question. Book clubs only describe their products as 'classic' or 'timeless' when they are uncertain if their customers have ever heard of this month's merchandise. All the other explanations, from 'spy' through 'historical' to 'war', diminish rather than describe. They are admissions that the appeal is limited and the values are less than universal. E. M. Forster said that *The Seven Pillars of Wisdom* was about the war in the desert in the way that '*Moby Dick* was about catching a whale'. The idea that Herman Melville had written a 'sea-faring' or 'nautical' novel never struck him. *Moby Dick* is not about ships, it is about life.

Two classifications are particularly patronizing. The description 'woman's novel' is offensive to its potential readers because the title gives an implied warning that either the subject or the characters are unlikely to be interesting to men. The term 'working-class novel' is, on the other hand, offensive to the book it describes; for it contains a note of surprise that the working class are worth writing about and registers clear astonishment that any of them are capable of writing with interest about themselves. It also includes a hidden threat that the novel was written with some terrible didactic purpose – to demonstrate that the nineteenth-century painters and decorators of London subsidized their employers or to show that the twentieth-century Lancashire mill workers remained human even when unemployed. The fact that the *Ragged Trousered Philanthropists* and *Love on the Dole* were both part-autobiographical adds to their 'significance' as well as their authenticity. We may read them with pleasure but we also read them for a purpose.

Stephen Reynolds initially intended to use his knowledge of the Sidmouth fishing community 'for the purposes of fiction'. But, according to the preface he wrote to the first edition of *A Poor Man's House*, he 'became unwilling to cut about the material, to modify the characters in order to meet the exigencies of plot, form and so on'. Perhaps more important he found himself 'in possession of conclusions, hot for expression, which could not be incorporated at all into fiction'. In consequence *A Poor Man's House* is a journal – not autobiography, for it is less about the author than what the author observes, and only fiction in that the names of the families amongst whom Reynolds lived have been changed. If Reynolds had remained true to his original intention, he might well have produced a 'working-class novel' that was forgotten as quickly as the rest of his work. As it turned out, he created an account of working class life that remains a revelation seventy years after its original publication.

A Poor Man's House is strongest when it chooses to reveal without attempting to instruct. 'At nine years old, Tony was put with old Cloade the grocer . . . and by the time he was twelve, he was earning four shilling a week, not a penny of which he ever saw . . . for his mother used to go to the shop every Saturday night and lay out all poor Tony's wages in groceries . . . Besides running errands he had to clean boots and knives and to scrub out and tidy up the bar, which in those days was attached to every Devon grocery . . . His possible working day was from 3.30 a.m. to 10.00 p.m.' Tony Widger – in real life Bob Woolley – escaped from the grocery business and became a fisherman, and it was with the Woolleys that Reynolds lodged when he moved, more or less permanently, to Sidmouth in 1906. He had made summer visits to the town since childhood and it was to Sidmouth that he went for comfort and consolation when he returned to England in 1903 after six months, theoretically spent studying at the *Ecole des Mines*, but in practice occupied by a disappointing exploration of literary Paris. During the three years between France and Devon he lived at home in Devizes and completed his first novel, *The Holy Mountain*. But it was only when he moved into the 'one little room at the back' of Bob Woolley's house that Reynolds began his successful writing. *The Holy Mountain* was only published after extracts from *A Poor Man's House* had appeared in the *Albany Review* and only then as part of the price John Lane was prepared to pay for the right to publish the story of the Sidmouth fishermen.

Reynold's attachment to Sidmouth and the sea is not easy to explain. Indeed, it may have been his apparently inexplicable interest in such romantic matters that caused 'a permanent quarrel to smoulder' between him and his conventionally prosperous father. As a young man he grew devoted to the work of Joseph Conrad, but if his education at Bloxham public school and Manchester University (where he read Chemistry) prepared him for his eventual life on the Devon coast, it was more an apprenticeship for his appointment as 'Resident Inspector of Fisheries for the Southwestern Area' than a preparation for work as the friend and emanuensis of the fishing families. And the succession of official appointments to fishing enquiries and advisory committees were the result, not the cause, of his fascination with the Woolleys and their neighbours. It was because of the years that he spent with them that Reynolds became an accepted authority on 'drifting for mackerel and herring, hooking mackerel, seining for mackerel, sprats, flat fish, mullet and bass, bottom line fishing for whiting, conger or pout, lobster and crab potting and prawning'.

It may, at least in part, be Reynolds's background that enabled him to become affectionately involved in the fishermen's lives yet still remain sufficiently detached to tell their true story. Although he thinks of the middle and working classes as 'two civilizations', neither seems to him superior to the other. 'To turn a typical poor man into a typical middle class man is not only to develop him in some respects and do the opposite in others: it is radically to alter him. The civilization of the poor may be more backward materially but it contains the nucleus of a finer civilization than that of the middle class.' Reynolds thinks of his fishing friends as being different but equal.

He has an unqualified – indeed, almost idolatrous – admiration for the fishing families' qualities and courage: 'When one thinks of the average educated woman's fear of childbirth, although she can have doctors, nurses, anaesthetic and every other alleviation, the contrast is very great, more especially as the fisherman's wife has good reason to anticipate much pain and danger in addition to the possibility of her money giving out.' But he has escaped the romantic attachment that prevents full perception. The 'poor

brave small serving girls' are, he notices, 'not fresh', the inevitable result of being 'boxed up too much'. As George Orwell
discovered in more desperate circumstances, nothing more
distresses the scrubbed middle-class social traveller than sudden
exposure to the great unwashed. Reynolds is as concerned about
their feelings as he is about his own senses. On the first day in his
new lodgings he goes down to tea after no more than a 'wash
over', because asking for a bath risked 'exposing the lack of
one'.

Tony Widger could 'eat his food with fishy hands', while
Reynolds turned 'against the best of food' if he could 'smell fish
on his fingers' – a severe disadvantage for poor fishermen whose
principal relaxation was eating. So fastidiousness was a crime as
well as a handicap.

'Yu li'l devil!' shouted his mother. 'Take yer hands off or I'll gie 'ee such a
one . . . Yu'd eat an eat till yu busted, I believe; an yu'm that cawdy
[finical] over what yu has gie'd 'ee.'

Attempts to reproduce regional dialects rarely succeed and perhaps the best that can be said for Stephen Reynolds's efforts is that
they cause no more embarrassment than the parallel failures of
more illustrious writers. Walter Morrell's account of his alterca-
tion with the colliery manager is sanctified by the reputation of
D. H. Lawrence and *Sons and Lovers*. But it is no less unconvinc-
ing.

'It'll never do, this 'ere' 'e says. 'You'll be havin' th' roof in, one o' these
days.' An' I says 'Tha'd better stan' on a bit o' clunch, then, an' hold it up
wi' they ead.'

But Reynolds, like Lawrence, seems to be attempting – however
inadequately – to reproduce the real opinions of real people –
people with whom he sympathizes. That is in part because he
genuinely identified with the fishermen and, despite his rejection
of socialism, developed a sort of philosophy based on what he
believed to be working-class values. He could not have produced
the sort of golf club anecdotes that George Orwell, despite his
ideological commitment, employed to raise a laugh:

'Enjoy yourself!' yelled the mother. 'What yer think I brought yer out 'ere for an' bought y' a trumpet an' all. D'ya want to go across my knee? You little bastard you *shall* enjoy yerself!'

Reynolds's philosophy is a crude version of what later turned into the demand for 'equality of opportunity'. 'The poor', he believed, were 'quite capable of fighting out their own salvation. A clear ring is all they want.' Pugilistic metaphors were much in vogue amongst the early proponents of a competitive social system in which it was hoped men (and sometimes even women) would scramble for success and prosperity unhampered by the formal restraints of law, wealth, or birth. Stephen Reynolds made the point that, fifty years earlier, had been made by opponents of the purchase of Commissions in the Army and the proponents of recruitment to the civil service by examination in much the same bellicose language as they used. 'When I say "a clear ring" I do not mean that one side should have seconds and towels provided and that the other side should be provided with neither.'

The idea of social *laissez-faire* is less attractive now than it was during the first decade of the century. But his feelings for the people about whose conditions he philosophized enabled him to produce an account of their life and work which retains a compulsive fascination. John Buchan believed that the story of Seacombe proved that Reynolds possessed a 'sympathy which is a kind of genius'. Arnold Bennett saw him as 'a new authentic talent' with 'a finished style'. Joseph Conrad thought that *A Poor Man's House* satisfied 'an intimate need of which one becomes aware only after it has been satisfied'. But the rapturous reception that the journal received in 1908 was Reynold's only real literary triumph. Determined to remain in Sidmouth with the Woolleys, he cut his connection with Ford Maddox Ford's *Literary Review* and spent the next four years writing essays about the places 'where man and sea face one another' and, in collaboration with Tom Woolley, 'a working class view of politics'. Of the four books he produced, before his writing ended in 1912, none enjoyed a critical reception remotely like that which welcomed *A Poor Man's House*.

The poor man, his house, and his habits have only a limited lesson to teach us about the condition of the English working class during the heady Edwardian days of imperial glory. For the Woolleys cum Widgers worked at a trade which was so untypical of the occupations that fed and clothed the poor in other places that they were impossible to place at the centre of a social document from which general conclusions could be drawn about industrial deprivation or agricultural disadvantage. *A Poor Man's House* is all the better for that – all the better for being a simple account of a single community. The sentimental – amongst whom Stephen Reynolds certainly numbered – will find it an heroic story of victory over hardship and adversity. The less romantically inclined will discover in *A Poor Man's House* a meticulous account of the life and work of a community which, because of the deep commitment which Stephen Reynolds felt towards the town of his adoption, fascinates his readers in the way that it fascinated him.

PREFACE

THE substance of *A Poor Man's House* was first recorded in a journal, kept for purposes of fiction, and in letters to one of the friends to whom the book is dedicated. Fiction, however, showed itself an inappropriate medium. I was unwilling to cut about the material, to modify the characters, in order to meet the exigencies of plot, form, and so on. I felt that the life and the people were so much better than anything I could invent. Besides which, I found myself in possession of conclusions, hot for expression, which could not be incorporated at all into fiction. *A Poor Man's House* consists then of the journal and letters, subjected to such slight re-arrangement as should enable me to draw the truest picture I could within the limits of one volume.

Primarily the book aims at presenting a picture of a typical poor man's house and life. Incidentally, certain conclusions are expressed which – needless to say – are very tentative and are founded not alone on *this* poor man's house. Of the book as a picture, it is not the author's place to speak. But its opinions, and the manner of arriving at them, do require some explanation; the right to hold such opinions some substantiation.

Educated people usually deal with the poor man's life deductively; they reason from the general to the particular; and, starting with a theory, religious, philanthropic, political, or what not, they seek, and too easily find, among the millions of poor, specimens – very frequently abnormal – to illustrate their theories. With anything but human beings, that is an excellent method. Human beings, unfortunately, have individualities. They do what, theoretically, they ought not to do, and leave undone those things they ought to do. They are even said to possess souls – untrustworthy things beyond the reach of sociologists. The inductive method – reasoning from the particular to the general – though it lead to a fine crop of errors, should at least help to counterbalance the psychological superficiality of the deductive method; to counterbalance, for example, the nonsense of those well-meaning persons who go routing about among the poor in search of evil, and suppose that they can chain it up with little laws. Chained dogs bite worst.

For myself, I can only claim – I only want to claim – that I have lived among poor people without preconceived notions or *parti pris*; neither as parson, philanthropist, politician, inspector, sociologist nor statistician; but simply because I found there a home and more beauty of life and more happiness than I had met with elsewhere. So far as is possible to a man of middle-class breeding, I have lived their life, have shared their interests, and have found among them some of my closest and wisest friends. Perhaps I may reasonably anticipate one type of criticism by adding that I have felt something of the pinch and hardship of the life, as well as enjoyed its picturesqueness. Since the book was first written, it has fallen to me, on an occasion of illness, to take over for some days all the housekeeping and cooking; and I have worked on the boats sometimes fifteen hours a day, not as an amateur, but for hard and – what is more to the point – badly-needed coin. It took the gilt off the gingerbread, but it didn't spoil the gingerbread!

Would it were possible to check by ever so little the class-conceit of those people who think that they can manage the poor man's life better than he can himself; who would take advantage of their education to play ducks and drakes with his personal affairs. For it is my firm belief that in the present phase of national evolution, and as regards the things that really matter, the educated man has more to learn of the poor man than to teach him. Even Nietzsche, the philosopher of aristocracy, went so far as to say that 'in the so-called cultured classes, the believers in "modern ideas", nothing is perhaps so repulsive as their lack of shame, the easy insolence of eye and hand with which they touch, taste, and finger everything; and it is possible that even yet there is more *relative* nobility of taste, and more tact for reverence among the people, among the lower classes of the people, especially among peasants, than among the newspaper-reading *demi-monde* of intellect, the cultured class.'

                                                        S.R.

Seacombe, 1908.

PREFACE TO THE NEW EDITION

WORKS of fiction are frequently cast into the form of journals, diaries, letters, autobiography, and so forth. In every respect they are written down as if they were works of fact, actually as well as imaginatively true; and on the extent of the illusion their success largely depends. But it was soon recognized by most of those who read *A Poor Man's House* that the book was a work of fact and not of fiction, a record and not an invention. At the same time, it has to be recognized also that there are different sorts and degrees of fact. Most are not so simple as that two and two make four, or a certain thing happened on a certain day. If an author is dealing with people, and not with mere measurements or bare events, then, however carefully he sticks to the fact, he cannot avoid the necessity of straining all his material through his own personality. Least of all can he avoid it in dealing with what he has lived through. Unconsciously, as well as consciously, he selects, suppresses, colours. He sinks detail in the general impression. Only so much space is at his disposal. He has the reader to think of; not merely how to express his meaning best, but how to convey it best. There are certain truths, not the least important nor the least essential to truth, that he knows the public simply won't stand in a book; and sometimes it is his duty to sail as close as possible to the wind of truthfulness without capsizing altogether. In short, his work cannot but be a mass of compromises, in which he is sole arbiter. He cannot reproduce; he must recreate. The personal factor creeps in whether he will or no.

Moreover, the reader does make a difference between works of fiction and works of fact. He may be more stirred by the first; he is more influenced by the second. If a novelist alters his opinions, it doesn't matter. His novels stand. But if a philosopher recants, if a divine repents of his theology, if a politician changes party, his followers, who have trusted in him, have a right to know it. Likewise, in a lesser degree, with the writer of a book in fact. His readers, who have been influenced by his book, though ever so little – influenced, maybe, by just the personal factor – have a right to ask, 'You said certain things – do you still believe them? You expressed certain opinions – have you acted upon them yourself?'

To answer properly would require another book. Five years ago, or more, while I was writing this one, a literary friend said to me, 'If your life down there, fishing and writing, is an enthusiasm, you'll grow out of it; but if it's a habit, I suppose you'll stay there.' Three years ago – very crowded years they've been – when I was finishing the book, I wrote of the New Year: 'Life has given me a New Year's Gift so good that I cannot free myself from a suspicion of its being too good. It has given me home.'

And the best answer I can make is perhaps this: that I am still here; more here, more tied, than ever. It is still home. Sometimes, of course, I have said to myself, 'I'll go. I'll break free. Why should I expose myself to endless troubles, rebuffs, and even enmities, when I've no need?' That I have said because very often I have been tired to death with trying to carry on two jobs at once, besides some half-a-dozen related schemes; and it is not exactly easy to do mental work among hand-workers, who neither adapt their daily life to it (why should they?), nor realize fully the conditions under which it has to be done. In the irritation and tiredness of the moment one is apt to forget the kindnesses of yesterday and the sure kindness of to-morrow. Usually one blames somebody else for miseries which have their origin in one's own self. At the back of everything there lies in wait that profound discouragement which arises from the fact that one's dearest projects move slowly – so much more slowly than one's life flits along. It is no holiday to be a buffer between two classes, continually subject on both sides to misunderstandings and suspicions, very cruel, very absurd, very excusable; nor is it sport to be kin to one class in education and one part of one's work, and to another class in feeling and the other part of one's work; though I for one, being troubled in mind, am more heartened by the touch of a friendly hand and the sound of a friendly voice saying, 'What the hell's the matter with 'ee?' than by any amount of intellectual analytical non-creature sympathy. But it means much loneliness and disappointment, towards whichever side one turns.

I mention these things not to complain; far from it; still less to blame; but for the purpose of showing that the opinions herein expressed have been tested and tried almost beyond endurance, and yet have survived the racket of it. One other test there is, even more conclusive. When I say to myself, 'Well, where else would you like to be? Is there anything else you'd like to do, anything else you are keen on?' the reply comes at once, 'Nowhere. Nothing. Nothing at all.' To up-anchor would be to go adrift, to become derelict. I fuss about noise, like most writers, yet write with my door wide open; not to hear what is said, but still to have in my ears the sound of voices which one day I shall never hear any more. And life is contradictory like that, so one finds when the first flush of youth is past. It's a complicated affair o' it, as 'Tony Widger' so often says. The hardest brick wall one bangs one's head against is, after all, oneself.

Therefore, nothing has been altered in this edition. There is nothing there I wish to unsay. Doubtless after more experience of fishing, writing, and living, I could revise it and touch it up and add to it, but I do not think I could better it as a whole. It was written in the springtime of an experience. The freshness and glow of that springtime I could not retrap, now in the sweats of summer. Outlines have become obscured by detail. Opinions are absorbed in the carrying of them out. It is as if a man should see a fair country that instantly imprinted itself on his mind's eye, and then should settle there to earn his living. Never again can he see it as he did at first. The question of whether the ten-acre field would do with a top-dressing will blot his view of younder hill; the tranquillity of evening will be disturbed by the best cow going dry or the sow overlaying her young; and walking under the open sky he will have in his mind the crops underfoot. Within short compass, he will not be able to give so accurate a picture of the country as he could have done at first. Its beauty will be the same; it will mean as much to him, and more; but with this difference: that instead of lying outside him, to be looked at and described in general, it will have become a part of his own life, not so easy to put into words. So, when I happen to look at *A Poor Man's House*, it reads like another man's work, with which I am almost astonished to find myself in enthusiastic agreement. And although the book has been at times rather warmly discussed by the people with whom it deals, most objections have carried as a tag, 'But 'tis true enough, what's said in this book, after that. An' it ought to be said, too!'

At present the air is full of social remedies, mostly quack. Real reform does not begin in electioneering speeches, nor in parliaments, nor yet in select societies for this, that, and t'other; nor yet, for that matter, in books; but in people's minds and feelings. Real justice between class and class has its root in sympathetic understanding, not in pettifogging laws and penalties, founded on so-called scientific investigation. Efficiency is a smaller thing than life. Few men knowingly and deliberately do injury. 'They know not what they do' was a greater and wider saying than the churches have made of it. It is true enough, of course, that no amount of sympathetic understanding will, of itself, provide food to eat, or a roof to cover one, or any improvement at all. Nor, on the other hand, is there likely to be any improvement without it. In the righting of wrong it comes, and must come, first; just as a good intention precedes a good deed, and a sense of justice is needful for justice to be done. Reform without understanding *is* quackery – in every sense of the word. If *A Poor Man's House* should do anything, however little, to rouse sympathy, aid understanding, and out of laughter bring good-fellowship, though only among a few, then, faults or no faults, the book will have been worth writing. I hope it may be the case.

S. R.

1911.

A POOR MAN'S HOUSE

I

Egremont Villas,
Seacombe, *April*.

I

THE sea is merely grinding against the shingle. The *Moondaisy* lies above the sea-wall, in the gutter, with her bottom-boards out and a puddle of greenish water covering her garboard strake. Her hunchbacked Little Commodore is dead. The other two of her old crew, George Widger and Looby Smith are nowhere to be seen: they must be nearly grown up by now. The fishermen themselves appear less picturesque and salty than they used to do. It is slack time after a bad herring season. They are dispirited and lazy, and very likely hungry.

These old lodgings of mine, with their smug curtains, aspidestria plant, china vases and wobbly tables and chairs . . .

But I can hear the sea-gulls screaming, even here.

2

Yesterday morning I met young George Widger, now grown very lanky but still cat-like in his movements. He was parading the town with a couple of his mates, attired in a creased blue suit with a wonderful yellow scarf around his neck, instead of the faded guernsey and ragged sea-soaked trousers in which he used to come to sea. What was up? I asked his father, and Tony had a long rigmarole to tell me. George had got a sweetheart. Therefore George had begun to look about him for a sure livelihood. George was not satisfied with a fisherman's prospects. 'Yu works and drives and slaves, and don't never get no forarder.' So George had gone to the chief officer of coastguards without saying a word to his father and had been found fit. George had joined the Navy. He was going off to Plymouth that very day at dinner-time.

It is like a knight of romance being equipped by his lady for the wars. But what must be the difficulty to a young fisherman of earning his bread and cheese, when all he can do for his sweetheart is to leave her forthwith! There's a fine desperation in it.

Tony seemed rather proud. 'They 'ouldn't think as I had a son old enough for the Navy, wude they, sir? I married George's mother, her that's dead, when I wer hardly olden'n he is. I should ha' joined the Navy meself if it hadn't been for the rheumatic fever what bent me like I am. 'Tis a sure thing, you see – once yu'um in it an' behaves yourself – wi' a pension at the end o'it. But I'm so strong an' capable-like for fishing as them that's bolt upright, on'y I 'ouldn't ha' done for the Navy. Aye! the boy's right. Fishing ain't no job for a man nowadays; not like what it used to be. They'll make a man of him in the Navy.'

In the evening, after dark, I saw Tony again. He was standing outside a brilliantly light grocer's shop, his cap awry as usual, and a reefer thrown over his guernsey. Something in the despondency of his attitude haled me across the road. 'Well, Tony? George is there by now?'

'Iss . . . I-I-I- w-wonder what the boy's thinking o'it now . . .'

The man was crying his heart out. 'I come'd hereto 'cause it don' seem 's if I can stay in house. Went in for some supper a while ago, but I cuden' eat nort. 'Tisn' 's if he'd ever been away from home before, yu know.'

'Come along down to the Shore Road, Tony.'

It seemed wrong, hardly decent, to let his grief spend itself in the lighted-up street. The Front was deserted and dark, for there was rain in the wind, and the sound of the surf had a quick savage chop in it. Away, over the sea, was a great misty blackness.

As we walked up and down, Tony talked between tears and anger – tears for himself and George, anger at the cussedness of things. He looked straight before him, to where the row of lamps divided the lesser from the greater darkness, the town noises from the chafing surf; it is the only time I have ever seen a fisherman walk along shore without a constant eye on the sea.

'He's taken and gone away jest as he was beginning to be o' some use wi' the boats, an' I thought he wer settling down. *I* didn' know what wer going on, not till he came an' told me he wer off.

But 'tisn' that, though I bain't so strong as I was to du all the work be meself; 'tis what he's a-thinking now he've a-lef' home an' 'tis to late to come back if he wants tu. He's ther, sure 'nuff, an' that's all about it.'

In the presence of grief, we are all thrown back on the fine old platitudes we affect to despise. 'You mustn't get down over it, Tony,' I said. 'That won't make it a bit the better. If he's steady – woman, wine and the rest – he'll get on right enough. He's got his wits about him; knows how to sail a boat and splice a rope. That's the sort they want in the Navy, I suppose. *He*'ll make his way, never fear. Think how you'll trot him out when he comes home on leave. Why, they say a Devon man's proper place is the Navy.'

'Iss, they du. *I* should ha' been there meself if it hadn' been for the rheumatics – jest about coming out on a pension now, or in the coastguards. I *be* in the Royal Naval Reserve, but I ain't smart enough, like, for the Navy. The boy . . .'

'He's smart and strong as they make 'em.'

'Aye! he's smart, or cude be, but he'll hae to mind what he's a-doin' there. *They* won't put up wi' no airs like he've a-give'd me. Yu've got to du what yu'm told, sharp, an' yu mustn't luke [look] what yu thinks, let 'lone say it, or else yu'll find yourself in chokey [cells] 'fore yu knows where yu are. 'Tis like walking on a six-inch plank, in the Navy, full o' rules an' regylations; an' he won't get fed like he was at home nuther, when us had it.'

'Why don't you go to bed and sleep, Tony?'

'How can I sleep wi' me head full o' what the boy's thinking o' it all!'

More walking and he calmed down a little.

'Come and have some hot grog for a sleeping draught, Tony, and then go home to bed.'

'Had us better tu?'

'Come along, man; then if you go straight to bed you'll sleep.'

'I on'y wish I cude. The boy must be turned in by this time. 'Tis like as if I got a picture of him in my mind, where he is, an' he ain't happy – *I* knows.'

When Tony went down the narrow roadway, homewards, he had had just the amount of grog to make him sleep: no more, no less. That father's grief – the boy gone to sea, the father left stranded ashore – it was bad to listen to. While going up town I wondered with how much sorrow the Navy is recruited. We look on our sailors rather less fondly than on the expensive pieces of machinery we send them to sea in. I don't think I shall ever again be able to regard the Navy newspaper-fashion. It seems as if someone of mine belongs to it . . .

Lucky George! to be so much missed.

This morning, when I saw Tony on the Front, he was more than a little awkward; looked shyly at me, from under his peaked cap, as if to read in my face what I thought of him. He had slept after all, and spoke of the hot grog as a powerful, strange invention, new to him as a sleeping draught. When, in talking, I said that I have only a back bedroom and a fripperied sitting room, and that my old lodgings do not please me as they used to, he clapped me on the shoulder with a jollity intended, I think, to put last night out of my mind. 'What a pity yu hadn't let we know yu cuden't find lodgings to your liking. Us got a little room in house where they sends people sometimes from the Alexandra Hotel when they'm full up. My missis 'ould du anything to make 'ee comfor'able. Yu an't never see'd her, have 'ee? Nice little wife, I got. Yu let us know when yu be coming thees way again; that is, if yu don' mind coming wi' the likes o' us. We won't disturb 'ee.'

Good fellow! It was his thanks. However I shall be going home to-morrow. Tony Widger lives, I believe, somewhere down the Gut, in Under Town, a place they call the Seacombe slum. You can see a horde of children pouring in and out of the Gut all day long, and in the evening the wives stand at the seaward end of it, to gossip and await their husbands. Noisy place . . .

II

A CARD from Tony Widger:

Dear Sir in reply to your letter I have let to the hotel which is full for the 28th july until the 6ᵗʰ Aus, but I have one little room to the back but you did not say about the time it would take you to walk down also John to Saltmeadow have let so you can have that room if you can manage or you can see when you come down their are a lot of People in Seacombe or you write and let me know and I will see if I can get rooms for you if you tell me about the time you will be hear from yours Truly Anthony Widger.

Risky; but never mind. There is always the sea. It is something to have the certainty of a bed at the end of a long day's tramp. Besides, I want to see Tony, and George too if by chance he is at home. And there may be a little fishing. And—

> And stepping westward seems to be
> A kind of *heavenly* destiny.

That's the real feeling at the back of my mind. *I want* to go west, towards the sunset; over Dartmoor, towards Land's End, where the departing ships go down into the sea.

III

I

AFTER a hundred miles of dusty road, it is good to snuff the delicately salted air. The bight of the Exe, where we crossed it by steam launch, was only a make-believe for the sea. How wonderfully the slight rippling murmur of a calm sea flows into, and takes possession of one's mind.

I stood by the shore and watched the boats, and was very peaceful. Then I went down the Gut to the house that I guessed was Anthony Widger's. Many children watched me with their eyes opened wide at my knapsack. A pleasant looking old woman – short, stout, charwoman-shaped – came out of the passage just as I raised my hand to knock the open door. 'Are you Mrs Widger?' said I.

'Lor' bless 'ee! I ben't Mrs Widger. Here, Annie! Here's a gen'leman to see 'ee.'

Mrs Widger, the afternoon Mrs Widger, is a quite slim woman who – strangely enough for a working man's wife – looks a good deal younger than she is. She has rather beautiful light brown hair and dresses tastefully. I am afraid she will not feel complimented if the old woman tells her my mistake.

Her manner of receiving me indicated plainly a suspended judgment, inclined perhaps towards the favourable. I was shown my room, a little long back room, with ragged wall-paper, and almost filled up by a huge, very flat, squashy bed. After a wash-over (I did not ask for a bath for fear of exposing the lack of one) I went down to tea.

Bread, jam and cream were put before me, together with fairly good hot tea from a blue, smoky, enamelled tin teapot which holds any quantity up to a couple of quarts. Mrs Widger turned two guernseys, a hat, several odd socks, and a boot out of a great chintz-covered chair which lacked one of its arms. To my *made* conversation she replied shortly:

'Dear me!' 'My!' 'Did you ever . . .' She was taking stock of me.

Presently she went to a cupboard, which is also the coal-hole, and brought out an immense frying-pan, black both inside and out. She heated it till the fat ran; wiped out it with a newspaper; then placed in it three split mackerel. 'For Tony's tea,' she explained. 'He's to sea now with two gen'lemen, but I 'spect he'll be in house sune.'

Voices from the passage: 'Mam! Tay! Mam, I wants my tay!'

A deeper voice: 'Missis, wer's my tay? Got ort nice to eat?'

It was Tony himself, accompanied by a small boy and a slightly larger small girl.

'Hullo, sir! Yu'm come then. Do'ee think you can put up wi' our little shanty? Missis ought to ha' laid for 'ee in the front room. Us got a little parlour, you know.—I be so wet as a drownded corpse, Missis!'

The two children stood on the other side of the table, staring at me as if I were a wild beast behind bars which they scarcely trusted. ''Tis a gen'leman!' exclaimed the girl.

'Coo'h! the boy ejaculated.

Tony turned on them with make-believe anger: 'Why don' 'ee git yer tay? Don' 'ee know 'tis rude to stare?'

'Now then, you children,' Mrs Widger continued in a strident voice, buttering two hunks of bread with astonishing rapidity. 'Take off thic hat, Mabel. *Sit* down, Jimmy.'

'Coo'h! Jam!' said Jimmy. 'Jam zide plaate, like the gen'leman, please, Mam Widger.'

'When you've eat that.'

I never saw children munch so fast.

Tony took off his boots and stockings, and wrung out the ends of his trousers upon the hearth-rug. He pattered to the oven; opened the door; sniffed.

'Her's got summat for my tay, I can see. What is it, Missis? Fetch it out – quick, sharp! Mackerel! Won' 'ee hae one, sir? Ther's plenty here.'

Whilst Mrs Widger was helping him to the rest of his food, he ate the mackerel with his fingers. Finally, he soaked up the vinegar with bread, licked his finger-tips and turned towards me. 'Yu'm in the courting chair, sir. That's where me an' Missis used to sit when we was courting, en' it, Annie? Du 'ee see how we've a-broke the arm? When yu gets a young lady, us'll lend 'ee thic chair. Didn' know as I'd got a little wife like thees yer, di 'ee? Ay, Annie!'

He turned round and chucked her under the chin.

'G'out, you dirty cat!' cried Mrs Widger, flinging herself back in the chair – yet not displeased.

It was a pretty playful sight, although Mrs Widger's voice is rather like a newspaper boy's when she raises it.

2

This morning, when I arrived downstairs, the kitchen was all of a caddle. Children were bolting their breakfast, seated and afoot; were washing themselves and being washed; were getting ready and being got ready for school. Mrs Widger looked up from stitching the seat of a small boy's breeches *in situ*. 'I've a-laid your breakfast in the front room.'

Thither I went with a book and no uncertain feeling of disappointment.

The front room looks out upon Alexandra Square. It is, at once, parlour, lumber room, sail and rope store, portrait gallery of relatives and ships, and larder. It is a veritable museum of the household treasures not in constant use, and represents pretty accurately, I imagine, the extent to which Mrs Widger's house-pride is able to indulge itself. But I have had enough at Salisbury of eating my meals among best furniture and in the (printed) company of great minds. The noise in the kitchen sounded jolly. Now or never, I thought. So after breakfast, I returned to the kitchen and asked for what bad behaviour I was banished to the front room.

'Lor'! If yu don't mind this. On'y 'tis all up an' down here . . .'

3

I went yesterday to see my old landlady at Egremont Villas. She asked me where I was lodging.

'At Tony Widger's, in Alexandra Square.'

'Why, that's in Under Town.'

'Yes, in Under Town.'

'Oh, law! I can't think how you can live in such a horrid place!'

On my assuring her that it was not so very horrid, she rearranged her silken skirts on the chair (a chair too ornamentally slight for her weight) and tilted up her nose. 'I must get and lay the table,' she said, 'for a lady and gentleman that's staying with me. *Very* nice people.'

Under Town has, in fact, an indifferent reputation among the elect. Not that it is badly behaved; far from it. The shallow-pated resent its not having drawn into line with their cheap notions of progress. If Under Town had put plate-glass windows into antique buildings . . . Visitors to Seacombe, not being told, hardly so much as suspect the existence of its huddled old houses and thatched cottages. The shingle-paved Gut runs down unevenly from the Shore Road between a row of tall lodging houses and the Alexandra Hotel, then opens out suddenly into a little square which contains an incredible number of recesses and sub-corners, so to speak, with many more doors in them than one can discover houses belonging to the doors. Two cottages, I am told, have no ground floors at all. Cats sun themselves on walls or squat about gnawing fish bones. A houdan cockerel with bedraggled speckly plumage and a ragged crest hanging over one eye struts from doorstep to doorstep. The children, when any one strange walks through the Square, run like rabbits in a warren to their respective doors; stand there, and stare. Tony Widger's house is the largest. Once, when Under Town was Seacombe, a lawyer lived here – hence the front passage. It has a cat-trodden front garden, in which only wall-flowers and some box edging have survived. Over the front door is a broken trellis-work porch. Masts and spars lean against the wall. The house is built of red brick, straight up and down like an overgrown doll's house, but the whole of the wall is weathered and toned by the southerly gales which blow down the Gut from the open sea. Those same winds see to it that Alexandra Square does not smell squalid, however it may look. At its worst it is not so depressing as a row of discreet semi-detached villas. It is, I should imagine, a pretty accurate mirror of the lives that are lived in it – poor men's lives that scarcely anybody fathoms. If one looks for a moment at a house where people have starved, or are starving . . . What a gift of hope they must possess – and what a sinking in their poor insides!

4

This morning they told me how my little hunchbacked Commodore died. He had been ailing, they said; had come to look paler and more pinched in his small sharp face. Then (it was a fisherman who told me this): 'He was in to house one morning, an' I thought as 'e were sleepin', an' I said, 'Harry, will 'ee hae a cup o' tay; yu been sleeping an't 'ee?' An' 'e says, 'No, I an't; but I been sort o' dreaming.' An' 'e said as he'd see'd a green valley wi' a stream o' water, like, running down the middle o' it, an' 'e thought as 'e see'd Granfer there (that us losted jest before 'en) walking by the stream. A'terwards 'e sat on 's mother's lap, like 's if 'e wer a child again, though 'e wer nearly nineteen all but in size; an' 'e jest took an' died there, suddent an' quiet like; went away wi'out a word; an' us buried 'en last January up to the cementry on land.'

So the *Moondaisy's* luckiest fisherman packed up and went.

5

It is astonishing how hungry and merry these children are, especially the boys. They rush into the kitchen at meal times and immediately make grabs at whatever they most fancy on the table.

'Yu little cat!' says their mother, always as if she had never witnessed such behaviour before. 'Yu daring rascal! Put down! I'll gie thee such a one in a minute. Go an' sit down to once.' Then they climb into chairs, wave their grubby hands over the plates, in a pretence of grabbing something more, and spite of the whacks which sometimes fall, they gobble their food to the accompaniment of incessant tricks and roars of shrill laughter. Never were such disorderly, hilarious meals! If Tony is here they simply laugh at his threats of weird punishment, and if he comes in late from sea, they return again with him and make a second meal as big as the first. Sometimes, unless the food is cleared away quickly, they will clamour for a third meal, and clamour successfully. What digestions they must have to gobble so much and so fast!

To judge by their way of talking, they divide the world into folk and gentlefolk. 'Who gie'd thee thic ha'penny?' Mrs Widger asked Jimmy.

'A man, to beach.'

'G'out!' said Mabel. ''Twas a gen'leman.'

'Well . . .'

'Well, that ain't a *man!*'

Usually, at breakfast time, the voices of Tony's small nieces may be heard coming down the passage: 'Aun-tieAnn-ie! AuntieAnn-ie!' Their tousled, tow-coloured little heads peep round the doorway. If we have not yet finished eating, they are promptly ordered to 'get 'long home to mother.' Otherwise, they come right in and remain standing in the middle of the room, apparently to view me. Unable to remember which is Dora and which Dolly, I have nicknamed them according to their hair, Straighty and Curley. What they think of things, there is no knowing; for they blush at direct questions and turn their heads away. So also, when I have been going in and out of the Square, they have stopped their play to gaze at me, but have merely smiled shyly, if at all, in answer to my greetings. Yesterday, however, they had a skipping rope. I jumped over it. Instantly there was a chorus of laughter and chatter. The ice was broken. This morning, after a moment or two's consideration behind her veil of unbrushed hair, Straighty came and clambered upon the arm of the courting chair – dabbed a clammy little hand down my neck, whilst Curley plumped her fist on my knee and stayed looking into my face with very wondering smiling blue eyes. By the simple act of jumping a rope, I had gained their confidence; had proved I was really a fellow creature, I suppose. Now, when I pass through the Square, some small boy is sure to call out, 'Where yu going?' And my name is brandished about among the children as if I were a pet animal. They have appropriated me. They have tamed that mysterious wild beast, 'the gen'leman.'

One boy, Jimmy – a very fair-headed, blue-eyed, chubby little chap, seven years old – Tony's eldest boy at home – seems to have taken a particular fancy to me. Whether it began with bananas, or with my giving him a pick-a-back to the top of the cliffs, I hardly know. At all events he has decided that I am a desirable friend. He has shown me his small properties – his pencil, and his boats that he makes out of a piece of wood with wing-feathers for sails and a piece of tin, stuck into the bottom, for centre-keel; – has told me what standard he is in at school; and one of the first things I hear whenever he comes into the house, is: 'Mam! Wher's Mister Ronals?'

To-day, on my way to the Tuckers' to tea, I passed Jimmy's school. The boys were just let loose. Jimmy left a yelling group of them to come along with me. Nearby the Tuckers' gate, I told him where I was going, and said *Good-bye*. Jimmy fell behind. But whilst we were at tea, I repeatedly saw a white head sneaking round the laurels outside the window, and blue eyes peeping. Miss Tucker had him in; whereupon, rather shyly, with hands horribly grubby from the school slates, Jimmy ate much bread and butter and many cakelets, and ended up by tucking three apples into his blouse. He came home very pleased indeed with himself.

Tony was almost angry. 'However come'd 'ee, Missis, to let 'em go out to a gen'leman's to tay in thic mess?'

'Stupid! How cude I help o'it?'

'What did 'ee think o'it, Jimmy?'

'The lady gie'd I dree apples!'

Tony, though shocked, was also pleased; Jimmy delighted. Every now and then he draws himself up with a 'Coo'h! I been out to tay wi' Mister Ronals!'

They have a strange way, these children, of placing their hands on one, smiling up into one's face, and saying nothing. It has the effect of making one feel their separate, distinct personalities, and, additionally, of making one feel rather proud of the approbation of those small personages who think so much and divulge so little.

6

There has been no fishing. Either the sea has been too rough to ride to a slingstone[1] for blinn and conger, or else too calm, so that the mackerel hookers[2] could not sail out and therefore no fresh bait was to be had. It is quite useless to fish for conger with stale bait. Tony tells me that I ought to be here in a month's time, when he will have fewer pleasure parties to attend to, and will go out for mackerel, rowing if he cannot sail. He says there will *have* to be a good September hooking season, because, though the summer has been fair, the fisherfolk have not succeeded in putting by enough money to last out the winter, should the herrings fail to come into the bay, as they have failed the last few years. I should like to *work* at the mackerel hooking with him. Indeed, although I am looking forward to a glorious tramp across Dartmoor, yet I am more than half sorry that I have a room bespoken at Prince Town for the day after to-morrow.

Putting aside one or two things that are unpleasant – a few disagreeables resolutely faced – it is wonderful how rapidly one feels at home here. The welcome, the goodfellowship, is so satisfying. This morning, the visitor from the hotel, who has Mrs Widger's front room, so far presumed on the fact that we were educated men among uneducated – both gen'lemen, Tony would say – as to remark flippantly though not ungenially, 'The Widgers are not bad sorts, are they? I say, what a mouth Mrs Widger's got!'

Mrs Widger has a noticeably wide mouth; I know that perfectly well; but I can hardly say how indignant I felt at his light remark; how insulted; as if he had spoken slightingly of someone belonging to me.

[1] A heavy stone used instead of an anchor over rocks, among which an anchor might get stuck and lost.
[2] After the end of July, the mackerel are mostly caught not in nets, but by trailing a line behind a sailing boat.

IV

I

WHEN I took leave of the Widgers, there was the question of payment for my board and lodging. We were just finishing breakfast; the children had been driven out, Mrs Widger was resting awhile, and the table, the whole kitchen, was in extreme disorder.

I asked Mrs Widger what I owed, and, as I had expected, she replied only: 'What you'm minded to pay.'

'Three and six a day,' I suggested.

'Not so much as that,' said Mrs Widger. ''Tisn't like as if us could du for 'ee like a proper lodging house.'

'Don' 'ee think, Missis,' said Tony, 'as we might ask 'en jest to make hisself welcome.'

It was out of the question, of course. The mackerel season has been so bad. Mrs Widger shot at Tony a look he failed to see. Otherwise, she did not let herself appear to have heard him.

The discussion hung.

'Say three shillings, then,' I suggested again.

'That 'll du,' returned Mrs Widger, allowing nothing of the last few minutes' brain-work to show itself in her voice.

Mrs Widger knows what it is to have to keep house and feed several hungry children on earnings which vary from fairly large sums (sums whose very largeness calls for immediate spending) to nothing at all for weeks together.

As I was setting out, Jimmy said to his mother: 'Don' 'ee let Mister Ronals go, Mam 'Idger.' He followed me to the end of the Gut; would have come farther had I not sent him back. That, and Tony's desire to make me welcome, brightened the bright South Devon sunshine. I kept within sight of the sea as long as possible. The little sailing boats on it looked so nimble. I have a leaning to go back, a sort of hunger . . .

2

I don't think I can remain here. To-morrow I shall move on, and tramp around the county back to Seacombe. The Moor is as splendid as ever, but this hotel life, following so soon on the life of Under Town . . . Though the good, well-cooked food, neither so greasy nor so starchy as Mrs Widger's, is an agreeable change, I sit at the table d'hôte and rage within. I am compelled to hear a conversation that irritates me almost beyond amusement at it. These people here are on holiday. Most of them, by their talk, were never on anything else. They chirp in lively or bored fashion, as the case may be, of the things that don't matter, of the ornamentations, the superfluities and the relaxations of life. At Tony Widger's they discuss – and much more merrily – the things that do matter; the means of life itself. Here, they say: 'Is the table d'hôte as good as it might be? Is the society what it might be? Is it not a pity that there is no char-à-banc or a motor service to Cranmere Pool and Yes Tor?' There, the equivalent question is: 'Shall us hae money to go through the winter? Shall us hae bread and scrape to eat?' Here, a man wonders if in the strong moorland air some slight non-incapacitating ailment will leave him: illness is inconvenient and disappointing, but not ruinous. There, Tony wonders if the exposure and continual boat-hauling are not taking too much out of him; if he is not ageing before his time; if he will not be past earning before the younger children are off his hands. Here, they laugh at trifles, keeping what is serious behind a veil of conventional manners, lest, appearing in broad daylight, it should damp their spirits. There, they laugh too, and at countless trifles; but also courageously, in the face of fate itself. By daring Nemesis, they partially disarm her. With a laugh and a jest – no matter if it be a raucous laugh and a coarse jest – they assert: 'What will be, will be; us can't but du our best, for 'tis the way o'it.' Here, they skate over a Dead Sea upon the ice of convention; but there, they swim in the salted waters, swallow great gulps, and nevertheless strike out manfully, knowing no more than anyone else exactly where the shore lies, yet possessing, I think, an instinct of direction. Here, comfort is at stake: there, existence.

Coming here is like passing from a birth and death chamber into a theatre, where, if the actors have lives of their own, apart from mummery, it is their business not to show them. It is like watching a game from the grand stand, instead of playing it; betting on a race instead of running it. The transition hither is hard to make. Retired athletes, we know, suffer from fatty degeneration of the heart; retired men of affairs decay. I have walked lately at five miles an hour with the Widgers, and I do not relish dawdling at the rate of two with these people here. Better risk hell for heaven than lounge about paradise for ever.

V

UNDER TOWN, SEACOMBE.
September.

I

A FINE tramp from Totnes – and such a welcome back! Jimmy met me threequarters of a mile up the road, very much farther than he usually strays from the beach. 'I thought as yu was coming this way 'bout now, Mister Ronals. Dad's been out hooking an' catched five dozen mackerel before breakfast. Mam's sick. I be coming out wiv yu t'morrow morning. Dad couldn't go out after breakfast, 'cause it come'd on to blow. I've 'schanged my pencil, what yu give'd me, for a knife wi' two blades.' So anxious was he to take me in house that he scarcely allowed me time to go down to the Front and look at the sea and at the boats lying among a litter of nets and gear the length of the sunny beach.

Mrs Widger hastened to bring out the familiar big enamelled teapot, flung the cloth over the table and began to cut bread and butter. 'Coo'h! tay!' exclaimed Jimmy. 'That's early, 'cause yu be come, Mister Ronals.'

'Be yu glad Mr Ronals's come back?' his mother asked.

'Iss . . .'

'What for?' I asked jocularly.

''Cause yu gives us bananas – an' pennies sometimes.'

''Sthat all yu'm glad for?' said Mrs Widger. 'Pennies an' bananas?'

'No vear!' said Jimmy; and he meant it.

All the while, Tommy (Jimmy's younger brother, about five years old) was sitting up to table, looking at the jam-jar with one eye and at me with the other. He squints most comically, and is a more self-contained young person than Jimmy. Four of the children are at home; Bessie, Mabel, Jimmy and Tommy; George and the eldest girl are away. Bessie and Mabel, too, are out the greater part of the day, either at school, or else helping their aunts, or minding babies (poor little devils!), or running errands for the many relatives who live hereabout. Both of them are more featureless, show less of the family likeness, than the boys. One cannot so easily forecast their grown-up appearance. At times, during the day, they come in house with a rush, but say little, except to blurt out some (usually inaccurate) piece of news, or to tell their step-mother that: 'Thic Jimmy's out to baych – I see'd 'en – playin' wi' some boys, an' he's got his boots an' stockings so wet as . . .'

'Jest let 'en show his face in here! *He* shan't hae no tea! He shall go straight to bed!' shouts Mrs Widger, confident that hunger will eventually drive Jimmy into her clutches.

The two girls, in fact, do not seem to enter so fully as the boys into the life of the household, though they are always very ready to take up the responsibility of keeping the boys in order.

'Jimmy! Tommy – there! Mother, look at thic Jimmy! Mother, Tommy's fingering they caakes!'

'I'll gie thee such a one in a minute! Let 'lone . . . Ther thee a't, Mabel, doin' jest the same, 's if a gert maid like yu didn't ought to know better.'

'Did 'ee ever hear the like o'it?' asks Tony. 'Such a buzz! Shut up, will 'ee, or *I'll* gie thee summut to buzz for! Wher's thic stick?'

The children merely laugh at him.

2

At supper to-night, Tony was talking about his second wedding and about his children, who, dead and alive, number twelve. 'Iss, 'tis a round dozen, though I'd never ha' thought it,' he said reckoning them up on his fingers. 'Ther be six living an' four up to the cementry, an' two missing, like, what nobody didn' know nort about, did they, Annie? Janie – that's my first wife, afore this one, – her losted three boys when they was two year an' ten months old, an' one year an' seven months, an' nine months old. An' her died herself when Mabel here was six months old, didn' 'er, Annie? An' yu've a-losted Rosie, an' the ones what never appeared in public. Our last baby, after Tommy, wer two boys, twinses. One wer like George an' one like Tommy most; one wer my child an' t'other wer yours, Annie. Six on 'em dead! Aye,

Tony've a see'd some trouble, I can tell 'ee, an' he ain't so old as what some on 'em be for their age, now, thru it all. But it du make a man's head turn like.'

Mrs Widger's gaze at him while he talked about the dead children was wonderful to see – wide-eyed, soft, unflinching – wifely and motherly at once.

'John,' Tony continued, speaking of his youngest brother who has only two children, 'John du say as a man what's got seven or eight children be better off than a man what's got on'y two, like he, 'cause he don't spend so much on 'em. 'Tis rot, I say! Certainly, he du spend so much on each o' his as us du on two o' ours p'raps; but I reckon a hundred pounds has to be wrenched an' hauled out o' these yer ol' rheumaticy arms o' mine for each child as us rears up.'

'Yes—'t has—gude that,' said Mrs Widger.

' 'Tisn' that I don' du it willingly. I be willing enough. But it du maake a man du more'n he'd hae to du otherwise, an' it wears 'en out afore his time. Tony's an ol' man now, almost, after the rate, though he bain't but forty or thereabout, an' s'pose us has six or a dozen more come along, Annie . . .'

'Gude Lord! 'Twon't be so bad as that, for sure. An' if 'tis, can't be helped. Us must make shift wi' 'em.'

Then they went on to talk about their wedding. Best remembered, apparently, are the *hot* wedding breakfast (an innovation then in these parts), the Honiton lace that Mrs Widger's mother made her, and the late arrival home from the village where they were married – a trick which procured them quietness, whilst depriving the people in the Square of an excitement they had stayed up half the night to witness. 'When us come'd home, 'twas all so dark and quiet as a dead plaace, an' the chil'ern asleep upstairs, an' all,' said Tony.

'Yes, 'twer,' Mrs Widger broke in, her eyes brightening at the recollection of the successful trick. 'But 'twer queer, like, wi' the children asleep upstairs what wer to be mine, an' wasn't. I did wonder to meself what I wer starting on. Howsbe-ever I wer fair maazed all thic day. *I* wasn' ready when Tony drove out to where us lived, not I.'

'No-o-o! Her had her sleeves tucked up like 's if her 'adn't finished her housework. Her wern't dressed nor nothin' to ree-ceive me.'

'I didn' know what I wer doing all thic day.'

'An' the parson, *I* had to pay for he, an' he give'd the money back to she 'cause her wer a nice li'l thing – bit skinny though. 'Twer a maazed muddle like. *I* ought to ha' had thic money be rights.'

'G'out! But I did the ol' parson up here. Us didn' hae no banns put up to Seacombe. I told the clergyman to our home that Tony'd been livin' there dree days, or dree weeks, or whatever 'twas, an' *he* didn' know no better. 'Twon't be the first lie I've told, says I to meself n'eet [nor yet] the last. I saved thee thic money, Tony.'

'Ah, yu'm a saving dear, ben' 'ee. Spends all my money.'

'Well for yu! I should like to know what yu'd do wi' it if yu hadn't had me to lay it out for 'ee.'

Tony did not wish to question that. The recollection of the wedding had put him in high spirits. He got up from his second supper (so long as food remains on the table he takes successive meals with intervals for conversation between them), and pirouetted round the table singing,

> Sweet Ev-eli-na, sweet Ev-eli-na!
> My lo-ove for yu-u
> Shall nev-ver, never die . . .

He dragged Mrs Widger out of her chair, whisked her across the room. 'There!' he said, setting her down flop. ''En't her a perty li'l dear!'

Once again, after another little supper, he got up and held Mrs Widger firmly by the chin, she kicking out at his shins the while. 'Did 'ee ever see the like o'it? Eh? Fancy ol' Tony marryin' thic! Wouldn' 'ee like a kiss o' it? I du dearly. Don' I, Missis?'

'G'out!' says Mrs Widger, speaking furiously, but smiling affectionately. 'G'out, you fule! Yu'm mazed!'

Tony returned to his third supper quite seriously, only remark-ing: 'I daresay yu thinks Tony a funny ol' fule, don' 'ee?'

That, I did not. Indeed, I begin to think them peculiarly wise. There is the spontaneity of animals about their play, and a good deal of the unembarassed movements of animals – with something very human superadded. One reads often enough about the lovelight in the eyes of lovers, and sometimes one catches sight of it. Either frank ridicule, or else great reverence, is the mood for witnessing so delicate and strong, so racial a thing. Yet this love-light, seen in the eyes of a man and wife who have been married ten years, and have settled down long ago to the humdrum of married life, seems to me a far finer manifestation of the hither mysteries, a far greater triumph. What freshness, what perpetual rejuvenation they must possess! The more one regards such a thing, the more magnificent and far-reaching it appears. No philosophical bulwark against trouble can compare with it. Such love ceases to be a matter for novels and selected moments and certain lusty ages; ceases to be exceptional. It is the greatest of those very great things, the commonplaces. Tony tells me that when he comes in at night, cold from fishing, Mrs Widger always turns over to the other side of the bed, leaving him a warm place to creep into. Mrs Widger says that no matter what time Tony comes in or gets up, he never fails to make, and take her up, a cup o' tay. So does their love direct the prosaic details of living in one house together. I do not think I am wrong in fancying that it percolates right down through the household, and even contributes to the restfulness I feel here, spite of unorderly children and the strident voices. 'Yu dang'd ol' fule!' can mean so much. Here it appears to be an expression of almost limitless confidence.

Mrs Widger has put me this time into the front bedroom, which overlooks the Square and has, through the Gut, a narrow view of the sea.

Tony's sister, who lives almost next door, is giving birth to a child this evening. I can see the light in her window – a brighter light than usual, – and the shadows passing across the yellow blind. Many other eyes are turned towards the window. There is a subdued chatter in the Square.

3

Little did I foresee what sleeping in the front bedroom means. Tony's sister gave birth to a boy about ten o'clock. On hearing that everything was as it should be, I went to bed, but, alack! not to sleep. For the subdued chatter grew into an uproar which continued till fully midnight. All the women in the neighbourhood seemed to have come this way; and they meg-megged, and they laughed, and when their children awoke they shouted up at the windows from outside. I heard snatches of childbearing adventures, astonishing yarns, interspersed with hard commonsense, not to say cynicism – the cynicism of people who cannot afford to embroider much the bare facts of existence or to turn their attention far from the necessities of life. 'Her'll be weak,' one woman said, 'an' for a long time – never so strong as her was before. 'Tis always worse after each one you has, 'cepting the first, which is worst of all, I say. But there, her must take it as it comes . . .'

Sundry other bits of good practical philosophy I perforce listened to; and at last, when everybody had turned in (I imagined their pleasant lightheadedness as they snuggled under the bedclothes in the stuffy cottage rooms – the witticisms and echoes of laughter that were running through their heads); when, I say, everybody had turned in, an offended dog in the hotel yard began to howl.

If it were not that the window of the back bedroom is over the scullery, the ash-heap and the main drain, I would ask to move back there.

In Under Town a birth makes the stir that is due to such a stupendous event.

4

The Widger's kitchen is an extraordinary room – fit shrine for that household symbol, the big enamelled tin teapot. At the NW. corner is the door to the scullery and to the small walled-in garden which contains – in order of importance – flotsam and jetsam for firewood, old masts, spars and rudders, and some weedy, grub-eaten vegetables. At the top of the garden is a tumbledown cat-haunted linhay, crammed to its leaky roof with fishing gear. No doubt it is the presence everywhere of boat and fishing gear which gives such a singular unity to the whole place.

The kitchen is not a very light room: its low small-paned window is in the N. wall. Then, going round the room, the courting chair stands in the NE. corner, below some shelves laden with fancy china and souvenirs – and tackle. The kitchener, which opens out into quite a comforting fireplace, is let into the E. wall, and close beside it is the provision cupboard, so situated that the cockroaches, having ample food and warmth, shall wax fat and multiply. Next, behind a low dirty door in the S. wall, is the coalhole, then the high dresser, and then the door to the narrow front passage, beneath the ceiling of which are lodged masts, spars and sails. The W. wall of the kitchen is decorated with Tony's Oddfellow 'cistificate,' with old almanacs and with a number of small pictures, all more or less askew.

There is an abundance of chairs, most of them with an old cushion on the seat, all of them more or less broken by the children's racket. Over the pictures on the warm W. wall – against which, on the other side, the neighbour's kitchener stands – is a line of clean underclothing, hung there to air. The dresser is littered with fishing lines as well as with dry provisions and its proper complement of odd pieces of china. Beneath the table and each of the larger chairs are boots and slippers in various stages of polish or decay. Every jug not in daily use, every pot and vase, and half the many drawers, contain lines, copper nails, sail-thimbles and needles, spare blocks and pulleys, rope ends and twine. But most characteristic of the kitchen (the household teapot excepted) are the navy-blue garments and jerseys, drying along the line and flung over chairs, together with innumerable photographs of Tony and all his kin, the greater number of them in seafaring rig.

Specially do I like the bluejacket photographs; magnificent men, some of them, though one strong fellow looks more than comical, seated amid the photographer's rustic properties with a wreath of artificial fern leaves around him and a broadly smiling Jolly-Jack-Tar face protruding from the foliage. Some battle-ships, pitching and tossing in fearful photographers' gales[1] and one or two framed memorial cars complete the kitchen picture gallery.

It is a place of many smells which, however, form a not disagreeable blend.

An untidy room – yes. An undignified room – no. Kitchen; scullery (the scullery proper is cramped and its damp floor bad for the feet); eating room; sitting room; reception room; storeroom; treasure-house; and at times a wash-house, – it is an epitome of the household's activities and a reflexion of the family's world-wide seafaring. Devonshire is the sea country – at every port the Devonian dialect. It is probably the pictures and reminders of the broad world which, by contrast, make Mrs Tony's kitchen so very homely.

5

Almost every evening, just now, Mrs Widger goes off to a Dutch auction of hardware and trinkets at the Market House. She usual-ly brings home some small purchase, worth about half the money she has paid; but if she were to go to an entertainment at the Seacombe Hall she would be not nearly so well amused as by the auctioneer and the other housewives, and at the end of the even-ing she would have nothing whatever to show for her money. Besides, the children would never go off to bed quietly if they imagined that she was going to a real entertainment. As she did not return very early last night, Tony and I got our own supper – bread, cheese, a great deal of Worcester sauce, and a pint of mother-in-law [stout and bitter] from the Alexandra. Then we drew up to the fire and smoked. John, healthy and powerful fellow, had been arguing in the daytime on the beach, that if a youth cannot do a man's work at seventeen, he never will. Tony disagreed. Twenty-five to thirty-five, he says, is a man's prime

[1] Composite pictures apparently; made from a photograph of a ship and of a bad painting of a hurricane.

for strength and endurance together. Nevertheless, he is sure that he often did more than a man's work long before he was seventeen, which led him to talk about his boyhood, when Granfer and Gran Widger had frequently not enough food in the house for their many children to eat. 'Us had to rough it when I wer a boy, I can tell 'ee,' says Tony. ' 'Twer often bread an' a scraape o' fat an' *Get 'long out o'it!'*

At nine years old, Tony was put with old Cloade, the grocer, now dead; and by the time he was twelve, he was earning four shillings a week, not a penny of which he ever saw or had as 'spending money'; for his mother used to go to the shop every Saturday night and lay out all poor Tony's wages in groceries. The only pocket-money he ever received was a copper or two 'thrown back' from what he could earn by going to sea for mackerel early enough to return to work by half-past six in the morning. Besides running errands, he had to clean boots and knives and to scrub out and tidy up the bar, which in those days was attached to every Devon grocery. Then he could go home to breakfast. And if old Cloade was going up on land, shooting, Tony had to get up and wake him at half-past three and to cork bottles or something of that sort before the master started out for his day's sport. And again, if Tony had fallen foul of any of the shop assistants during the day, had cheeked them perhaps, or stayed overlong at meals, then, waiting till closing time at eight or nine in the evening, they would send him a couple of miles inland, to the top of the hills, with a late parcel of groceries. His possible working day was from 3.30 a.m. to 10.0 p.m.

The chief part of his work, when he was not cleaning up or running errands, was the sorting of fruit and the cracking of sugar. Every nail of his fingers has come off more than once on account of the damage done them by the sugar-cracker. Better than any national event, he recollects the introduction of cube sugar. 'When they tubs o' ready-cracked sugar fust come'd down to Seacombe, 'twer thought a gert thing—an' so 'twas.'

Nearly every year an attack of (sub-acute?) rheumatic fever gave him a painful holiday, during which he crawled about the crowded cottage at home on his hands and knees. The one advantage of his irregularly long hours was that, if work were slack, he could linger over his meals. It was the assistants who kept a sharp eye on his movements. Them he hated – and cheeked. 'The more I done, the worse they treated me. An' as I grow'd up an' did often enough more'n a man's work, so I got to know it. One day I stayed home more'n an hour to breakfast, an' one on 'em asted me wer I'd a-been, an' I said as I'd had me half-hour to breakfast, an' he said as I'd had an hour an' a half, an' I told 'en 'twern't no business o' his an' dared 'en to so much as touch me or I'd knock his head in, which I could easily ha' done – an' there wer the master standin' by! 'Fore I knowed, he gie'd me one under one yer wi' one hand, an' one under t'other yer wi' t'other hand; knocked me half silly; an' said if he had any more o' my chake he'd send me going thereupon. 'Iss, I said, 'an I *will* go, an' if I can't pick up a livin' on the baych wi' fishin' (I 'adn't no boats then, n'eet for years a'ter), an' if I couldn't pick up a livin' wi' fishin', I'd go to sea. An' I took an' lef' the shop, an' went wi'out me pay due nor nort further about it.

'Well, I should think as I stayed away two or dree days, saying as, if I couldn' live *by* the sea, I'd go off *tu* sea. By'm-by, ol' Mr Cloade – I could al'ys get on all right wi' he hisself—'twer they assistants . . . Mr Cloade come'd down to baych an' said as he'd rise me wages be two shillings, from four shillings to six a week. So I went back. But 'twern't for long, for I wer turned seventeen then, an' strong, an' I knowed that six shillin's a week, every penny o' which mother laid out in groceries – p'raps givin' me dreepence for meself latterly – that wern't no wage for me doing more'n a man's work, early an' laate, at everybody's beck an' call. 'Twern't vitty.

'It come'd soon a'ter . . . I wer sorting oranges, an' one o' the assistants called like they al'ays did: "Widger, Widger! *Widger*! Yer, Widger!" 'Twer al'ays, 'Widger! Widger!' in thic show – blarsted row! "I wants 'ee to take thees yer parcel to Mr Brindley-Botton's (what used to live to Southview House) in time for lunch. Hurry up!"'

Tony, in short, put a couple of the bruised oranges into his pocket, ran off, and delivered his parcel at Southview House. On the way back, he ate one of the oranges and, boyishly, threw the peel about outside Mr Brindley-Botton's side gate. He heard someone shouting to him and – but without turning his head – he shouted 'Hell about it!' airily back. Then, as it was the dinner hour, he loitered on the Green Patch to play marbles with some other lads, and to share the second bruised orange. On returning to Cloade's:

'Whu did I see but Mr Brindley-Botton's coachman wi' a little packet in white paper. 'Twas thic orange peel, all neatly done up, an' a li'l note saying as I'd a-been cheeky to him, which I hadn't, not knowingly. Mr Cloade, he called me into his little office, asted me what I'd been doing, where I went, an' where I got the oranges.

'"Bought 'em," says I.

''Twas a lie, an' I hadn't no need for to tell it, seeing I was al'ays free to take a bruised orange or two when I wer sorting of 'em. On'y I wer frightened. "Where did you get them?" he asked.

'"Up to Mrs Ashford's for a penny," says I.

'"Did you?"

'"Yes, sir," says I.

'"Are you telling me a lie? I can find out, mind."

'"No, sir," I said.

'"Be you sure you ain't telling of a lie?"

'Then I broked down, an' I said they was bruised ones what I'd a-took. Father, he wer working to Mr Cloade's then, fishing being bad, an' the master called he. *He* walloped me – walloped me with a rope's end. An' I swore as I'd never go back no more, an' I didn't. Every time Father tried to make me, I up an' said as I'd go to sea.

'Ay! for all I'm a man now, I 'ouldn't like to work like I did then – more'n a man's work an' less'n a boy's pay, an' hardly a penny for meself. I tells John *he* don't know what 'tis to work like I did then. *I* 'ouldn't du it no more.'

But, with his father's boat, Tony did work far harder – hooking mackerel at dawn, in with a catch and out to sea again, or up on land hawking them round; out drifting all night; crabbing, lobster-potting, shrimping,[1] wrinkling,[2] or taking out frights,[3] wet and dry, rough and calm, day and night. 'Aye, an' I be suffering from it now. Thees yer bellyache what thins me every summer an' wears a fellow out, don't come from nothing but tearing about then. I wer al'ays on the tear, day an' night, in from sea to meals an' out again 'fore I'd had time to bolt down two mouthfuls. Often I wer so tired that Father'd hae to call me a dozen times afore I cude wake up, an' then I'd cry, *cry*, if I wer ten minutes laate to work – when I had summut to du on land, that was. Half the day I wer more asleep than awake, wi' bein' out fishing all night. But I didn't let 'em see it. Not I! Rather'n that, I'd go up to the closet an' catch off there for five minutes, before they shude see I wern't fit to du me work. An' I never had nort o' me own for years, for all I done. Whether I earned two pound, or thirty shillings, or nothing at all, I never had so much as a penny for pocket-money, to call me own. I had to take it all in house – aye! an' tips too, when I got 'em. Father, he wern't doing much then, an' ther were seven younger'n me. That's where my earnings went. An' me, as did the work, was wearing Mother's boots an' Father's jacket.'

When Tony was indisputably grown up, one half of what he earned went, according to custom, to the boatowner, in this case his father, though frequently he had to pay for repairs and new gear. That went on for years after he was married—'hauling an' rowing an' slaving an' pulling me guts out wi't!'—until, in fact, the present Mrs Widger insisted on his buying boats of his own.

Our talk shifted to Tony's first wife, who died (and Tony almost died too) as the result of the landlord's taking up the drains, and leaving them open, in the height of a hot summer. Tony told me about her people and her native place, a fishing village along the coast. He showed me photographs of her, and a framed, pathetically ugly, imitation cameo memorial, which is getting very dirty now. I knew he loved her very much. He nearly went out of his mind when she died, leaving him with four young children. The untidy little kitchen, with its bright fire, its deep

---

[1] Prawning.   [2] Periwinkle gathering.
[3] Freights, *i.e.* pleasure parties.

shadows and its white clothes hung along the line; Tony's drooping figure, bent over the hearth in an old blue guernsey: the
contrasting redness of his face, and the beam of light from a
cracked lamp-shade falling across his wet, memory-stuck blue
eyes . . . The kitchen seemed full of the presence of the long-dead
woman whom Tony was still grieving for in some underpart of
his mind. 'Iss, her was a nice woman,' he said, 'a gude wife to me;
a gude wife: I hadn't no complaint to make against she.'

The one shabby sentence hit into me all his sorrow, that which
remains and that which has sunk into time.

The Mrs Widger that is, returned from the Dutch auction with
an elaborate badly-plated cruet. 'Al'ays using up my saxpinces
what I has to slave for,' said Tony.

'G'out! 'Tis jest what us wants.'

'You won't never use it.'

'We'll hae it out on thy birthday – there! Will that zatisfy thee?'

'Not afore then? I wer born at the end o' the year, an' that's why
I al'ays gets lef' behind.'

'Not a day before thy birthday! What'll yu be saying if I buys
sauces to put in all they bottles?'

'Cut glass, is it?'

'No! What d'yu think?'

'What a woman 'tis! Gie yer Tony a kiss then.'

'G'out yu fule!'

The wise fool took a kiss. We had a second supper and hot
grog. We were merry. But when I said *Good night*, I saw in Tony's
eyes a recognition that I had understood (so he felt, I think) some
part of what he seldom, if ever, brings up now to talk about.

Only a yarn about a man's first wife . . . If so, why did I go to
bed feeling I had been privileged beyond the ordinary? Wives die
every day; worn out, most of them. There came into my mind's
eye with these thoughts a picture of the open sea; yet hardly a
picture, for I was there in the midst of it. On the waves and
low-lying clouds, and through the murk, was the glimmer of a
light which, I felt, would make everything plain, did it but
increase. For a moment it flickered up – and there, over the story

sea, I saw death as a kindly illusion. I do not understand the
wherefore of my little vision, nor why it made my heart give one
curious great thump . . .

A cats' courtship beneath my window broke it off.

6

Five or six years ago, when I was ill and left Seacombe, as I
thought, for good, I did not relish selling the *Moondaisy*. I was too
fond of her. So I gave her to the two men who had asked for the
first and second refusals of her, and neither of whom possessed a
small sailing boat. But I reckoned without those superficial beach
jealousies which overlie the essential solidarity of the fishermen.
Neither man used her much. Neither man looked after her. She
was a bone of contention that each feared to gnaw. While the poor
little craft lay on the beach, or in the gutter above the sea-wall, the
mice ate holes into her old sail and her gear was distributed
half-way over Under Town.

Granfer, however, had in his cottage an old dinghy sail that fits
the *Moondaisy*. Her yard and boom were in his linhay, the sheet
and downhaul in Tony's. One oar, the tholepins, and the ballast
bags have not yet been found. I bent on the sail, spliced the sheet
to the boom; borrowed tholepins from Uncle Jake,[1] ballast bags
and a mackerel line with a very rusty hook from Tony, an oar
from John – and, at last, put to sea.

The wind – westerly, off land – was too puffy for making the
sheet fast. I held it with one hand and tried to fish with the other.
In order not to stop the way of the boat and risk losing the lead on
the sea-bottom, I wore her round to lew'ard, instead of tacking to
wind'ard. A squall came down, the sail gybed quickly, and the
boom slewed over with a jerk, just grazing the top of my head.
Had that boom been a couple of inches lower, or my head an inch
or two higher . . . I should have been prevented from sailing the
Moondaisy home, pending recovery from a bashed skull. Everything aboard that was loose, myself included, scuttled down to
lew'ard with a horrid rattle. A malicious little gush of clear green

---

[1] Granfer's brother, Tony's uncle.

water, just flecked with foam, spurted in over the gun'l amidships. I wondered whether I could have swum far with a
cracked skull: the *Moondaisy's* iron drop-keel would have sunk
her, of course. Why I was fool enough to wear the boat round so
carelessly, I don't know.

Anyhow, I wound up the mackerel line; my catch, nil. Such an
occurrence makes one very respectful towards the fisherman who
singlehanded can sail his boat and manage five mackerel lines at
once – one on the thwart to lew'ard and one to wind'ard; a bobber
on the mizzen halyard and two bobbers on poles projecting from
the boat. He must keep his hands on five lines, the tiller and the
sheet; his eyes on the boat's course, the sea, the weather and the
luff of the sail. Probably I know rather more of the theory of
sailing than he does; but, when a squall blackens the sea to
wind'ard, whilst I am thinking whether to run into the wind or
ease off the sheet; whilst by doing neither or both, I very nearly
capsize, or else stop the boat's way and lose my mackerel leads on
the bottom – he, almost without thinking, does precisely what is
needful, and another mackerel is hooked long before I should
have brought the boat up into the wind again.

The greatest charm of sailing lies in this: that it is the art of
making a boat move by dodging, by taking advantage of, a score
of possible dangers. Except when running before the wind, it is
the capsizing-power of the wind which propels the boat. The
fisherman is an artist none the less because his skill seems partly
inborn; because he sails his boat airily and carelessly, yet grimly –
for life and the bread and cheese of it. The 'poor fisherman' for
whom appeals to charity are made, as if he were a hardworking,
chance-fed, picturesque but ignorant and helpless creature, is
more than a trader, more than a skilled labourer in a factory. To a
peculiar extent he sells himself as well as his skill and his goods.
He lives contingently on his own life.

7

All that day the wind out in the Channel was blowing fresh from
the sou'west, as we could see by the blackness of the horizon and

the saw-edged sea-line beyond the outer headlands. During the afternoon, a ground-sea crept into the bay, silently rolling in like an unbidden unannounced guest who will not name his business. And when, at the turn of the tide, the breeze in-shore also backed to the sou'west a busy lop was superposed on the long heaving swell.[1] About half-past seven, the Widgers were gathered together near their boats.

'What time be it high tide?' asked Granfer. ''Bout ten, en' it?'

'Had us better haul the boats up over?' said Tony. 'Tides be dead, en't they?'

'No-o-o,' replied Uncle Jake. 'They 'en making.'

''Tis goin' to blow, I tell 'ee,' said Granfer. 'See how brassy the sun's going down. Swell coming in too. Boats up be boats safe.'

'Hould yer bloody row,' said John. 'What be talking 'bout? Plenty o' time to haul up if the sea makes.'

'All very well for yu,' Tony protested, 'living right up to Saltmeadow. If the sea urns up to the boats in the night yu won't be down to lend a hand, no, not wi' yer own boats. 'Tis us as lives to the beach what has to strain ourselves to bits hauling your boats up over so well as our own.'

'Let 'em bide, then!'

'Looks dirty, I say,' said Granfer. 'Might jest so well haul up as bide here talking about it. *I* shan't sleep till I knows the boats be all right.'

'Thee't better lie awake then. An't got no patience wi' making such a buzz afore you wants tu.' With that, John shouldered his coat and strode homewards. The rest of us pulled the boats up, John's included, till their stems touched the sea-wall, and we

---

[1] A *lop* is a short choppy sea raised by the immediate action of a breeze. A *swell* consists of the long heaving waves which follow, and sometimes precede, a storm. The diverse action of different sorts of waves on a shingle beach is interesting. Short seas (*i.e.* short from crest to crest), even when they are very high, have not nearly the force or *run* of a long, though much lower groundswell; that is they neither run so far up the beach nor so greatly endanger the boats. All kinds of waves possess more run at spring than at neap tides. A lop on a swell at spring tide is therefore the most troublesome of all to the fishermen.

placed the two sailing boats, John's and Tony's, close beside the steps, handy for hauling up over if need should be.

Tony and Granfer went in house. Uncle Jake watched them go with an ironical smile on his wrinkled old face. 'Don't like the looks o' this yer lop on a ground-swell,' he said. 'There! Did 'ee see how thic sea licked the baych? Let one o' they lift yer boat. . . . My zenses! 'Tis all up wi' it, an' I should pick it up in bits, up 'long, for firewood. – Well, John's gone hom along . . .'

John is the youngest, handsomest and most powerfully built of the Widgers; the most independent, most brutal-tongued and most logical, though not, I fancy, the most perceptive. The inborn toughness, the family tendency to health and strength, which made fine men of the elder Widgers in spite of their youthful exposure and privations, has, in the case of John who underwent fewer hardships, resulted in the development, unimpeded, of a wonderful physique. 'Never heard o' John being tired,' says Uncle Jake.

Premature toil did not bend him; what he is the others had it in them to be, and by their labour helped to make him. Because his spirit has never been so buffeted, let alone broken, by hard times, he is also the most self-reliant. And like the majority of lucky men, he takes fate's forbearance as his due and adds it to his own credit. Fair-headed, blue-eyed, his clean-shaven face deeply and clearly coloured; a combination of the Saxon bulldog type with the seafaring man's alertness; his heavy yet lissome frame admirably half-revealed by the simplicity of navy-blue guernsey and trousers, – it is one of the sights of Seacombe to see him walk the length of the Front with his two small boys. He lacks, however, the gift of expressing himself, except when he is angry – and then in a torrent of thrashing words. He communicates his good-will by smiling all over his face with a tinge of mockery in his eyes and the bend of his long neck; whether mockery at oneself or at things in general is not evident. (It is mainly, I think, by smiling at one another that we remain the very good friends we are.) In any discussion, his 'Do as yu'm minded then!' is his signal for making others do as *he* is minded. The advantages possessed by him – health, strength, clear-headedness, and good looks – he knows how to use, and that without scruple. He is never hustled by man or circumstance; seldom gives himself away; and seldom acknowledges an obligation. What one might reasonably expect him to do in return for help or even payment, he carelessly, deliberately, leaves undone, and performs instead some particularly nice action when it is least of all anticipated. His opinion is respected less because it is known, than because it isn't known, and by playing in the outer world with a crack football team he adds to his prestige here. 'What du John say?' is often asked when it doesn't matter even what John thinks. Without gratitude for it, unconsciously perhaps, he exacts from others a sort of homage, which is certainly not rendered without protest. 'There's more'n one real lady as John could ha' married if he'd a-been liked,' I heard Granfer say over his beer one day. 'The way they used to get he to take 'em out bathing in a boat . . . Put 'en under the starn-sheets, I s'pose—he-he-he-he-he! But they real ladies du tire o' gen'lemen sometimes. Some on 'em had rather have a strong fellow like John. He married out o' the likes o' us, as 'twas. Her what he married used to eat wi' the gen'leman's family what her come'd yer with; sort o' companion-nurse her was.'

Once, when the *Moondaisy* was mine, John charged me sixpence for putting me ashore from the steamer, after he had been earning money with my boat that very same day. There is no meanness in his face, and I wondered who had taught him so to distinguish between the borrowing of a private boat and the use of a craft that was on the beach for hire – a perfectly sound distinction. Probably it was some commercial-minded lodger or beach-chatter, from whom he picked up the opinion that nowadays, to get on, you must run with the hare and hunt with the hounds – a precept which he quotes with cynical gusto but carries out only so far as suits his feelings. He aims at being businesslike, but the businesslike side of his character is the more superficial. Pride will not allow him to boggle over bargains. 'Take it, or leave it,' is his way. Most up-to-date in what he does do, he is no pioneer, and follows a lead grudgingly when innovations are in question. Most progressive outwardly, he is the most conservative at heart. A reader of his daily paper, he speaks the broadest Devon of them all; scrupulously groomed after the modern way, and a smoker of cigarettes (he was laughed out of a pipe I've heard say), he still wears the old-fashioned seaman's high-heeled shoes. Tobacco is his obvious, his humane, weakness. What his other weaknesses are, I don't know. He strikes one as master of his fate, never yet wrecked, nor contemplating it. Did such a misfortune occur . . . who knows what would happen? He is now, in his youth, so full of strength.

About ten o'clock, Tony, who was snoozing in the courting chair (Mrs Widger had gone on to bed) woke up with a 'How about they boats?' I went out to look.

The sea was covered with that pallid darkness which comes over it when the moon is hidden behind low rain-clouds. Out of the darkness, the waves seemed to spring suddenly, without warning at one's very feet. Every now and then, when a swell and a lop came in together, their combined steady force and quick energy swept right up the beach, rattling the pebbles round the sterns of the boats. For the better part of an hour I waited. Then, after a sea had thrown some shingle right into a boat, I called Tony.

''Tis past high water, en' it?' he said sleepily.

'Thee't better come out an' see for thyself!'

He dragged himself up and out. ''Tis al'ys like thees yer wi' the likes o' us. 'Tis a life o'it!'

'Aye,' he said, 'the say's goin' down now sure 'nuff. Better git in house again. Raining is it?'

A sea lifted Tony's and John's sailing boats; was sweeping them down the beach. We rushed, one to each boat, and hung on. Another sea swept the pebbles from under our feet – it felt as if the solid earth were giving way.

'Those was the high tide waves,' said Tony. 'If us hadn' a-come out both they boats 'ould ha' been losted. Yu've a-saved John his – all by chance. Aye! that's like 'tis wi' us, I tell thee. Yu never knows. – Be'ee going to bed now?'

I stayed out a little while longer: the loss of boats means so much to men whose only capital they are. Just after Tony had gone in, the clouds parted and the moonlight burst with a sudden glory over the sea. In the moonglade, which reached from my feet to the far horizon, the waters heaved and curled, most silvery, as if they were alive. That was the wistful gentle sea from which, but a moment or two before, we had wrested back our property – that sea of little strivings within a large peace. I thought at the time that there was surely a God, and that as surely He was there. For which reason, I was glad, when I came in house, that Tony had gone on to bed.

This morning John asked me: 'Whu's been moving my boat?'

'The sea, last night.'

'Oh . . .'

'I'm going to make a salvage claim on your insurance company.'

'H'm?'

'Happened to be out here and hung on, or else she'd have been swept down the beach.'

'Did you?'

'That's it – while yu were snug.'

'Have 'ee got a cigarette on yu? – Match ? – Thank yu.'

8

When I came into the kitchen early last evening, there was an old woman sitting bolt upright in the courting chair. At least, I came to the conclusion that she really was old after a moment or two's watchfulness. Her flowered hat, her shape – though a little angular and stiff, – her gestures and her bright lively damson-coloured eyes were all youthful enough. But one could see that her inquiet hands, which were folded on her lap, had been worn by many a washing-day. Her skin, though wrinkled, was taut over the outstanding facial bones, as if the wrinkles might have opened out and have equalized the strain, had age not hardened them to brown cracks – and the tan of her complexion had old age's lack of clearness. As so often happens when the teeth remain good in spite of receding gums, her mouth was tightly stretched semicircular-wise around them, and the lips had become a long, very long, expressionless line, shaded into prominence, as in a drawing, by a multitude of lines up and down, from chin and nose;—a Simian jaw, remindful of the Descent of Man. All the accumulated hand-to-mouth wisdom of generations of peasantry seemed to lurk behind the old woman's quick eyes; to be defying one.

I was introduced to her – Mrs Pinn, Mrs Widger's mother. She was bound to shake my proffered hand; she did it, half rising, with a comic mixture of respect and defiance; then sat back in the courting chair as if to intimate, 'I knows how to keep meself to meself, I du!'

I went outdoors, leaving them to talk; helped Tony haul up the beach his lumpy fourteen-foot sailing boat, the *Cock Robin*, and returned with him to supper.

'Hullo, Gran Pinn!' he roared. 'Yu here! Didn' know I'd got a new maate for hauling up, did 'ee? Have her got 'ee yer drop o' stout eet? Us two'll take 'ee home if yu drinks tu much.'

'Oh yu . . .' screeched Mrs Pinn with facetious rage followed by a swift collapse into company manners again.

'Thees yer be my mother-in-law, sir.'

'Mr Whats-his-name knaws that, an' I knaws yu got he staying with 'ee—there!'

'Well then, gie us some supper then.'

Mrs Pinn—'twas to be felt in the air – had been hearing all about me. Beside her glass of stout and ale, she looked a little less prim and defiant. But she was still on company manners. She sat delicately, on the extreme edge of a chair, by the side of, not facing, her plate of bread, cheese and pickles; approached them; mopped up, so to speak, a mouthful and a gulp; then receded into mere nodding propinquity. Her supper was a series of moppings-up. Me she kept much in her eye, and to my remarks ejaculated 'Aw, my dear soul!' or 'Did yu ever?' I said with feeble wit, in order to grease the conversation, that stout and bitter, being called *mother-in-law*, was just the thing for Mrs Pinn.

'Aw, my dear life!' she exclaimed, taking a mouthy sip. 'What chake to be sure!'

It was Mrs Widger who, with a glint of amusement in her eyes, came tactfully to my rescue.

About ten o'clock, Mrs Widger took down two glasses and the sugar basin, and set the conical broad-bottomed kettle further over the fire. Mrs Pinn glanced at the top shelf of the dresser where my whiskey bottle stands. Her bright eyes kept on returning to that spot. I should have liked to ask Mrs Pinn to take a glass, but knew I could not afford to let it be noised abroad that 'there's a young gen'leman to Tony Widger's very free with his whiskey.' I dared not make a precedent I should have to break; the breaking of which would give more disappointment than its non-creation. Equally well, I knew that it was no use going to bed without something to make me sleep . . . I told Tony I would go out and look at the weather.

'Yu must 'scuse me 'companying of 'ee 'cause I got me butes off. My veet *du* ache!'

On my return, the bright eyes were still travelling to and fro, from bottle to glasses. I yawned, Tony yawned noisily, Mrs Widger capaciously. Mrs Pinn was herself infected. ''Tis time I was home . . . Oh, Lor'!' she yawned.

She went; and when I asked Tony to share my customary nightcap, it was with ill-hidden glee that he replied as usual: 'Had us better tu?'

His native politeness prevented him from saying anything, however, and Mrs Widger showed not a sign of having observed the little victory, so meanly necessary, so galling in every stage to the victor.

Tony declares that he will really and truly start mackerel hooking to-morrow morning – 'if 'tis vitty,' and 'if the dirfters an't catched nort,' and 'if' tis wuth it,' and 'if he du.'

9

A creaking and shaking in the timbers of the old house, very early this morning, must have half awakened me; then there was a muffled rap on my door. 'Be 'ee goin' to git up?'

'Yes . . . 'Course . . . What time is it?'

The only answer was a *pad-pad-pad* down the stairs. I looked out over the bedclothes. The window, a grey patch barred with darker grey, was like a dim chilly ghost gazing at me from the opposite wall. By the saltiness of the damp air which blew across the room and by the grind of the shingle outside, I could tell that the wind was off sea. The sea itself was almost invisible – a swaying mistiness through which the white-horses rose and peeped at one, as if to say, 'Come and share our frolic. Come and ride us.'

Tony, sleepy and sheepish in the eyes, was pattering about the kitchen in his stockings (odd ones), his pants and his light check shirt. The fire was contrary. We scraped out ashes; poked in more wood and paper. Soon a gush of comfortable steam made the lid of the kettle dance. The big blue tin teapot was washed out, filled and set on the hob. The cupboards and front room were searched for cake. Tony went upstairs with a cup o' tay for the ol' doman and came down with a roll of biscuits. (Mrs Widger takes the biscuits to bed with her as maiden ladies take the plate basket, and for much the same reason.)

Faint light was showing through the north window of the kitchen. 'Coom on!' said Tony. 'Time we was to sea.' He refilled the kettle, hunted out an old pair of trousers, rammed himself into a faded guernsey and picked up three mackerel lines[1] from the

[1] The fishermen's line is very different from the tackle makers' arrangements. It varies a little locally. At Seacombe, the upper part consists of 2–3 fathoms of stoutish conger line, to take the friction over the gunwale, and 5–6 fathoms of finer line, to the end of which a conical 'sugarloaf' lead is attached by a clove hitch, the short end being laid up around the standing part for an inch or so and then finished off with the strong, neat difficue (corruption of *difficult?*) knot. A swivel, or better still simply an eyelet cut from an old boot, runs free, just above the lead, between the clove hitch and difficue knot. To the eyelet is attached the 'sid'—*i.e.*, two or three fathoms of fine snooding; – to the sid a length of gut on which half an inch of clay pipe-stem is threaded, and to the gut a rather large hook. The bait is a 'lask,' or long three-cornered strip of skin, cut from the tail of a mackerel. The older fishermen prefer a round lead, cast in the egg-shell of a gull, because it runs sweeter through the water, but with this form the fish's bite is difficult to feel on account of the jerk having to be transmitted through the heavy bulky piece of lead.

The lines are trailed astern of the boat as it sails up and down, where the

dresser. He took some salted lasks from the brine-pot, blew out the lamp – and forth we went. After collecting together mast, sails and oars from where they were lying, strewn haphazard on the beach, we pushed and pulled the *Cock Robin* down to the water's edge, and filled up the ballast-bags with our hands, like irritable, hasty children playing at shingle-pies. 'A li'l bit farther down. Look out! Jump in. Get hold the oars,' commanded Tony. With a cussword or two (the oars had a horrid disposition to jump the thole-pins) we shoved and rowed off, shipping not more than a couple of buckets of water over the stern. Tony scrambled aboard over the starboard bow, his trousers and boots dripping. ''Tis al'ays like that, putting off from thees yer damn'd ol' baych. No won'er us gits the rhuematics.' He hung the rudder, loosed the mizzen. I stepped the mast, hoisted the jib and lug, and made fast halyards and sheets. Our undignified bobbing, our impatient wallowing on the water stopped short. The wind's life entered into the craft. She bowed graciously to the waves. With a motion compounded of air and water, wings and a heaving, as if she were airily suspended over the sea, the *Cock Robin* settled to her course. Spray skatted gleefully over her bows and the wavelets made a gurgling music along the clinker-built strakes of her.

Tony put out the lines: tangled two of them, got in a tear, as he calls it, snapped the sid, bit the rusty hook off, spat out a shred of old bait, brought the boat's head too far into the wind, cursed the flapping sail and cursed the tiller, grubbed in his pockets for a new

mackerel are believed to be. When well on the feed they will bite, even at the pipe clay and bare hook, faster than they can be hauled inboard. River anglers and even some sea fishers are disposed to deny the amount of skill, alertness and knowledge which go to catching the greatest possible number of fish while they are up. It is often said that the mackerel allows itself to be caught as easily by a beginner as by an old hand. One or two mackerel may: mackerel don't. In hooking, as opposed to fishing fine with a rod, the sporting element is supplied by fish, not *a* fish; by numbers in a given time, not bend and break. The tackle brought to the sea by the superior angler, who thinks he knows more than those who have hooked mackerel for generations, is a wonder, delight, and irritation to professional fishermen: it is constructed in such robust ignorance of the habits, and manner of biting, of mackerel, and it ignores so obstinately the conditions of the sport. Likewise the fish ignore *it*.

hook, and made tiny knots with clumsy great fingers and his teeth. 'An't never got no gear like I used tu,' he complained, and then, standing upright, with the tiller between his legs and a line in each outstretched hand, he unbuttoned his face and broke into the merriest of smiles. 'What du 'ee think o' Tony then, getting in a tear fust start out? Do 'ee think he's maazed – or obsolete? But we'll catch 'em if they'm yer. Yu ought to go 'long wi' Uncle Jake. He'd tell 'ee summut – and the fish tu if they wasn't biting proper!'

By the time the lines were out, the dun sou'westerly clouds all around had raised themselves like a vast down-hanging fringe, a tremendous curtain, ragged with inconceivable delicacy at the foot, between which, and the water-line the peep o' day stared blankly. The whitish light, which made the sea look deathly cold, was changed to a silvery sheen where the hidden cliffs stood. From immaterial shadows, looming over the surf-line, the cliffs themselves brightenend to an insubstantial fabric, an airy vision, ruddily flushed; till, finally, ever becoming more earthy, they upreared themselves, high-ribbed and red, bush–crowned and splashed with green – our familiar, friendly cliffs, for each and every part of whom we have a name. The sun slid out from a parting of clouds in the east, warming the dour waves into playfulness.

'Twas all a wonder and a wild delight.

As I looked at Tony, while he glanced around with eyes that were at once curiously alert and dreamy, I saw that, in sptie of use and habit, in spite of his taking no particular notice of what the sea and sky were like, except so far as they affected the sailing of the boat, – the dawn was creeping into him. Many such dawns have crept into him. They are a part of himself.

'Look to your lew'ard line!' he cried, 'they'm up for it!'

He hauled a mackerel aboard, and, catching hold of the shank of the hook, flicked the fish into the bottom of the boat with one and the same motion that flung the sid overboard again; and after it the lead. Wedging the mackerel's head between his knees, he bent its body to a curve, scraped off the scales near its tail, and cut a fresh lask for the living fish. He is a tenderheart by nature, but now: 'That'll hae 'em!' he crowed.

The mackerel bit hotly at our new baits.[1] Before the lines were properly out, in they had to come again. Flop-flop went the fish on the bottom-boards as we jerked them carelessly off the hooks. Every moment or two one of them would dance up and flip its tail wildly; beat on the bottom-boards a tattoo which spattered us with scales; then sink back among the glistening mass that was fast losing its beauty of colour, its opalescent pinks and steely blues, even as it died and stiffened.

Suddenly the fish stopped biting, perhaps because the risen sun was shining down into the water. The wind dropped without warning, as southerly winds will do in the early morning, if they don't come on to blow a good deal harder. The *Cock Robin* wallowed again on the water. 'We'm done!' said Tony. 'Let's get in out o'it in time for the early market. There ain't no other boats out. Thees yer ought to fetch 'levenpence the dizzen. We've made thees day gude in case nort else don't turn up.'

While I rowed ashore, he struck sail, and threw the ballast overboard. Most pleasantly does that shingle ballast plop-rattle into the water when there is a catch of fish aboard. We ran in high upon a sea. Willing hands hauled the *Cock Robin* up the beach: we had fish to give away for help. The mackerel made elevenpence a dozen to Jemima Caley, the old squat fishwoman who wears a decayed sailor hat with a sprig of heather in it. 'Yu don' mean to say yu've a catched all they lovely fish!' she said with a rheumy twinkle, in the hope of getting them for tenpence.

''Levenpence a dozen, Jemima!'

'Aw well then, yu must let I pay 'ee when I sold 'em. An't got it now. Could ha' given 'ee tenpence down.'

With a mackerel stuck by the gills on the tip of each finger, I came in house. The children were being got ready for school.

---

[1] Undoubtedly, if the mackerel are only half on the feed, a fresh lask is better than any other bait, better than an equally brilliant salted lask. It is the shine of the bait at which the fish bite, as at a spinner, but probably the fresh lask leaves behind it in the water an odour or flavour of mackerel oil which keeps the shoal together and makes them follow the boat.

When I returned downstairs with some of the fishiness washed off, Mrs Widger was distributing the school bank-cards and Monday morning pennies. (By the time the children leave school, they will have saved thus, penny by penny, enough to provide them with a new rig-out for service – or Sunday wear.) There was a frizzling in the topsy-turvy little kitchen.

'Mam! Vish!'

'Mam! I wants some vish. Mam 'Idger . . .'

'Yu shall hae some fish another time.'

'No-o-o!'

'Go on!'

'Well, jam zide plaate then.'

Jimmy's finger was in the jampot.

'Yu daring rascal!' shrieks Mam Widger. 'Get 'long to school with 'ee! Yu'll be late an' I shall hae the 'spector round. Get 'long – and see what I'll hae for 'ee when yu comes back.'

'Coo'h! Bulls' eyes! Ay, mam? Good bye, Dad. Good bye, Mam. Bye, Mister Ronals. Gimme a penny will 'ee?'

'God damn the child – that ever I should say it – get 'long! *I'll* hae a bull's eye for 'ee. Now go on.'

A tramp of feet went out through the passage.

Mrs Widger shovelled the crisp mackerel from the frying-pan into our plates. Tony soused his with vinegar from an old whis-key bottle. We lingered over our tea till he said: 'Must go out an' clean they ther boats – the popples what they damn visitors' children chucks in for to amuse theirselves, not troubling to think us got to pick every one on 'em out be hand, an' looking daggers at 'ee when you trys to tell 'em o'it so polite as yu can. Ay, me – our work be never done.'

'No more ain't mine!' snapped Mrs Widger, moving off to her washtub.

10

For the last two or three days there has been a large flat brown-paper parcel standing against the wall on the far side of my bed. I have wondered what it was.

This evening, after we had all finished tea, while Tony was puffing gingerly at a cigarette (he is nothing of a smoker) with his chair tilted back and a stockinged foot in Mrs Widger's lap, Jimmy said, as Jimmy usually says: 'Gie us another caake, Mam 'Idger.' He laid a very grubby hand on the cakelets.

'Yu li'l devil!' shouted his mother. 'Take yer hands off or I'll gie 'ee such a one . . . Yu'd eat an eat till yu busted, I believe; an yu'm that cawdy [finical] over what yu has gie'd 'ee . . .'

Tony took up the poker and made a feint at Jimmy, who jumped into the corner laughing loudly. With an amazing contrast in tone, Mrs Widger said quietly: 'Wait a minute an' see what I got to show 'ee, if yu'um gude.'

She went upstairs with that peculiar tread of hers – as if the feet were very tired but the rest of the body invincibly energetic, – and returned with the flat parcel. She undid the string, the children watching with greedy curiosity. She placed on the best-lighted chair an enlargement of a baby's photograph, in a cheap frame, all complete. 'There!' she said.

'What is ut?' asked Tony. 'Why, 'tis li'l Rosie!'

'Wer did 'ee get 'en?' he continued more softly. 'Yu an't had 'en give'd 'ee?'

'Give'd me? No! Thic cheap-jack . . . But 'tisn' bad, is it?'

'What cheap-jack?'

'Why, thic man to the market-house – wer I got the cruet.'

'O-oh! I didn' never see he . . . What did 'ee pay 'en for thic then?'

'Never yu mind. 'Twasn't none o' yours what I paid. What do 'ee think o'it?'

''Tisn' bad – very nice,' remarked Tony, bending before the picture, examining it in all lights. 'Iss; 'tisn' bad by no means. Come yer, Jimmy an' Tommy Do 'ee know who that ther is?'

'Rosie!' whispered Jimmy.

'What was took up to cementry,' added Tommy in a brighter voice.

'Iss, 'tis our li'l Rosie to the life (mustn' touch), jest like her was.'

A moment's tension; then, 'A surprise for 'ee, en' it?' Mrs Widger enquired.

'My ol' geyser!'

The children' riot began again. 'Our Rosie . . .' they were saying. Mam 'Idger, slipping out of Tony's grasp, carried the picture off to the front room. She was sometime gone.

Wordsworth's *We are Seven* came into my mind:

> 'But they are dead; those two are dead!
> Their spirits are in heaven!'
> 'Twas throwing words away; for still
> The little maid would have her will,
> And said, 'Nay, we are seven!'

I knew, of course, intellectually, that the poem records more than a child's mere fancy; but never before have I felt its truth, have I been caught up, so to speak, into the atmosphere of the wise, simple souls who are able to rob death of the worst of its sting by refusing to let the dead die altogether, even on earth. Rosie is dead and buried. I perceive also – I perceived, whilst Tony and the children stood round that picture – that Rosie is still here, in this house, hallowing it a little. The one statement is as much a fact as the other; but how much more delicately intangible, and perhaps how much truer, the second.

II

While we waited for Tony to come in to supper, Mrs Widger told me about Rosie's death. 'It must be awful,' she said, 'to lose a child fo them as an't got nor more. I know how I felt it when Rosie was took. Nothing would please me for months after but to go up to the cementry, to her little grave. 'Most every evening I walked up after tea – didn' feel as if I could go to bed an' sleep wi'out. Tony had to fend for hisself if he wanted his supper early. Ther wasn't no reason, but it did ease me, like, to go up there, an' it heartened me a little for next day's work. 'Twas a sort o' habit, p'raps. What broke me of it was my bad illness. [When the twins, 'what nobody didn' know nort about,' were born.] At first, I used to think o' Rosie, when I were lyin' alone upstairs, most 'specially at night time if Tony wer out to sea an' it come'd on to blow a bit. I used to think, if ort happened to Tony . . . Our room to the top o' the house, sways when it do blow. I don't trouble me head about Tony when he's to sea ordinary times – expects 'en when I sees 'en – but then I wer weak, like, an' full o' fancies. An' after I got about again I wer much too weak to go to cementry: I used to faint every time I come'd downstairs. Howsbe-ever, I did come down again, an' Tony used to go out and get me quinine wine and three-and-sixpenny port an' all sorts o' messes, to put me on me legs wi'out fainting. 'Twas thic illness as broke me o' going up to Rosie's grave.'

'You walk up now on Sunday evenings . . .' I hazarded, recollecting that then the children run wild for a couple of hours and come in tired and dirty to cry for their mam.

'Yes . . .' said Mrs Widger.

I saw that I had trespassed into one of the little solitary tracts of her life.

'One day,' she continued, backing the conversation with an imperfectly hidden effort, 'when Dr Bayliss come to see me, Tony was asleep in the next bed, snoring under the clothes after a night to sea. Dr Bayliss didn' say nort, 'cept he said: 'Your husband's a fisherman, isn't he, Mrs Widger?' But I saw his shoulders ashaking as he went out the door, an' that evening he sent me a bottle o' port wine out o' his own cellar, an' it did me a power o' gude. Tony – he was that ashamed o' hisself, though I told 'en 'twasn't nothing for a doctor to see 'en . . .'

At that moment Tony returned. He really was ashamed of the doctor finding him in bed, whether as a breach of manners or of propriety was not plain. Possibly the latter. He has an acute sense of decency, though it rules and regulations are not the same as those of the people he calls gentry. Our conversation here would hardly suit a drawing-room. Tony, if he comes in wet, thinks nothing of stripping down to his shirt. But, curiously enough, one of his chief complaints about the people who hire boats, is their occasionally unclean conversation. 'The likes o' us 'ould never think of saying what they du. Me, I didn' know nort about

half the things they say till I wer grow'd up an' learnt if from
listening to the likes o' they. Yu'd hear bad language wi' us an'
plain speaking, but never what some o' they talks about when
they got no one to hear 'em 'cept us they hires, an' they thinks us
don't matter.' Tony is right, I believe. Most of the impropriety I
used to hear at school, university, and in the smoking room,
though often little but a reaction against silly conventions, a tilt
against whited sepulchres, – was well-named *smut*. It was furtive,
a distortion of life's facts and inimical therefore to life. Impropriety here, on the other hand, is a recognition of life's facts, an
expression of life, a playful ebullition.

Tony, when he came in, enquired of Mam 'Idger what she had
done with the picture. 'Did Rosie die in the summer?' I asked,
remembering how the children will run out to the milkman with
a dirty can unless a sharp eye is kept upon them, and how also the
larder is fixed up over the main drain.

'Her died late in the autumn with convulsions from teething,'
Mrs Widger replied. 'An' her didn't ought to ha' died then but for
Dr Brown. When her was took ill, proper bad, I sent one of the
maidens for Dr Bayliss, but he was out to the country for they
didn' know how long. So off I sends the maid to Dr Brown, an'
he sends back a message as he cuden' attend Dr Bayliss's patients
wi'out Dr Bayliss asked him. Certainly 'twas late; but my blood
jest boiled, an' I took Rosie into Grannie's an' goes up myself.
Rosie didn' belong to no doctor. Her'd never had one. Howsbe-
ever, Dr Brown says to me the same as he'd told the maid, that he
cuden' come. An' then he says, "My good woman, I *won't*
come!" Jest like that! My flare was up; I wer jest about to let fly my
mind at 'en—an' I remembered Rosie lying in convulsions to
Grannie's, an' flew out o' his house like a mad thing. Rosie wer all
but dead. Her was gone when Dr Bayliss come'd next morning.'

'Aye!' added Tony. 'That wer it. Some doctors be kind, an'
some don't trouble nort about the likes o' us when they got
visitors to run a'ter. I don' say they treat the likes o' us worse'n
other people; I don' know: oftentimes they'm so kind as can be;
but when they don't behave like they ought to, other people has
the means to make 'em sorry for it, an' us an't. They knows that.

Us can't do nort an' that's the way o'it. Rosie didn' never ought to ha' died.'

'No-o-o!' said Mrs Widger.

One can see the tigress in most women, in every mother, if one waits long enough. I saw it in Mrs Widger then. If she ever has the whip hand of Dr Brown . . .

12

This mackerel hooking, which is a two-man job though Tony could and would do it by himself were I not here, has most fortunately raised me out of the position of a mere lodger, a household excrescence, tolerated only for the sake of certain shillings a week. It has provided me with a niche of my own, which I occupy – at sea the mate on a mackerel hooker, on shore a loafer 'ready to lend a hand,' and in the house a sort of male Cinderella. It is far pleasanter, I find, to be a small wheel in the machine than to remain seated on a mound of pounds, shillings and pence – beflunkeyed, as if in a soulless hotel!

Tony cannot fill his spare time by reading: it makes his longsighted eyes smart. On account of that, and of nights at sea, with rest taken when and where possible, he has developed an amazing talent for 'putting it away'; that is, for sleeping. He can turn out perfectly well at any hour, if need be, but at ordinary times he is most content to follow somebody else's first. I on my part, sleeping indifferently well, wake usually before dawn, and greatly dislike waiting for an early cup o'tay.

About half-past four I jump out of bed, creep downstairs and chop wood. That warms me. Then with a barbaric glee, I scrape the ashes, sending clouds of dust over the guernseys and boots that have been set near the fire to dry. No matter; being light and fire-dry, it will brush off the one and shake out of the other. People who never light fires at dawn can have no idea of the exhilaration to be obtained from a well-laid, crackling, flaming fire.

Tony appears at the door, half-dressed, yawning and stretching his arms on high. 'Yu an't been an' made tay, have 'ee?' he says with delighted certainty. The cups are filled. He takes up Mam 'Idger's cup and returns with the paper roll of 'Family Biscuits.' We forage for tit-bits, feed standing, yawn again, and go out to 'see what to make o'it.'

Unless the sea is broken by the wind, there is about it just before dawn a peculiar creeping clamminess. It seems but half awake, like ourselves. It has no welcome for us. 'Can't you wait,' it seems to say, 'till I begin to sparkle?'

Tony looks out over. 'Had us better tu?' he asks with a shiver.

'Why not?'

'Shove her down then. There's macker out there!'

By the time the sun is rising (it never rises twice the same) south of the easternmost headland, Tony has worked himself into a tear over self-tangling lines, and has been laughed out of it again. We are perhaps a mile or two out, and if the mackerel are biting well, we are hauling them in, swiftly, silently, grimly; banging them off the hook; going *Tsch!* if they fall back into the sea; cutting baits from fish not dead. If, however, they are not on the feed, we sing blatant or romantic or sentimental songs (it is all one out there), and laugh with a hearty sea-loudness. And if the mackerel will not bite at all we invent a score of reasons and blame a dozen people and things. But there we are – ourselves, the sea, and the heavenly dawn – the sea heaving up to us, and ourselves ever heaving higher, up and over the lop. It exalts us with it. We hardly need to talk. A straight look in the face, a smile . . . We are in the more immediate presence of one another. Did we lie to each other with our tongues, the greater part of our communications would yet be truth.

We sail or row home, turn the mackerel out on the beach, count them back into the box, wash the blood off them, and stoop low, turning them over and over, whilst we haggle for our price. The other day, with the exuberance of the sea still upon me, I slapped old Jemima Caley's rusty shoulder and lo! she rose her price one penny.

'Damme!' she said, 'I'll gie 'ee ninepence a dozen if I has to go wi' out me dinner for't! They *be* fine fish.'

'*Sweet* fish, Jemima!'

'Lor' bless 'ee, yes!'

But she hawked them at twopence-halfpenny or threepence a pair according to the customer. And now, her wry sly smile, peeping from underneath her battered hat-brim, meets me at every back-street corner.

Soap and water, the buzz of the children, their mother's loud voice, and mackerel for breakfast . . . It is all quite prosaic and perfectly commonplace, it is far from idyllic; yet it would need the touch of a poet to bring out the wonder, the mystery, of it all: to light up the door of the soul-house through which we pass to and fro, scarce knowing.

Tony comes in early to dinner after a morning's frighting. His object is to get an hour or so for sleep before the visitors come out from their later lunch. Mam 'Idger says we are lazy; that she 'don't gie way to it, she don't!' (She did a couple of days ago.) When the after-dinner tea is finished, Tony makes a start for 'up over!' Mrs Widger enquires if I have some writing to do – and asks also if I would like to be awakened before tea-time!

Never does sleep at night come so graciously as that afternoon snooze, while the sound of the sea and the busy noises of the square float gently in at the windows; float higher and higher; float right away. About half-past two, Tony goes down to take somebody out for a sail or to paint his boats. I frequently do not hear him.

13

Is there not more than one signification to the words 'And I, if I be lifted up, will draw all men unto Me?' There are times when the mind is lifted up by a master-emotion, arising one hardly knows how, nor whither leading; a feeling that takes charge of one, as a big wave is said to take charge of a boat when it destroys steerage-way; an emotion so powerful that it does but batten on all which might be expected to clash with it. These are the periods when day and night are enveloped in one large state of mind, and life ceases to be a collection of discrete, semi-related moods. These are the dawns of the soul, the spring seasons of the spirit. The world is created afresh.

Everything, and nothing, is prosaic. 'Tis *all according*. But it is startling indeed how suddenly sometimes the earth takes on a new wonderfulness, and Saint Prosaic a new halo. What, to put it in the plainest manner possible, am I doing here? Merely fishing and sailing on the cheap (not so very cheaply); roughing it – pigging it, as one would say – with people who are not my people and do not live as I have been accustomed to do. Yet, as I know well *all* the time, this change from one prosaic life to another has brought about a revelation which, like great music, sanctifies things, makes one thankful, and in a sense very humble; incapable of fitting speech, incapable of silence.

14

Astonishment at, and zest in, these Under Town lives; the discovery of so much beauty hitherto unsuspected and, indeed, not to be caught sight of without exceptional opportunity, sets one watching and waiting in order to find out the real difference of their minds from the minds of us who have been through the educational mill; also to find out where and how they have the advantage of us. For I can feel rather than see, here, the presence of a wisdom that I know nothing about, not even by hearsay, and that I suspect to be largely the traditional wisdom of the folk, gained from contact with hard fact, slowly accumulated and handed on through centuries – the wisdom from which education cuts us off, which education teaches us to pooh-pooh.

Such wisdom is difficult to grasp; very shy. My chance of observing it lies precisely in this: that I am neither a sky-pilot, nor a district visitor, nor a reformer, nor a philanthropist, nor any sort of 'worker,' useful or impertinent; but simply a sponge to absorb and, so far as can be, an understander to sympathize. It is hard entirely to share another people's life, to give oneself up to it, to be received into it. They know intuitively (their intuitions are extraordinarily acute) that one is thinking more than one gives voice to; putting two and two together; which keeps alive a lingering involuntary distrust and a certain amount, however little, of ill-grounded respectfulness. (Respectfulness is less a tribute to real or fancied superiority, than an armour to defend the poor man's private life.) Besides which, these people are necessary to, or at least their intimacy is greatly desired by, myself, whereas their own life is complete and rounded without me. I am tangential merely. They owe me nothing; I owe them much. It is I who am the client, they the patrons.

We are told enough nowadays that capital fattens on labour, naturally, instinctively, without much sense of wrong-doing, and has so fattened since the days when Laban tried to overreach Jacob. What we are not so often told is that the poor man not less instinctively looks upon the gen'leman as legitimate sport. 'An 'orrible lie' between two poor people is fair play from a poor man to a wealthier, just as, for instance, the wealthy man considers himself at liberty to make speeches full of hypocritical untruth when he is seeking the suffrage of the free and independent electors or is trying to teach the poor man how to make himself more profitable to his employer. It is stupid, at present, to ignore the existence of class distinctions; though they do not perhaps operate over so large a segment of life as formerly, they still exist in ancient strength, notwithstanding the fashionable cant – lip-service only to democratic ideals – about the whole world kin. There is not one high wall, but two high walls between the classes and the masses, so-called, and that erected in self-defence by the exploited is the higher and more difficult to climb. On the one side is a disciplined, fortified Gibraltar, held by the gentry; then comes a singularly barren and unstable neutral zone; and on the other side is the vast chaotic mass. In Under Town, I notice, a gentleman is always *gen'leman*, a workman or tramp is *man*, but the fringers, the inhabitants of the neutral zone, are called *persons*. For example: 'That *man* what used to work for the council is driving about the *gen'leman* as stays with Mrs Smith – the *person* what used to keep the greengrocery shop to the top of High Street afore her took the lodging house on East Cliff.' It is, in fact, strange how undemocratic the poor man is. (Not so strange when one realizes that far from having everything to gain and nothing to lose by a levelling process, he has a deal to lose and his gains are problematical.) I am not sure that the doesn't prefer to regard the gen'leman as another species of animal. Jimmy and Tommy have a name of their own for the little rock-cakes their mother cooks. They call them *gentry-cakes* because such morsels are fitted for the – as Jimmy and Tommy imagine – smaller mouths of ladies and gentlemen. The other afternoon Mable told me that a boat she had found belonged not to a boy but to a *gentry-boy*. Some time ago I begged Tony not to *sir* me; threatened to punch his head if he did. It discomforted me to be belaboured with a title of respect which I could not reasonably claim from him. Rather I should *sir* him, for he is older and at least my equal in character; he has begotten healthy children for his country and he works hard 'to raise 'em vitty.' Against my book-knowledge he can set a whole stock of information and experience more directly derived from and bearing upon life. I don't consider myself unfit to survive, but he is fitter, and up to the present has done more to justify his survival – which after all is the ultimate test of a man's position in the race. At all events, he did cease *sir-ing* me except on ceremonial occasions. At ordinary times the detested word is unheard, but it is still: 'Gude morning, sir!' 'Gude night, sir!' And sometimes: 'Your health, sir!' At that the matter must rest, I suppose, though the *sir* is a symbol of class difference, and to do away with the symbol is to weaken the difference.

But at the same time, I am lucky enough to possess certain advantages. I have, for instance, managed to preserve the ability to speak dialect in spite of all the efforts of my pastors and masters to make me talk the stereotyped, comparatively inexpressive compromise which goes by the name of King's English. Tony is hard of hearing, catches the meaning of dialect far quicker than that of standard English, and I notice that the damn'd spot *sir* seldom blots our coversation when it is carried on in dialect. Finally there is the great problem of self-expression. There, at any rate, I am well to windward.

The cause of the uneducated man's use of the word *like* is interesting. He makes a statement, uses an adjective, and – especially if the statement relates to his own feelings or to something unfamiliar – he tacks on the word *like,* spoken in a peculiarly explanatory tone of voice. What does the word mean there? Is it merely a habit, a 'gyte,' as Tony would say? And why the word *like*?

When a poet wishes to utter thoughts that are too unformulated, that lie too deep, for words—

> Break, break, break,
> On thy cold grey stones, O Sea!
> And I would that my tongue could utter
> The thoughts that arise in me—

he has recourse to simile and metaphor. Take, for example, the transience of human life, a subject on which at times we most of us have keen vague thoughts that, we imagine, would be so profound could our tongues but utter them.

Blake's Thel is a symbol of the transience of life.

> O life of this our Spring! why fades the lotus of the water?
> Why fade these children of the Spring, born but to smile and fall?

'Thel, the transient maiden, is . . . What is Thel?' says Blake, in effect. Thel cannot be described straightforwardly. 'What then is Thel *like*?'

> Ah! Thel is like a water bow, and like a parting cloud,
> Like a reflection in a glass, like shadows on the water,
> Like dreams of infants, like a smile upon an infant's face,
> Like the dove's voice, like transient day, like music in the air.

Shakespeare, in a corresponding difficulty, uses one convincing simile:

> Like as the waves make towards the pebbled shore
> So do our minutes hasten to their end;
> Each changing place with that which goes before,
> In sequent toil all forwards do contend.

Drummond of Hawthornden exclaims:

> This Life, which seems so fair,
> Is like a bubble blown up in the air
> By sporting children's breath . . .

Bacon speaks more boldly and concisely. He forsakes simile for metaphor, leaving the word *like* to be understood.

> The World's a bubble, and the Life of Man
> Less than a span . . .

Were Tony to try and express himself by the same means, he would say: 'The world's a bubble, like, and the life of man less than a span, like.'

Like, in fact, with the poor man as with the poet, connotes simile and metaphor. The poor man's vocabulary, like the poet's, is quite inadequate to express his thoughts. Both, in their several ways, are driven to the use of unhackneyed words and simile and metaphor; both use a language of great flexability;[1] for which reason we find that after the poet himself, the poor man speaks most poetically. Witness the beautiful description: 'All to once the nor' easter springed out from the land, an' afore us could down-haul the mainsail, the sea wer feather-white an' skatting in over the bows.' New words are eagerly seized; hence the malaprop-isms and solecisms so frequently made fun of, without apprecia-tion of their cause. *Obsolete* has come hereto from the Navy, through sons who are bluejackets. Now, when Tony wishes to sum up in one word the two facts that he is older and also less vigorous than formerly, he says: 'Tony's getting obsolete, like.' A soulless word, borrowed from official papers, has acquired for us a poetic wealth of meaning in which the pathos of the old ship, of declining years, and of Tony's own ageing, are all present with one knows not what other suggestions besides. And when *obsolete* is fully domesticated here, the *like* will be struck off.

---

[1] The flexibility and expressiveness of dialect lies largely in its ability to change its verbal form and pronunciation from a speech very broad indeed to something approaching standard English. For example, 'You'm a fool,' is playful; 'You'm a fule,' less so. 'You're a fool,' asserts the fact without blame; while 'Thee't a fule,' or 'Thee a't a fule!' would be spoken in temper, and the second is the more emphatic. The real differences between 'I an't got no-thing,' 'I an't got ort,' and 'I an't got nort,'—'Oo't?' 'Casn'?' 'Will 'ee?' and 'Will you?'—'You'm not,' 'You ain't, 'You bain't, and 'Thee a'tn't,'—are hardly to be appreciated by those who speak only standard English. *Thee* and *thou* are used between intimates, as in French. *Thee* is usual from a mother to her children, but is disrespectful from children to their mother.

In short, every time Tony uses *like*, he is admitting, and explaining that he has expressed himself as best he could, but inadequately notwithstanding. He has felt something more delicately, thought upon something more accurately, than he can possibly say. He is always pathetically eager to make himself plain, to be understood. One knows well that touching look in the eyes of a dog when, as we say, it all but speaks. Often have I seen that same look, still more intense, in Tony's eyes, when he has become mazed with efforts to express himself, and I have wished that as with the dog, a pat, a small caress, could change the look into a joyfulness. But it is just because I am fond of him that I am able to feel with him and to a certain extent to divine his half-uttered thoughts; to take them up and return them to him clothed in more or less current English which, he knows, would convey them to a stranger, and which shows him more clearly than before what he really was thinking. That seems to be one of my chief functions here – thought-publisher. Evidently grateful, he talks and talks, usually while the remains of a meal lie scattered on the table. 'Aye!' he says, at the end of a debauch of *likes*. 'I don' know what I du know. Tony's a silly ol' fule!'

He does not believe it; nor do I; for I am often struck with wonder at the thoughts and mind-pictures which we so curiously arrive at together.

15

The old feudal class-distinctions are fast breaking down. But are we arriving any nearer the democratic ideal of *Liberté, Égalité, Fraternité?* In place of the old distinctions, are we not setting up new distinctions, still more powerful to divide? There is to-day a greater social gulf fixed between the man who takes his morning tub and him who does not, than between the man of wealth or family and him who has neither. New-made and pink, the 'gentleman' arises daily from his circle of splashes, a masculine Venus from a foam of soap-suds. (About womenfolk we are neither so enquiring nor so particular.) For the cults of religion and pedigree we have substituted the cult of soap and water, and 'the prominent physician of Harley Street' is its high priest. Are you a reputed atheist? Poor man! doubtless God will enlighten you in His good time. Are you wicked? Well, well . . . Have you made a fortune by forsaking the official Christian morality in favour of the commercial code? You can redeem all by endowing a hospital or university. But can they say of you that somehow or other you don't look quite clean? Then you are damn'd!

The cottage where the heroine of the 'nice' book lives is always spotlessly clean. A foreigner who adopts the bath-habit, is said to be just like an Englishman. It is the highest praise he can earn, and will go further in English society than the best introductions.

Cleanliness is our greatest class-symbol. In living with people who have been brought up to different ways of life, a considera-tion of cleanliness is forced upon one; for nothing else rouses so instantaneously and violently the latent snobbery that one would fain be rid of. Religiously, politically, we are men and brothers all. Yet still – there *are* men we simply cannot treat as brothers. By what term of contempt (in order to justify our unbrotherliness) can we call them? Not *poor men;* for we have *Poor but honest* too firmly fixed in our minds, and we would all like a colonial rich rough diamond of an uncle to appear suddenly in our family circle. Hardly *men of no family;* for men of no family are received at court. Not *workmen;* for behold the Carlylese and Smilesian dignity of labour! Not *the masses;* for the masses are supposed to be our rulers. What then can we call these people with whom we really cannot associate on equal terms? Why, call them THE GREAT UNWASHED. O felicitous phrase! O slave of the conscience! That is the unpardonable social sin. At the bottom of our social ladder is a dirty shirt; at the top is fixed not laurels, but a tub! The bathroom is the inmost, the strongest fortress of our English snobbery.

Cleanliness as a subject of discussion is, curiously enough, con-sidered rather more improper than disease. Yet it has to be faced, and that resolutely, if we would approach, and approaching, understand, the majority of our fellow-creatures.

Chemically all dirt is clean. Just as the foods and drinks of a good dinner, if mixed up together on a dish, would produce a filthy mess, so conversely, if we could separate any form of dirt into the pure solid, liquid and volatile chemical compounds of which it is composed, into pretty crystals, liquids and gases, exhibited in the scientific manner on spotless watch-glasses and in thrice-washed test-tubes, – we might indeed say that some of these chemicals had an evil odour, but we could not pronounce them unclean. Prepared in a laboratory, the sulphuretted hydrogen gas which makes the addled egg our national political weapon, is a quite cleanly preparation. Dirt is merely an unhappy mixture of clean substances. The housewife is nearest a scientific view of the matter when she distinguishes between 'clean dirt' and 'dirty dirt,' and does not mind handling coal, for instance, because, being clean dirt, it will not harm her. Cleanliness is a process by which we keep noxious microbes and certain poisons outside our systems or in their proper places within. (It has been shown that we cannot live without microbes, and that there exist normally in some parts of the body substances which are powerfully poisonous to other parts.) Rational cleanliness makes for health, for survival. It is, ultimately, an expression of the Will to Live.

Far, however, from being rational, our notions on cleanliness are in the highest degree superficial. We make a great fuss over a flea; hardly mention it in polite company; but we tolerate the dirty housefly on all our food. We eat high game which our cook's more natural taste calls muck. We are only just beginning to realize the indescribable filthiness of carious teeth, than which anything more unclean, a few diseases excepted, can scarcely be found in slums. Even in this great age of pseudo-scientific enlightenment, we do not have a carious tooth extracted until it aches, though we have a front tooth cleaned and stopped on the first appearance of decay. What the eye doth not see . . . Yet we presume to judge men by their deviation from our conventional standards of cleanliness.

My lady goes to the doctor for her headaches and *crises de nerfs*. 'Dyspepsia and autotoxaemia,' says the doctor. 'Try such-and-such a diet for a month, then go to Aix-les-Bains.' But how would my lady be ashamed did he tell her plainly: 'Madam, though I observe that you bathe frequently, your cleanliness, like your beauty, is only skin-deep. You are fair without and foul within. Your alimentary canal is overloaded and your blood is so unclean that it has poisoned your nervous system. Eat less, take more exercise and drink plenty – of water. Try to be as clean as your gardener.' It has been remarked that the labourer who sweats at his work is, in reality, far cleaner than the bathing sedentary man, for the labourer has a daily sweat-bath, whereas the other only washes the outside of him: the cleanliness of the latter is skin-deep, and of the former blood-deep. Once stated, the fact is obvious. Moreover, the labourer has the additional advantage of being self-cleansing, whereas the sedentary man, for his inferior kind of cleanliness, requires a bath and all sorts of apparatus. No doubt, in time we shall learn to value both kinds of cleanliness, each at its worth. The Martians of fiction, when in a fair way to conquer the earth, succumbed before earthly microbes to which they were unaccustomed, against which they had not acquired immunity. If by antiseptics they could have kept these microbes at bay, they would have done well, but if, like mankind, they had possessed self-resistance against them (that is, if they had been self-cleansing) it would have been still better. There is no paradox in saying that, practically, it is very difficult for a healthy person to be genuinely unclean; and that ideally, in the surgeon's eyes, we are all, rich man and tramp, so unclean that there is little to choose between us, and every one of us requires a comprehensive scrubbing in an antiseptic tub.

But just as the habit of aiding nature by eating predigested food is bad, so too rigid a habit, too great a need of cleanliness is a positive disadvantage in the struggle for existence. Harry Stidston says fleas are loveable little creatures. I have had to learn to put up with one or two sometimes. Tommy makes his mother undress him in the middle of dinner to find one. In other words, Harry Stidston can do his work and live under conditions which would put me to flight, and I have a like advantage over Tommy. Again, Tony can do with an occasional bath and can eat his food with fishy hands, while I am a worm and no man without my daily bath, or at least a wash-over, and, except at sea, turn against the best of food if I can smell fish on my fingers. The advantage is Tony's. It is good to be clean, but it is better to be able to be dirty.

The upshot is half-a-dozen – maybe unpleasant – truths, without recognition of which the latter-day citadel of snobbery cannot be stormed, nor the poor man and his house appreciated at their worth; namely:—

1. *Ideally:* We are all so unclean that there is little to choose between us.
2. *Scientifically:* Cleanliness, as practised, is conventional and irrational.
3. Blood-cleanliness is better than skin-cleanliness.
4. To be self-cleansing is better than to be cleansed by outside agents.
5. It is hard for a healthy, active person to be really unclean.
6. *Practically:* The need of cleanliness is a weakness.

According to the orthodox standards, this house of Tony's is by no means so clean as the rose-embowered cottage of romance. It was not hygienically built. The children gain health by grubbing about outside, then come in house and demonstrate their healthy appetite by grabbing. I could wish at times that they were a little more conscious of their noses. We cannot, try how we will, get wholly rid of fleas, because fleas flourish in beaches, boats and nets. There are several things here to turn one's gorge, until prejudices are put aside and the matter regarded scientifically. For, as one may see, the effective cleanliness of this household strikes a subtle balance between more contending needs than can be fully traced out. If, for instance, Mrs Widger came down earlier and scrupulously swept the house, her temper would suffer later on in the day. If she did not sometimes 'let things rip,' and take leisure, her health, and with it the whole delicate organisation of the household, would go wrong. Of a morning, I observe she has neck-shadows. Horrid! Perhaps, but being a wise woman, pressed always for time, she postpones her proper wash until the dirty work is done. Were we to kill off the wauling cats which make such a mess of the garden, the neighbourhood would lose its best garbingers. Baked dinner is never so tasty as when the tin, hot from the oven, is placed upon a folded newspaper on the table. Tony and the children tear fish apart with their fingers. It does not look nice, but that is the reason why they never get bones in their throats, for, as a fish-eating instrument, sensitive fingers are much superior to cutlery and plate, and so on . . .

I used to think that I was pigging it here. Now I do not.[1]

16

The dawns are later now. We do not need to get up quite so early, and usually, just as we are drinking our cup o' tay, we hear a pattering of naked feet on the staircase. Jimmy, the Dustman still in his eyes, appears at the door. He has an air of being about to do something important. He picks out his stockings and old grey suit from the corners where they were left to dry. He does not ask to have his boots laced up nor complain of their stiffness. Then with his coat exceedingly askew on his shoulders, he demands: 'Tay! please.'

'What do *yu* want? Git up over to bed again.'

'I be comin' hooking wiv yu.'

'Be'ee? Yu'll hae to hurry up then.'

When the sea is not too loppy nor the wind too cold, Jimmy goes with us. The soft-mouthed mackerel need hauling up clear of the gunwale with a long-armed swing, beyond Jimmy's power to give, and therefore as a rule he is not at first allowed to have a

---

[1] On the moral aspect of cleanliness I have not touched. Miss M. Loane, a Queen's Nurse, in her remarkable book *The Next Street but One*, observes 'Cleanliness has often seemed to me strangely far from godliness. Where the virtue is highly developed there is often not merely an actual but an absolute shrinkage in all sweet neighbourly charities. If an invalid's bedroom needs scrubbing and there is no money to pay for the service, or if a chronic sufferer's kitchen is in want of a 'thorough good do-out,' if two or three troublesome children have to be housed and fed during the critical days after an operation on father or mother, do I look for assistance from 'the cleanest woman in the street?' Alas, no; whether she be wife, widow, or spinster, I pass her by, careful not to tread on her pavement, much less her doorstep, and seek the happy-go-lucky person whose own premises would be better for more water and less grease, but from whose presence neither husband nor child ever hastens away.'

line; for fish represent money and mackerel caught now will be eaten as bread and dripping in the winter. Jimmy sits huddled up on the lee side for'ard. He becomes paler, looks plaintively, and sighs a big sigh or two.

'What's the matter, Jim-Jim? Do 'er feel leery?'

If Jimmy volunteers a remark, nothing is the matter. But if he merely answers 'No-o-o!' he means *yes*, and in order to stave off sea-sickness he must be given a line.

Then is Jimmy 'proper all right.' Then does he brighten up. 'How many have us catched?' he asks. The sight of him fishing in the stern-sheets re-assures me as to his future, about which I am sometimes fearful, just as some men are depressed by a helpless baby because they foresee, imaginatively, the poor little creature's life and all possible troubles before it. When I watch Jimmy in house, rather naughty perhaps, or when I hear Bessie, fresh from the twaddle that they put into her head at school, saying, 'If Dad'd earn more money, mother, us could hae a shop an' he could buy me a pi-anno;' or when, as I am out and about with the boats, a grubby small hand is suddenly slipped into mine and a joyful chirping voice says, 'What be yu 'bout?' – then, and at a score of other times, I am fearful of what they may be led to do with Jimmy; fearful lest they may put the little chap to an inland trade where he is almost bound to become a lesser man than his father, be removed from the enlarging influence of the sea, and have it given him as the height of ambition to grow up a dram-drinking or psalm-smiting, Sunday-top-hatted tradesmen. Then I desire savagely to have the power of a God, not that I might direct his life – he can sail his own boat better than I, – but that I might keep the ring clear for him to fight in, and prevent foul play. What indeed would I not do to remove some of the guilt of us educated men and women who force our ideas on people without asking whether they need them, without caring how maimed, stultified and potent for evil the ideas become in process of transmission, without seeing that for the age-old wisdom of those whom we call the uneducated we are substituting a jerry-built knowledge – got from books – which we only half believe in ourselves? New lamps for old! The pity of it! The farce!

But when I watch Jimmy fishing, I grow confident that the sea has its grip on him; that it will drag him to itself as it dragged his father from the grocery store; that whatever happens, it will always be part of his life to keep trivialities, meannesses and education from quite closing in around him.

17

The Fisher Father and Child

As I pulled the boat across a loppy sea—
The bumping and splashing boat,
With the sail flapping round my head,
And the pile of mackerel amidships ever growing larger and
     lovelier in the light—
And the sun rose behind the cliffs to eastward, and the sky became
     lemon-yellow
(A graciously coloured veil twixt the earth and all mystery
     beyond),
And the wavelets sparkled and darted like ten thousand fishes at
     play in the ambient dawn,—
It seemed that the sky and the sea and the earth gathered them-
     selves together,
And became one vast kind eye, looking into the stern of the boat,
At the father and boy.
Navy-blue guernsey, and trousers stained by the sea, scarce hid-
     ing the ribbed muscles;
Tan-red face, the fresh blood showing through;
Blue eyes, all of a flash with fishing and the joy of hauling 'em in;
     now on the luff of the sail (out of habit, there being hardly
     a sail-full of air), now to wind'ard, and again smiling on
     the child;
Big pendulous russet hands, white in the palms from salt water,
     and splashed with scales—
Hands that seem implements rather, appearing strangely no part
     of the man, but something, like the child, that has grown
     away from him and has taken a life of its own—

Strong for a sixteen-foot sweep, delicate to handle the silken
     snood of a line—
A man that the winds and the spray have blown on, gnarled and
     bent to the sea's own liking,
The Father!

And the boy—
Like delicate dawn to the sunset was the child to his father—
A sturdy slight little figure, as straight as the mast,
A grey and more gently coloured figure, glancing round with the
     father's self-same gestures softened, and with childish
     trustful sea-blue eyes;
Pattering with naked feet on the stern-sheets, and hauling the fish
     with a wary cat-like motion . . .
O splendid and beautiful pair!
O man of the sea! O child growing up to the sea!
You have given yourselves to the waters, and the waters have
     given of their spirit to you.
And I know when you speak that the sea is speaking through you,
And I know when I look at the sea, 'tis the likeness of your souls,
And I know that as I love you, I am loving also the sea—
O splendid and beautiful portions of the sea!

18

Mrs Pinn has put aside her respectful defiance, has ceased addres-
sing me as *sir*, and turns out to be a most jolly old woman,
possessed of any amount of laughing *camaraderie*. She frankly
explains the change thus: 'I used to think yu was reeligious. Yu du
look a bit like a passon [parson] sometimes. Do 'ee know 't? – No,
not now; be blow'd if yu du! Yu'm so wicked as the rest of 'em, *I*
believe, but yu ben't like they ol' passons. I'll 'llow yu'm better'n
they.' My own recollection, however, runs back to the evening
when she brought her damped-down washing round, and I
turned the mangle for her. It is hardish work. 'Tis a wonder how
she, an old woman, can do it when, if births are scarce, she is
reduced to taking in washing for a week or two. Tony calls her the

Tough Old Stick. Excellent name! I can picture her in her cottage up on land, bringing up her long family with much shouting, much hard common sense, some swearing and a deal of useful prejudice. Now, in her second youth – not second childhood – she is mainly a lace-worker and midwife. One night, Tony and myself broke into her cottage, locked the door behind us and helped ourselves to what supper we could find – which was pickled beetroot and raw eggs. Grannie Pinn climbed in upon us through the little window, and afterwards, to gain breath, she sat down to her lace pillow. Her dexterity was marvellous. She *threw* the bobbins about. I could not follow them with my eyes. She makes stock patterns only; refuses to be taught fresh patterns at her time of life, and cannot read them up for herself because she has never learned to read. The butterfly is her masterpiece. Working from early morning till evening's gossip-time, she can earn no less than nine pennies a day. What the lace-selling shop makes out of her, the lace-selling shop does not state.

As a midwife, no doubt, she earns more. She must be full of tonic sayings. I am told that when her patients are dying, she takes away the pillow 'so that they can die more proper like,' and also in order that they may get the dying over quicker. What scenes the Tough Old Stick have must been present at! Yet she is spryer by far than those who keep clear of tragedy. When I ask her to tell me truly how many patients she has killed off in her professional career, her eyes glitter and she bursts out: 'Aw, yu! What chake yu got, to be sure!'

She has her share of professional pride, but nevertheless I should like to know how many corpses she really has laid out for burial – and what she thought the while.

Usually she comes in just before supper-time:

'Ain't yu gone yet? I know; yu got some mark or other to Seacombe. Come on! which o' the young ladies is't? Out wi' it! Which on 'em is't?' When I tell her that she is the best girl in Seacombe and that I won't give her the chuck until she finds me a mark as youthful as herself and a hundred times as rich, she says:

'Then yu'm done! her won't hae nort still, 'cause I an't got nort, an' a hundred times nort be nothing – he-he-he! I knaws thiccy.'

The jokes, 'tis true, are poor. But the Tough Old Stick's enjoyment franks them all. You may fling a stinging fact in her face; tell her, if you like, that she could find plenty of marks for herself because, being old, she will have to die soon and then the poor fellow would be free again. 'I know't!' she says, and flings you back another stinging fact. Admirable Old Stick! She never flinches at a fact, howsoever grisly it be.

Above all, she revels in a little mild blasphemy; hardly blasphemy – imaginary details, say, about hell, in the manner of Mark Twain. 'Aw, my dear soul!' she exclaims. 'How yu du go on! Aw, my dear soul! Yu'm going to hell, sure 'nuff yu be!'

But her horror is only a pretence. She does not take such matters seriously. Indeed, few things have surprised me so much as the thoroughgoing agnosticism that prevails here. Uncle Jake is the religious member of the Widger family. For the rest, religion is the business of the clergy who are paid for it and of those who take it up as a hobby, including the impertinent persons who thrust hell-fire tracts upon the fisherfolk. 'Us can't 'spect to know nort about it,' says Tony. ''Tain't no business o' ours. May be as they says; may be not. It don't matter, that I sees. 'Twill be all the same in a hundred years' time when we'm a-grinning up at the daisy roots.'

Nevertheless, he is not atheistical, nor even wholly fatalistic. When his first wife was lying dead, he saw her in a dream with one of her dead babies in her arms, and he is convinced that that meant something very spiritual, although what it meant he does not care to enquire. The agnosticism refers not so much to immortality or the existence of a God, as to the religions, the nature of the God, the divinity of Christ, and so on.

'Us don' know nort about that, n'eet does anybody else, I believe, an' all their education on'y muddles 'em when they comes to weigh up thic sort o' thing.'

If the sparrows themselves had been acquainted with 'Are not two sparrows sold for a farthing? and one of them shall not fall to the ground without your Father,' their attitude towards religion might have resembled Tony's – a mixture of trust and *insouciance*, neither of them driven to any logical conclusion and both tempered by fatalism. 'When yu got to die, yu got tu,' says Tony, and it makes little difference to him whether the event has been decreed since the beginning of time, or whether it is to be decreed at some future date by a being so remote as God. The thing is, to accept the decree courageously.

The children go to Sunday School, of course; it is convenient to have them out of the way while Sunday's dinner is being cooked and the afternoon snooze being taken. Besides, though the Sunday School teaching is a fearful hotch-potch of heaven, hell and self-interest, the tea-fights concerts and picnics connected with it are well worth going to. But the household religion remains a pure *sparrowism*, and an excellent creed it is for those of sufficient faith and courage.

Of how the Sunday School teaching is translated by the children into terms of every day life, we had a fine example two or three weeks ago. Jimmy came home full of an idea that 'if you don' ast God to stop it, Satant 'll have 'ee,' and Mrs Widger asked him: 'What's the difference then between God an' Satant?'

'Ther ain't nort.'

'Yes, there is. What does God du?'

'God don't do nort unless yu asks Him.'

'An' what does Satant du?'

'Oh – I know! – Satant gets into yer 'art, an' gives 'ee belly-ache an' toothache.'

Not many days afterwards, Tommy was being sent to bed for getting his feet wet. 'Yu daring rascal! I'll knock yer head off if yu du it again. Yu'll die, yu will! An' what'll yu du then?'

'Go to heaven, o' course.'

'An' what do you think they'll say to 'ee there? Eh?'

Tommy was puzzled.

'You can ask 'em to send us better weather.' I suggested.

'Tell 'ee what I'll do,' said Tommy with a prodigiously wise squint. 'I'll take up a buckle-strap to thiccy ol' God, if 'er don't send better weather, an' then yu won't none on 'ee get sent to bed for wet feet!'

19

At a corner near here, there is a very blank cottage wall, and in the centre of it a little window. Behind the closed window, all day and every day, sits an old woman at her lace pillow. Some portraits – Rembrandt's especially – give one the impression that a shutter has suddenly been drawn aside; that behind the shutter we are allowed to watch for a moment or two a face so full of meaning as to be almost more than human. The same impression is given me by the old lace-maker in the window when I pass to and fro, and catch sight of her face so still, her hands so active, her bobbins so swift and, because of the intervening glass, so silent. How nervously the hands speed with the bobbins, how very deliberately with the pins that make the pattern! How hardly human it is!

One evening, however, the window was open, children stood round in a group, and I heard the small click of the bobbins through the still air. The children were laughing, delighted with the old woman's swiftness. She that had been a picture, was becoming a living being.

No doubt, she is working at her lace pillow now. She has several mouths to feed. I wonder does she earn as much as Grannie Pinn?

20

This long time I have wished to go congering all night, but have been unable to do so for want of a mate. It is more than one man's work to haul a boat up the beach in daytime, let alone the middle of the night or at early dawn. If the *Moondaisy's* old crew was here . . .

Ah! those were days – when George and the Little Commodore and the Looby and myself used to row out with a swinging stroke at sundown to Elm-beech-tree[1] and Conger Pool. The choosing of the mark; the careful heaving of the sling stone; the blinn,

[1]   A spot found by getting an elm-tree on the cliffs in a line with a beech-tree up on land.

skate, pollack, spider-crabs, and conger eels, we used to catch; the fights with the conger in the dark or by the light of matches or of an old lantern that blew out when it was most wanted; the absurd way the crew turned up their noses at my nice tomato sandwiches and gobbled down stringy corned beef; their quiet slumber round the stern seats and my solitary watch amidships over all the lines, and at the sea-fire trailing in the flood-tide; their crustiness when I awoke them to shift our mark and their jubilation when a whopper was to be gaffed; the utter peacefulness of the night after they had gone to sleep again; our merry row home and hearty beaching of the boat; the cup of hot tea . . . It is all clean gone. George is in the Navy and the Little Commodore is under a glass box of waxen flowers up on land. Did I bring back a catch alone, perhaps the old boat would be stove in.

Tony, however, has been saying that, on the rough ground a mile or so out, good-sized conger can be caught by day. On Saturday, therefore, I collected gear from the Widger linhays, borrowed a painter and anchor, and, the wind being easterly, I luffed the *Moondaisy* out a mile and a half south-east. There I dropped anchor.

Tony had given me two mackerel for a bait, one fresh and the other somewhat otherwise; that is to say it was merely fishmonger fresh – quite good enough for eating but hardly good enough for conger who, though they have a reputation for feeding on dead men, will only touch the freshest of bait. With the fresh mackerel I caught one large conger (it ripped in the sail a hole that took Mam Widger an hour to mend) and two dog-fish. Nothing at all would bite at the stale mackerel. The easterly sea was making a little and skatting in over the bows. Besides which, the *Moondaisy* began to drag her anchor. My hand to jaw-and-tail fight with the conger had made me a little unsteady; had made my muscles feel as if they might string up with cramp; which is not good for stepping a heavyish mast and sailing a boat. So I stepped the mast and set sail, to make sure, and ran homewards with the wind almost abeam.

We decided to save the conger for Sunday's dinner.

Mrs Widger made a most savoury stew of it, and when Tony

came in as usual, asking, 'Be dinner ready Missis?' she placed the
stew on the table.

Tony's face fell.

'Be this my dinner, Annie?'

'Iss, for sure.'

'*Thees?*'

'What d'yu think then?'

'*Thees!* Wer's yer baked spuds?'

'Do' ee gude to hae a change. Ther's some cold taties to the
larder if you likes to get 'em.'

'*Thees!* Why, I wish thees yer conger hadn't never been catched!'

'G'out! – Now then, you children . . .'

Tony picked over the fish, going *Tsch!* for every bone his
fingers came across.

'Thee't look so sulky as an ol' cow,' said Mam Widger.

'Well, what do 'ee think? Thees yer . . . Did 'ee ever see the like
o'it?'

Presently it occurred to him to peep inside the oven. His face
brightened. 'I know'd her 'ouldn't du me out o' me Sunday
dinner. Bring it out, Missis. Sharp! Gie thiccy stuff to the cat.
Baked spuds! What's Sunday wi'out baake? 'Tain't no day at all! I
couldn' ha' put away an hour after thic.'

For the remainder of the meal, when Tony was not eating, he
was singing; and several times he chucked Mam Widger under the
chin, and she retorted: 'G'out, yu cupboard-loving cat!'

21

This is the recipe for baked dinner:

Turn out the children and turn on the oven. Into the middle of a
large baking tin place a saucer piled up with a mixture of herbs
(mainly parsley), one sliced onion and breadcrumbs, the whole
made sticky with a morsel of dripping. Round about the saucer
put a layer of large peeled potatoes, and on top of all, the joint. Set
the baking tin on the hob and into it pour just enough warm water
to run over the rim of the saucer. Soon after the water boils,

transfer the whole to a fairly quick oven. When the meat is brown outside, slow the oven down. Serve piping hot from the oven, placing the tin on a folded newspaper and the joint, if large, on a hot plate.

To dish up hot bake in the ordinary way would be to let the nature out of it. The smell is a wonderful blend, most hunger-provoking. True, the joint, unless port or veal, is apt to be a little tough, but the taties are a delicious shiny brown, their soft insides soaked through and through with gravy. Bake is a meal in itself. Pudding thereafter is a work of supererogation – almost an impertinence.

Mrs Widger's cookery, though sometimes a little greasy for one who does no great amount of manual labour and undergoes no excessive exposure, is far from bad.

Food reformers; patrons of cookery schools where they try, happily in vain, to teach the pupils to prepare dishes no working man would adventure on; physical degenerates who fear that unless the working man imitates them, he will become as degenerate as they are, and quite unfit to do the world's rough work – forget that whereas they have only one staple food, if that, namely bread, the poor man has several staple dishes which he likes so well that he is loth to touch any other.

One day we did have at my suggestion a rather fanciful supper. Tony tasted, ate, and cleared the dish. Then he asked: 'An't 'ee got nort to make a meal on, Missis? no cold meat nor spuds?' He believes in the theory that good digestion waits on appetite rather than on digestible or pre-digested foods; that the meal which makes a man's mouth water is the best to eat; and that solid foods give solid strength. And if the same dish can make his mouth water nearly every day in the week, how much more fortunate is he than fickle gourmets!

When I first came here, I used periodically to run after the flesh-pots. I used to sneak off to tea at a confectioner's. Now I seldom feed out of house – simply because I don't want to. We start the day about sunrise with biscuits and a cup of tea which I make and take up myself. (Mam Widger and Tony look so jolly in bed, her indoor complexion and white nightgown beside his blue-check shirt and magnificently tanned face, that I've dubbed them 'The Babes in the Wood.') For breakfast, we have fried mackerel or herrings, when they are in season; otherwise various mixtures of tough bacon and perhaps eggs (children half an egg each) and bubble and squeak.[1] Sometimes the children prefer kettle-broth,[2] but they never fail to clamour for 'jam zide plaate.' Bake, hot or cold, and occasionally (mainly for me, I think) a plain pudding, or on highdays a pie, make up the dinner that is partaken of by all. But before the pudding is eaten, Tony and myself are already looking round to see that the kettle is on a hot part of the fire, and when the children are gone off to school, Mam Widger throws us out a cup o' tay each, with now and then a newly baked gentry-cake. Tony, who would like meat or a fry of fish for tea, has usually to content himself with bread and butter. The children go off to bed with a biscuit or a small chunk of cheese, and we may eat the same with pickles, or else fried or boiled fish if there is any in the house . . . Supper, in fact, is the meal of many inventions, including all sorts of crabs, little lobsters, and such unsaleable fish as dun-cow [dog-fish], conger, skate or weever, together with dree-hap'orth, or a pint, of stout and bitter from the Alexandra. Just before turning in, Tony and myself have a glass of hot grog.

From such a list of our fare, it would seem as if we over-ate ourselves as consistently as the *en pension* visitors at the hotels. (Mrs Widger, who has done a good deal of waiting, frequently tells us how manfully the visitors endeavour to eat their money's worth at the *tables d'hôte*). Tony's appetite – his habit of pecking at the food after a meal is over and the way he, and the children too if they have the chance, mop up pickles and Worcester sauce – is a continual joy to me. We do not drink much alcohol. On the other hand, the children are curiously discouraged from drinking cold water. Skim milk, tea, stout, ale, or even very dilute spirit is considered better for them – a prejudice which dates probably from the days before a pure water supply. Since, however, I who

[1] Fried mixed vegetables.
[2] Bread broth with butter, or dripping, and water instead of milk. A dash of skim milk is sometimes added.

am known to possess a contemptible digestion, have been seen to drink down several glasses of cold water daily, and to take no hurt, the ban on it has been more or less removed.

The above-mentioned goodies are distributed, it is true, over a good many days in the year, and I fancy that my being here drives up the scale of living somewhat. At all events, we do not go short. Waste on the one side, mainly arising from small eyes being bigger than small stomachs, is more than counterbalanced by a wonderful ability to swallow down gristle, rinds and hard bits without apparent harm. Granfer, indeed, says that he 'wouldn't gie a penny a pound for tender meat that don't give 'ee summut to bite at.' The children clamour always for 'jam zide plaate.' Without that or the promise of it, they often refuse to eat anything. They do not believe me when I tell them that they have more food than ever I did at their age; that I had to eat a piece of bread and a potato for each slice of meat; that jam and butter together was not thought good for me except on birthdays and Sundays. 'G'out!' they say. 'Ye lie!' Sometimes their mother is irritated into calling them 'cawdy li'l devils.' It does seem almost a pity that they have not had any of the discipline of starvation. The Yarty children who go half the day, and only too often whole days, on empty stomachs, are certainly as happy as ours: they never cry because dinner is not so good as they expect, and if we give them half a pie their earth is straightway heavenly. Tony thinks now and then how hard it will go with his children if the money runs short, as it has done and may easily do again. 'I mind the time,' he says, 'when I used to come in hungry and kneel down beside me mother wi' me head across her lap, crying! Her crying too; mother 'cause her hadn't got nort to eat in house, and me 'cause her didn't get nort, and 'cause her cuden't get nort, not even half an ounce o' tay, not havin' no money in house to get it with. An' then I used to go out an' try an' earn something, twopence maybe, just to stay us on.'

And that it is which has helped to make Tony the man he is.

22

Seldom does one catch the exact moment of an abrupt change in nature. Yesterday, however, I watched a wonderful thing – the oncoming of a sudden storm.

Uncle Jake had been holding forth on the beach. 'Us ain't had no equinoctial gales thees year, not proper like us used to. This season's going to break up sudden and wi' thunder, an' when it du, look out! I'd rather be here now than out in the offing, for all the sea's so calm. Ah!' pointing to a dinghy that was shoving off the beach, 'the bwoys 'ould laugh in me faace if I was to go an' say, "Don go. 'Tisn't fit." But *I* knows.'

I left him gazing seaward over the stern of his drifter, and walked up to the Western Cliffs. The air, scarcely a breath from the north-east, was oppressive in the extreme; very warm, too, for autumn. The sea was almost unruffled; the sky to westward magnificently heaped up with what Uncle Jake calls wool-packs. A fog crept over all the southern horizon, dimming with its misty approach the eastern headlands and making the sea like a dulled mirror. I felt, rather than heard, distant thunder.

The fog lifted. It hung low in the sky, a sulky blue cloud. Beneath it, the sea, still unruffled, was of a dense blue that, so it seemed, would have been black altogether but for its transparency and the refracted light within it.

Going on, I walked for some distance beneath a semi-arch of the wind-bowed lichenous thorns that grow upon the cliff-edge.

Without any warning – maybe there was a little hum in the air – a leafless bough, like a withered arm with its sinews ragged out, bent over across my path. The seagulls screamed and screeched; they flocked out from the cliff-ledges, and with still wings they towered up into the sky. Every twig and leaf began to play a diabolic symphony. Where the hedge ended I was blown back upon my heels. – It was more than half a gale of wind from the south-east.

The horizon was become clear; jagged like a saw. Divergent strings, marvellously interlaced on the water, streamed in with the wind, broadened into ribands fluttering over green-grey patches. The whole sea trembled, as if life were being breathed into it. White spots, curling wavelets, dotted it; then broke abroad as white-horses in full mad landward career. The whistle in the grass rose louder and shriller; the boughs bent further and let fly their autumn foliage horizontally into the wind; the gulls screeched wildly and more wildly; the chafing of the surf below took possession of the air . . .

I saw the dinghy put about and run for shore.

When I got back, Uncle Jake was still watching.

'Ah!' he said. 'Ah! Ah! I don't like they centre-keel boats wi' bumes [booms]. They'm all right for fine weather, but . . . Ah! They'm going' to gybe if they ain't careful. There! Did 'ee see? Why don't they ease their sheet off more? If the wind catches thic sail the wrong side . . . Did 'ee see that? Thic bume was all but coming over. Gybe, gybe, yu fules! Yu'm capsized if yu du, wi' thic heavy bume. Look'se! Have 'em got their drop-keel up, I wonder? Not they! They thinks that's the same as extra ballast. 'Twon't make no difference if a sea takes charge of 'em. Ah! did 'ee see the leach o' the sail flutter? Nearly over! Let 'em gybe, if they'm set on it. 'Twill upset they.—O-ho! They'm goin' to haul down an' row for it. Best thing the likes o' they can du. They calls me an ol' fule for joggin' along in my ol' craft while they has drop-keels and bumes, all the latest. I've a-know'd thees yer sea for fifty year an' more, an' I say, I tell thee, that two oars be better than two reefs any day. Le'but the seas take charge o' one o' they boats running afore the wind . . . All up! They spins like a top, an' gybes . . . 'Tis all up! Howsbe-ever, they'm saafe now, if they don't sheer broadside coming ashore. But *they* won't learn their lesson; not they. They maakes fun o' us as knows.

'There! the wind be softening now. I've a-know'd they thunder-puffs come down on 'ee like a hurricane. If they lasted long . . . 'Tis blowin' out in the Channel still. The horizon's black – see? 'Twill back, an' blow from the nor'east to-night, in here, but 'twill be east to south-east in the Channel, an' wi' thees flood tide runnin' up against it, yu'll see the say make!'

23

It did blow during the night; it must have been rough out in the Channel; then the wind dropped to a light breeze. But before ever Tony and myself were out of doors we heard the heave and thump of the long easterly swell.

We hauled the *Cock Robin* down to the water's edge, put in five bags of ballast ('Doesn't look's if it's blow'd itself out,' said Tony) and a spare oar – and stood and looked.

'Be it wuth it?' he questioned.

'Not much wind now, is there?'

'Can the two o'us shove off in thees yer swell? Can ee see any o' the other boats shoving down?'

'No . . .'

'There won't be much frighting to-day, for sure. Must make the day gude if us can. Yer's a calm. Jump in quick. Shove! Shove, casn'! Row. Lemme take an oar. Keep her head on. *Pull* – thic west'ard oar!'

We were fairly afloat outside the surf-line, both of us very red in the face. We upsailed – and away. After a few minutes' worry, deciding whether the mainsail and mizzen without the foresail would be enough, on a sea so much bigger than the wind, and looking for the *Cock Robin's* chronic leak, the bouncing, tumbling and splashing, the heave up and the mighty rushes down, put us both in high spirits. We decided to hoist the foresail after all. 'Let her bury her head if her wants to!'

Accordingly, I went for'ard to hook the foresail's tack to the bumkin [short iron bowsprit]. The thimble was too small. As I sat on the bow and leaned out over, my hand all but dipped into the waves. A stream of water did once run up my sleeve. Looking round and seeing Tony smile, I yelled back aft: 'What be smiling 'bout, Tony?' He replied: 'I was a-gloryin' in yer pluck.'

Which was very pleasant to hear – for a moment.

My position on the bow of the boat was absolutely safe, and I knew it. There was no risk at all, except of a bruise or a wetting. My toe was firmly hooked under the for'ard thwart, and short of my leg breaking, I could not have lost my hold. Besides, even had

I fallen overboard, I could easily have swum round while Tony 'bouted the boat. Tony was deceived. There was no pluck.

His words set me thinking, and I had to recognise rather bitterly, that what I call pluck did not form a great part of my birthright. I find myself too apprehensive by nature; imagine horrid possibilities too keenly; and indeed would far rather hurt myself than think about doing so. I suppose I have a certain amount of courage, for I am usually successful in making myself do what I funk; but I like doing it none the better for that. And up to the present, I have not failed badly in tight corners. On the contrary, I find (like most nervy people) that actual danger, once arrived, is curiously exhilarating; that it makes one cooler and sharper, even happy. One has faced the worst in imagination, and the reality is play beside it.

In the dictionary, *courage* is defined as 'The quality which enables men to meet danger without fear.' *Pluck* is merely defined as courage. There is, or ought to be, an essential difference between the meaning of the two words. Courage is a premeditated matter, into which the will enters, whilst pluck is an unpremeditated expression of the personality, an innate quality which, so to speak, does not need to be set in operation by the will. Courage rises to the occasion; pluck is found ready for it. Would it not, therefore, be more correct to say that *pluck* is the quality which enables men to meet danger without fear: and that *courage* is the quality which enables men to meet danger with fear overcome? The greatest courage might go farther than the greatest pluck, but for occasions on which either can be used, pluck, the more spontaneous, is also the superior. Most of us are irregularly, erratically plucky; one man with horses, who funks the sea; another man at sea who is afraid of horses. One man who fears live fists may think nothing of watching by the dead. Another who stands up pluckily in a fight, refuses to go near a corpse. One of the pluckiest men I know 'don't like dogs.' Pluck runs in streaks, but courage, to whatever degree a man possesses it, runs through him from top to bottom.

All the churches in the world may talk about sin and virtue, and make most admirable and subtle distinctions. We know very well in our hearts that pluck and courage are the great twin virtues, and that cowardice is the fundamental sin. The perfectly plucky and courageous man would never sin meanly; he would have no need to do so. He, and not the beefy brute or the intellectual paragon, would be Superman. The Christ, it often seems to me, keeps his hold on the world, and will keep it, not because he was God-man or man-God, not because he was born normally or abnormally, not because he redeemed mankind or didn't, not because he provided a refuge for souls on their beam-ends, but because, of all the great historic and legendary figures, he is the one who convinces us that he was never afraid. In him, as we picture him, courage and pluck were the same thing, and perfect.

But the present point is, or points are: How many men whose pluck and courage I have admired so much, have deceived me as I deceived Tony? And what combination of pluck and courage is it which enables these fishermen to follow their constantly dangerous occupation with equable mind; which, indeed, enables so many working men to follow their dangerous trades? For it is one thing to approach danger by way of sport, and another to work for a livelihood *in* danger.

One's analytics fail. It is, however, stupid merely to say, 'Ah, they are inured to it. Familiarity has bred contempt.' Seafaring men realise the dangers of the sea a good deal better than anyone else. Familiarity with the sea does not breed contempt; the older the seaman the more careful he is. I have met old seamen, heroes in their day, whom one would almost call nervous on the water. And in any case, what a state of mind it is – to be *inured* to danger! to be on familiar terms with the possibility of death! to be able to flout, to play with, to live on, that which all men fear!

24

I have been up the coast to have dinner and a chat with my old coastguard friend, Ned Luscombe, the man who taught me knots and splices during the night watches when I was a visitor here years ago. To go to his house now is very pleasant. For a long time after their first baby died on the day they entered a new house, before even the beds were up, it seemed as if Mrs Luscombe, a gentle, delicate woman, 'with the deuce of a will of her own,' Luscombe says, was going to decline and die too. The new baby, which was to have killed her, has put new life into her instead. They are touchingly proud of it, and very happy altogether. I do like to see married couples happy.

Luscombe himself is rather an extraordinary man; short, vivacious and solid; full of generous impulses, yet very well able to look after his own interests. It was he who dared the neighbourhood, and caused his wife to invite often to their house a crippled girl that had been raped by a scoundrel and then given the cold-shoulder by everyone else. Something of a sea-lawyer, he is one of the sharpest-brained – I don't say deepest-thinking – men I have ever come across. Hardly educated at all as a boy, he races through books (he read my Cary's *Dante* in a week), extracts the main gist of them, and is always learning some new thing, from shorthand to cooking, though he has no need to do much but behave himself for a pension. Almost harshly honest, he yet brinks out with pride a large edition of Pope that he 'nicked' from the second-hand bookstall of a heathen Chinee at Singapore. That little episode will not make a very big blot, I imagine, on the Book of Judgment. If I remember aright, the British Navy was then occupied in protecting land or concessions that the nation itself had 'nicked' from the heathen.

Luscombe's opinion on books, men and things, unless it has been borrowed from a newspaper, is always well worth hearing. His light of nature, by which he judges, is exceptionally powerful.

While we were smoking in his front room – furnished with a curious mixture of cheap English things and beautiful Eastern curios – a steward from one of the great liners came in. He began talking about the behaviour in a gale of a rich snobbish Jew and the behaviour of Jews generally on shipboard, and was inclined to take up the high, superior, patriotic attitude that Jews, not being Englishmen, were necessarily a nuisance in a storm. 'Well,' said Luscombe, 'all I know is, when a man tells me he's never been afraid of anything anywhere, I tells him to his face, "You'm a damn'd liar!" One day, in a pub at Plymouth, there was a man – a bluejacket too – boasting he'd never known what fear was, and I up and asked him, "Eh, chum? Did you say *Never?*"

'"Never!" he says. "Never in me life!"

'"You'm a liar then," says I.

'"We'll see," says he – goodish-sized chap.

'"You'm a bloody liar," says I, "and what's more, you ain't truthful."

'So we squared up there and then, and the bung and his men hyked us out into the street and we was having our scrap out when the police came up. He ran! "Eh, Mr Liar!" I yelled after him. "Did you say you was never afraid?"

'If I hadn't wasted time doing that, I shouldn't have got caught either. Very nearly landed me in chokey, that did. We was ship-mates afterwards, me and that man, and very good friends. He's a warrant officer now.'

Thence the conversation passed naturally to promotion from the ranks. 'I don't believe in it, not as a general rule,' said Lus-combe. 'Officers ought to be officers, and men ought to be men, and a ship's always more comfortable when both keep their places. Rankers as officers are apt to be bullies: that we all know jolly well. And besides that, the likes of us can't keep our kecker up the same as gen'lemen, and therefore I says we ain't fit for the quarter-deck, not yet awhile. 'Tisn't that the lower deck ain't so brave as the quarter-deck, because it is; only it can't keep it up so long; it gets discouraged like, when 'tis a long job, specially when 'tis one of those waiting-an-doing-nothing jobs. We ain't bred up to it, and our fathers wasn't, and there's no good to be got out of trying to pretend 'tisn't so.'

We argued on. Luscombe would not yield an inch of his posi-tion. I can't say off hand how far history bears him out, but I fancy that he is right to this extent: the lower deck has less flexibility of mind. It cannot view a depressing situation from so many sides at once. It is not, for instance, so quick to see the underlying humour of an emergency; not so ready to appreciate the so-called irony of fate. It cannot so easily turn round and laugh at itself and its predicament. So, though the lower deck's courage may be fully as great as, or greater than, that of the upper deck, it is applied more constantly, with less mental diversion, and therefore it tires sooner. Hence, it *may* not be so effective.

The argument undoubtedly has a true bearing on that sort of promotion which, in the prevailing educational cant, is called giving every poor boy (by free education, scholarships and other lures) his chance of climbing to the top of the ladder – as if success in life were one great tall ladder instead of many ladders of varying builds and heights. In attempting to justify modern educational policy, its victims are egged on too fast into a field of commercial, intellectual, or emotional stress for which they lack the fundamental grit, or rather for which the fundamental grit they do possess is not adapted, nor can be adapted in a generation. Their spirit, fine and valuable for the old purpose perhaps, is not suited to the new. Therefore, of good workmen *in posse* we make bad clerks and shopmen *in esse*; of good clerks detestable little bureaucrats or mean-minded commercial men, and so on. Possible wives and mothers we turn into female creatures. And Merrie England swarms with makeshift folk and breakdowns.

Happily nature, heredity, sometimes intervenes, and at adolescence the sharp boy, the pride of the examination room, develops into quite a nice commonplace young man, like the missionaries' nigger boy, and is saved, if he be not already committed to an unsuitable career. Otherwise, what mental deformity and slaughter! It was well said that education – what is called education – was the cruellest thing ever forced upon the poor. Mam Widger agrees. She knows her two boys are above the average in brains, but she says: 'I'd far rather for them to fend for themselves an' make gude fishermen like their father or gude sailors like their uncles, than for 'em to be forced on by somebody else to what they ain't fitted for. 'Tis God helps them as helps themselves, they du reckon, but I can't see as he helps them as is pushed.'

25

Uncle Jake allows us fine weather for the Regatta. 'But when it du break up, after this yer logie [dull, hazy, calm] spell, look out!' he says. 'Iss; look out!'

The day before yesterday, we were having a yarn together on the Front. 'Must go t'morrow an' pick Jemima Cayley some wrinkles [periwinkles],' he said. 'I got a lot o' work to do wi' my taties up to my plat [allotment], but I promised Jemima her should hae'em for Regatta, an' her shall, if I lives to get 'em. Her says my wrinkles be twice so heavy as anybody else's what her has – an' so they be, proper gert gobbets! They t'other fellows don' know where to go for 'em, but I du – master wrinkles, waiting there for Jake to pick 'em. On'y I ain't goin' to tell they beer-barrels where 'em be. Not I! – Wude yu like to come? Nobody goes where I goes.'

'Where's that?'

'Ah! Down to Longo. Yu'll see, if yu comes.'

'Haven't yu got a mate for it then?'

'*Mate!* I'd rather go be myself than wi' some o' they bladder-headed friends o' brewers. *They* don' like wrinklin' wi' Jake; makes 'em blow too much when they has to carry a bushel o' wrinkles, like I've a-done often, over the rocks an' up the cliff, two or dree miles home. They Double-X Barrels can't du that. Lord! can't expect 'em to. – *We'll* go in the *Moondaisy* t'morrow, an' then if we can't sail home, we can row, an' if it comes on a fresh wind, we'll haul her up to Refuge Cove an' go'n look how my orchards be getting on.'

It is good to hear Uncle Jake talk about the work that nobody else will do. (The exposure alone would be too much for many of them.) His face wrinkles up within its grey picture-frame beard, his keen yet wistful eyes open wide, and he draws up that youth-ful body of his – clad in faded blue jumper and torn trousers – on which the head of a venerable old man seems so incongruously set. He is the owner of a big drifter which hardly pays her expenses; he feels that taking out pleasure parties is no work for a fisherman—'never wasn't used to be at the beck an' call o' they sort o' people when I wer young'; – and therefore he picks up a living, laborious but very independent, between high and low tide mark for many miles east and west of Seacombe. Nobody learns exactly when or where he goes, nor what little valuables are in the old sack that he carries. He seldom sleeps for more than two hours on end; has breakfast at midnight, dinner in the early morning, and tea-supper only if it happens to be handy; and he feeds mainly on bread, cheese, sugar and much butter, with an occasional feast of half a dozen mackerel at once, or a skate or a small conger. Singularly straightforward in all his dealings, a little of the old West-country wrecking spirit yet survives in him, and he enjoys nothing better than smuggling jetsam past the coast-guards. Social position saves no one from hearing what Uncle Jake thinks. His tongue is loaded with scorn and sarcasm, but his heart holds nothing but kindness. He will jeer and taunt a man off the Front, and give him money round the corner or food in house. His nicknames are terrible – they stick. Few would care to turn and fight such an old man, and if they did he would almost certainly knock them into the dust or throw them into the sea. He is childless; and, since her illness several years ago, his wife, an untidy woman with beautiful eyes, has been scatterbrained and more trouble than use, a spender of his savings. He nursed her himself for many months. He does most of the housework now. He may remark on his wife, if he knows you very well, but about the childlessness he never talks.

At eight in the morning we made sail with the wind just north of east. The little *Moondaisy* was full of sacks, old boots and gear. Past Refuge Cove we sailed, past Dog Tooth Ledge, and across the out-ground of Landlock Bay, which holds the last long stretch of pebble beach for some miles down. Uncle Jake pointed to the western end of it. 'If ever yu'm catched down here by a sou'wes-ter, yu can al'ays run ashore, just there – calm as a mill-pond no matter how 'tis blowing. Yu can beach there when yu can't beach to Seacombe for the roughness o' the sea. Aye, I've a-done it! But yu can't get out o' Landlock Bay, though I mind when you could climb up the cliff jest to the east'ard o' thic roozing [landslip]. Howsbe-ever, 'tis a heavy gale from the south-east on a long spring tide as'll drive 'ee out o' thic cave there where the beach urns up. Now yu knows that: 'tisn't all o'em does.'

Similar bits of lore or reminiscence did he give me about every few yards of the coastline. Most merrily had the easterly wind and a following sea brought us down. Now we drew near the rocks, where at high tide the land drops sheer to the water. In the dry sunshine, such a sparkle was on the waves, such a shimmer on the high red cliffs, that it was hard to follow Uncle Jake when he said, as if he revered the place, ''*Tis* an iron-bound show! '*Tis* a shop! Poor devils, what gets throwed up here! But I know wher ther's some fine copper bolts waiting for me. I'll hae 'em! I've had some on 'em, an' I'll hae the rest when they rots out o' the timbers. Year '63 that wreck was – lovely vessel, loaded wi' corn. I mind it well. '*Twas* a night!'

We ran the *Moondaisy* ashore at Brandey-Keg Cove – a little beach running up into a deep gloomy cave where the smugglers used to store their cargoes and haul them up over the cliff. 'Us can walk down to Lobster Ledge an' west from there to Tatie Rock. I knows where they master gobbets be, if nobody an't had 'em – an' nobody an't. They don' like this iron-bound shop. They leaves it to Jake. But they wuden't, if they know'd what was here.'

I ate some of my breakfast while Uncle Jake was changing his boots and shifting his outer clothing. He would accept only one of my small cheese sandwiches. 'I got some bread and butter here,' he said, but I 'took partic'lar notice,' as Tony puts it, that he ate none of the bread and butter. And he refused to take a second sip of my tea because his sensitive nose detected that there had been whiskey in the bottle.

As we walked along the rocks, he placed above high-tide mark what bits of wreckage he could find, and kept a sharp look-out for any rabbits which might have fallen over the cliff. The only two we found, however, had been partially eaten by sea-gulls and rats. 'Let 'em hae 'em an' welcome,' said Uncle Jake. 'The winter's coming. I can't think how they poor gulls lives when all the sea round about is a hustle o' froth. I al'ays feeds 'em when I can. Don't yu think that *they* gets hungry tu?'

At Lobster Ledge – a jumble of peaked rocks with pools between – he left his sack conspicuously on the top of a high stone, and hopped – seemed to hop – down to a pool. 'They'm here!' he cried. I heard them clatter-clatter into his old cake tin, and then a tin-full rattle into his sack. On those rocks, where few can step at all without great care, he raced about, bent down double, and jumped and glided as actively as an acrobat – a veritable rock-man. 'Come here!' he called. 'Jest yu turn over thic stone. Ther's some there. My senses, what gobbets they be! If they ther fuddle-heads what goes nosing about Broken Rocks, on'y know'd . . .'

Underneath the stone, clinging to it and lying on the bed of the pool, were so many large winkles that instead of picking them out, I found it quicker to sweep up handfuls of loose stuff and then to pick out the refuse from the winkles. When Uncle Jake came across an unusually good pocket he would call me to it and hop on somewhere else. There was an element of sport in catching the dull-looking gobbets so many together. I soon got to know the likely stones – heavy ones that wanted coaxing over, – and discovered also that the winkles hide themselves in a green, rather gelatinous weed, fuzzy like kale tops, from which they can be combed with the fingers. They love, too, a shadowed pool which is tainted a little, but not too much, by decaying vegetable matter. Uncle Jake likes the stones turned back and then replaced 'as you finds 'em.'

I emptied my baler, holding perhaps a quart, into the ballast-bag. How one's back ached! How old and rheumaticy had one's knees suddenly become! Uncle Jake feels nothing of that, for all his sixty-five years. He still skipped from pool to pool. He flung me a lobster. 'There! put that in your bag for tay. Tide's dead low. The wind's dying away: sun's burnt it up. Shuden' wonder if it don't come in sou'west, an' if it du we'll hae a fair wind home along. – Well, how du 'ee like it? Eh?'

'All right.'

'Ah! yu ought to be down here in the winter, like I been, when you got to put your hands wet into your pockets to get 'em warm enough to feel the gobbets – aye, to hold 'em! Then carry 'em five mile home on your back to make 'ee warm again.'

So we went on: grab, grab, grab! clatter-clatter! rattle! We talked less and worked harder, because we were tired. The tide crept up. The wind veered to south-east and strengthened. ''Tis time to be off out of thees yer,' said Uncle Jake. 'The lop'll rise when the flid tide makes. Yu may know everything there is to know about fishing, but,' he added grimly, 'if yu don' know when to be off, 'twill all o'it be no gude to 'ee some day. Blast thees wind! We'll hae to row home now, or ratch out a couple o' miles to fetch in.'

We shouldered our sacks for the half-mile walk to the *Moon-daisy*. Walk . . . Scramble! Uncle Jake seemed to glide from rock to rock, but with two or three stone weight awkwardly perched on my shoulder, the wet running down my neck and an arm going numb, I slithered down the weed-covered slopes in a very breakneck fashion. I rather felt for the bladderheads who refuse to go wrinkling far from home.

Afloat again, we used the winkles for ballast in place of shingle. The lop *had* made, and was against us. We rowed up Landlock Bay to the western side of Dogtooth Ledge. Uncle Jake made an exclamation and stood up. 'What's that? Whoever's that? There! down there to Lobster Ledge! A gen'leman an' lady, looks so. How did us come to miss they? Look! They'm sittin' down, the fules! – Hi, yu! Hi! Hi! – They'm catched. When yu see the water washing over the Dog's Tooth, yu can't get round the ledge wi'out swimming. – Hi, yu! Hi! – They'm in for a night o'it sure, till the tide falls, if we don' take 'em round to Refuge Cove. Ther's nowhere there where they be, to get upon land. – Hi! Hi! Yu! – They'm mazed. An' her an't got no stocking on nuther. – Hi! hi! Hurry up! – Can't bide here all day. The flid and the sea's making fast.'

They came on at a leisurely pace. The Dog's Tooth was continuously awash. Spray broke on it. 'D'yu know,' said Uncle Jake when they were near enough, 'that yu'm catched by the tide? Yu'm in for a night o'it on this yer beach, wi'out yu swims round the ledge or lets we row yu to the lane in Refuge Cove. Yu can't get up on land herefrom.'

'Oh . . .' said the man. 'We'd better come on board your boat then.'

It took Uncle Jake nearly half-an-hour to row the three-quarters of a mile across the tide-rip on the ledge and into Refuge Cove. I carefully refrained from doing anything to lead them to suppose that they were aboard other than a fishing boat. It was Uncle Jake's expedition: his the prospective reward. When I helped the man ashore, he put some coppers into my hand. 'There's threepence for the old man's tobacco,' he said with an air of great benevolence. I was too surprised to speak: I pushed off and then burst into a laugh.

'What did 'er give 'ee?'

'Threepence. *Threepence!* For your tobacco!'

'Thank yu. I don't use tobacco. Yu'd better keep thic donation. They'd ha' catched their death o' cold there all night, an' there ain't no other boats down here along, nor won't be. That's what they reckons their bloody lives be worth, an' that's what the lives of the likes o' they *be* worth, tu! Dreepence! My senses . . .'

We roared with laughter. It put heart into us for our stiff row home against wind, wave and tide. When I went for'ard to place the cut-rope ready, Uncle Jake had to call me aft again: in spite of his strength the boat was being beaten to leeward.

It was nearly four o'clock when we had hauled up and were carrying the winkles on our backs down one of the untidy little roadways into Under Town. No dinner or high-tea was waiting for Uncle Jake. The house was unswept. How draggled the little bits of fern in the old china pots looked! The fire was out; the hearth piled up with ashes; and on the table stood a basin of potatoes in water, most of them unpeeled.

Uncle Jake came to a standstill, acutely alive in the midst of a domestic deadness. He raised himself upright beneath his load of winkles. 'That's what I got to put up wi',' he said. 'An't had a bite since breakfast at four by the clock this morning, 'cept thic sandwich o' yours. 'Tis a wonder how I du put up wi' it. I don' know for sure.'

'Thees is what I got to put up wi'!' he repeated when Mrs Jake came in from a neighbour's.

'I forgot,' she said with a gay high-pitched little laugh which had in it a tang of acquiescent despair – the echo of a mind that has ceased fighting anything, even itself.

'Forgot! Yu forgets!' Then in a softer tone: 'Gie us the quart cup.'

He emptied my winkles out upon the stone floor, knelt down, and measured them back into the ballast-bag: 'one – two – three –

four, that's one – five – six – seven – eight, that's two pecks – nine
– ten – half a peck over; good for you, skipper!' He had four pecks
himself, together with several small lobsters which he threw out
to me.

'But you'll eat those . . .'

'No, I shan't. Don't want 'em. Take 'em in home for yer tay.'

Then he hunted out of an inside breast-pocket a screw of
newspaper, and from it took a half-crown piece:

'That's your share.'

'But . . .'

'Go on! If you hadn' a-come I should ha' been the poorer by
more'n that, an' that's what one o' they beery bladderheads
would ha' had if they'd a-come – on'y I won't hae 'em 'long wi'
me. Better yu to hae it than one o' they, to gie to the brewer. I
wishes 'ee to take it. Yu've earned it, an' thank yu for your help. *I*
done all right out o'it.'

26

The Regatta has gone off well. The day was fine, the wind
nor'west and not too squally. There was a brave show of bunting;
very many people and several bands came down to the short
Front; and there were races on the water, in the water, and, in the
evening, on land. The sea sparkled. The place was all of a flutter.
Uncle Jake, irritated by the invasion of his beach, became most
scornful over the abundance of high starched collars, and the kid
gloves of the shop-assistants. Some of the young Seacombe
braves collected round to tease him and, if possible, to work him
into one of his famous passions. But they dared not so much as
nudge him; he is too earnest, too vigorous. He lashed them off
with his tongue. And when a dinghy capsized through trying to
sail off the wind in a squall, it was the old man who was quickest
at the water's edge with a punt, and first on the spot, although a
four-oared boat raced out to the rescue.

Some of the Widgers won races, I believe. One takes no great
note of prizes: they are too small. The Regatta is not primarily an
affair of fisherfolk; to take any great part in it would be to neglect

their own work; and when they do race, they have a neat method of defeating the patronage of the townsfolk who provide prize-money in order that they and the visitors may enjoy the spectacle of fishermen (in fisher phrase) pulling their insides out for nort. The prize-money is pooled and divided among all the competitors. In consequence, the races are rowed and sailed with great dignity, and many of the visitors excite themselves halfway to delirium over the extreme – the make-believe closeness of the finishes. It is not very sporting perhaps, but indulgence in the sporting spirit is for those who can afford it. The Seacombe fisherfolk can't.

A confounding number of the Widger family and its connexions arrived by boat, road and rail. Two or three grand teas were provided one after the other. Mrs Widger – looking really very young, alert, and pretty – packed the children off to the beach with gentry-cakes in their hands. Well she did so, for every chair in the kitchen was occupied by some relative, and the display of best clothes was most alarming. Worst of all, one party had brought the family idiot – a simpering, lollopy creature, stiff in the wrong places, who could not feed himself properly. With a vigorous tapping of the forehead, he was pointed out to me. 'He's a little deeficient, you know, sir – something lacking.' The idiot, finding himself the centre of attraction, fairly crowed with delight. 'Ou-ah!' he went. 'Ou-ah! ou-ah!'

On the pretext that a boat wanted hauling up, I escaped, with a piece of bread and jam in my hand, like the children.

A man of slightly unsober dignity accosted me in the Gut, and asked if Jim somebody-or-other was within. 'Him and me don't speak, nor eet meet,' he explained. 'I won't hae nort to do wi' he, nor enter the house where he is, for all we be related. – Come an' have a drink 'long wi' me, sir; now du; I asks 'ee. – 'Tis safer, yu know, for us not to meet.'

For the second time I lied, and escaped.

Uncle Jake ran up from the beach. 'Yer!' he said, 'there's a race to Saltmeadow, a veteran's race, for men over fifty. Yu come wi' me, an' I'll go in for it – an' beat the lot, I will. I knows I can.' Off we went, Uncle Jake in a high excitement. At the centre of the big oblong ring, two clean-built jumpers, men in the heyday of their strength, were making a local record for the high jump. Uncle Jake shouted out praise and sympathy to them. We found our way to where the veterans were grouped together, encouraging each other to enter with much foul language – which made them feel young again, no doubt. What a lot they were! some aged to thinness, others become fat and piggish. Only Uncle Jake appeared quite sound in wind and limb. He took off his boots and stockings, walked into the ring with a fine imitation of the athlete's swagger combined with a curious touch of shyness. 'Go it Uncle Jake!' they shouted. At the end of the first lap, he found himself so far ahead that he threw his old round sailor's cap high into the air and caught it, and he skipped along to the winning-post like a young lamb. A great cheer was echoed from cliff to cliff. Uncle Jake has not spoken his mind all his life for nothing. Seacombe does not unanimously like him, but it has the sense to be rather proud of him. A veterans' race is usually a sad spectacle, a grotesque *memento mori*: for Uncle Jake 'twas a triumph.

The next great sight of the evening was to watch the fishermen from other villages put off to their boats. Most of them were 'half seas over', some nearly helpless. They were thrown aboard from punts and had their sails hoisted for them; or, if they did it themselves, it was with most comic jerks. The gods, who un-doubtedly have a tenderness for drunkards – why not? – must have looked after them, for no news has come of any accident.

On returning in house, I met Tony with several of his men relatives. He drew me aside. 'Maybe I'll come home drunk to-night, but I promise 'ee I won't disturb 'ee, an' if yu hears ort – well, yu'll know, won' 'ee?'

For some reason not easily to be fathomed his kindly warning made me feel ashamed of my own sobriety, ashamed that I dared not 'go on the bust' with him. I firmly believe that it does a man good to 'go on the bust' occasionally. It develops fellow-feeling. And besides, who has the right to cast a stone at a man for snatching a little jollity when he may, be it alcoholic or not? The truth is, that Tony, who has no craving for drink, was prepared to plunge into the fastest current of the life around him, and to take his chance, whilst I, for niggardly, self-preservative, prudential reasons, was not.

However, he came home quite sober.

27

Up-country, next week, I shall greatly miss my window overlooking Alexandra Square. I have lived (rebelliously) in suburban streets where only clattering feet, tradesmen's carts and pitiful street singers broke the monotony; in a Paris *chambre à garçon, au sixième*, where the view was roofs and the noise of the city was attenuated to a murmur; in country houses which looked out on sweeps of hill, down, vale and sea, so changeable and lovely that they were dreamlike and as a dream abide in the memory . . . Here I have quick human life just below my window, and – up the Gut – a view of the sea unbroken hence to the horizon; a patch of water framed on three sides by straight walls and on the fourth by the sky-line; a miniature ocean across which the drifters sail to the western offing, and the little boats curvet to and fro, and

> The stately ships go on
> To their haven under the hill.

There is always, here, a sound of the sea. When, at night, the Square is still, it seems to advance, to come nearer, to be claiming one for its own.

But the Square, though still at night compared with daytime, is never dead, never absolutely asleep. Fishermen returning from sea crunch on the gravel. Lights in the windows (most of the people seem to burn night lamps) give it a cosy appearance; the cats make one think that fiends are pouring out of hell, through a hole in the roadway. Peep o' day is the stillest time of all. The cats seat themselves on walls. Sparrows chirp sleepily. Some rooks and a hoary-headed jackdaw come down from the trees nearby, quarter the roadway for garbage, and fly away croaking. Busy starlings follow. If the weather is hard and fish offal scarce on the beach, the gulls will pay us a supercilious visit. About six o'clock the children begin singing in bed, and soon afterwards one hears the familiar conversation of families getting up. 'Edie! what for the Lord's sake be yu doing? Yu'll catch your death o' cold. Johnnie, if yu don't make haste, I'll knock your head off, I will!' A child or two may cry, but on the whole their merriment does not seem greatly damped by their mothers' blood-curdling threats. I hear also, but not very often, the shrill wailing monotone, the weep dissolved in a shout, of a woman upbraiding her man for the previous night.

The children being dressed, but not washed (it is useless to wash the average child very long before sending it off to school), they run out to the beach to see what there is to be seen and to inspect the ash-buckets for treasure. An ash-bucket is Eldorado to them. If nothing is happening, are they at a loss for something to do? By no means. They come in house, fetch out tin cans, and beat them in a procession round the Square.

The milkmen arrive, then several greengrocers. One would think that Under Town lived on vegetables. The explanation is that the greengrocers can come here, and in tidying up their carts, can throw their refuse upon the roadway, as they would not be allowed to do in 'higher class' streets. They swear genially at the housewives, and are forgiven.

So the work and gossip of the day goes on, with a slight quieting down in the afternoon and an incredible amount of conversation after work, in the evening.

On Sundays, the great fact of best clothes lends a different and, to my mind, a less pleasant – a harder – tone to the children's voices. But their merriment cannot be wholly suppressed. Did those who dislike the Salvation Army wish to illustrate its short-comings, they could find a biting satire ready-made by the children of Under Town. A fat small boy comes round here, who has attentively studied the meetings; who can copy the canting, up-and-down, gentle-explosive, the *Behold I am saved, ye sinners!* tone to a nicety. He marches at the head of a band of serious infants who bear rags, tied to sticks and parasols, as banners. Every now and then he circles them to a standstill for an harangue about blood, fire and Jesus. (It is the gory part which delights him.) Then the procession re-forms, imitating brass instruments as unbroken voices can, and singing a Salvation hymn. They are earnest, the children; except Tommy Widger, whose irrepressible spirit causes him to march in the rear with a mocking dance and an infinitely grotesque squint. He is a pagan. He can turn the children's serious imitation into roaring Aristophanic farce. He represents the healthful laughing element of an age wherein rest from sorrow is too much sought in fever. He infects us all with jollity.

The back-door of the Alexandra, which opens on the Gut, is my home comedy. It is strangely fascinating; sad in a way, but very human; for nothing on earth, except one or two of the very great things of life, is so democratic as the back-door of a public house. Soon after breakfast, or even before, the tradesmen sneak round for their pick-me-ups. Then the housewives go for their jugs of ale and stout. Some people never enter the Alexandra except by the back way. They march down the Gut as if on important business; then, in the twinkling of an eye, they are gone within. One worn little woman, who wears a loose cape and a squalid sailor hat, walks up and down the Gut till it is completely clear, then jumps into the door, and closes it very quietly. When she comes out again it as a rabbit comes from a bolt-hole when a ferret is just behind. She runs five yards, stands still, looks up and down, and tries very hard to walk home unconcernedly. Sunday evenings, she hangs about outside until the bar is opened. With the turn of the key, in she goes. Once a servant, gossiping with her sailorman, kept the little woman outside for fully ten minutes after the lock was shot back. Poor little woman, how great her craving must be!

Last week, I saw a policeman standing at the top of the Gut. Up he looked; down he looked; Seacombe was orderly. Stepping as if to arrest a malefactor, he marched down the Gut . . . Where was the policeman? A battered billycock and a rakish pipe looked round the corner, then withdrew. The battered billycock knew where the policeman was. The price of a glass, and billycock would have been there too.

I was glad; for a few days before that the same policeman had arrested a man by flinging him halfway across the street into the mud. It was only a tramp. His witnesses, being poor people, dared not volunteer to give evidence on his behalf, and would not have been believed had they done so. He was sentenced to fourteen days: drunk and incapable, abusive moreover. A drunkard cannot legally be arrested unless he is also incapable or disorderly. It used to be a trick of the police to shadow a harmless *Weary Willie* until he happened to stumble, or even to butt him down themselves. He then becomes drunk and incapable within the meaning of the act, for, if the magistrate should doubt, is there not dirt on his clothes? Obviously, circumstantially, he was incapable. *He*, of course, must be a poor man. The trick is not safe with tradesmen. These things are commonplaces amongst the poor.

But billycock hat will not forget!

28

Yesterday morning early there was a great excitement along the beach. Drift-boats could be seen in the offing. 'I tell thee what 'tis,' they said, 'the whiting be in an' us chaps an't been out to look for 'em. Us don't du nort nowadays like us used tu.' Later on, however, we heard that the Plymouth drifters had been out after an autumn shoal of mackerel, had caught some thousands and had made good prices. The season for mackerel drifting here usually ends with July or August, but good October mackerel, mixed with herring, have occasionally been caught. Tony, John and myself decided to put to sea. When the other boats saw our fleet of nets being hauled aboard (in a furious hurry), they fitted out too.

We shoved off just before dark. The wind was strongish WSW. – off land, that is – so that inshore the sea was almost calm, except for the swell running in from outside. What it was like outside the white horses and the wind-streaks showed. Hardly had we gone half a mile before we heard the queer clutching noise which meant that a strong puff of wind had compelled Tony to let the sheet fly. The squall past, he hauled it in again, put his legs across the stern and hung on. We sailed eight miles from land in ten minutes under the hour – speed, that, for a twenty-two-foot open boat with its mainsail reefed! Where we downhauled to shoot the nets, the sea, unsheltered by cliffs and headlands, was – as Tony beautifully put it – 'rising all up in heaps'. Whilst I was trying to keep the boat before the wind, for net-shooting, a great comber plopped over the stern right upon my back. The sky was weird. Great wind-drifts of rain-cloud constantly spread out from the west, and wolves, higher up in the sky, were driving across the moon. We heated tea, but did not try to sleep. Tony and John kept up a curious dialogue. 'What do 'ee think o' it, then?'

''Tisn't vitty. I said so all along.'

'If a skat o' rain comes – and 'tis raining on land, seems so – the wind'll back out to sou'west, an' us'll hae to rin for it. A perty lop'll get up tu, an' we'm more'n a mile from land.'

'Us'll haul in be 'leven. No gude hanging on out here. If the wind *du* back . . .'

I have never heard them talk so much about the weather. And all the while, the sky drove into splendid cloud-forms, all windy, nearly all rainy. We lost the Eddystone light, then lost the Seacombe light and recovered the former, as a storm drifted along shore. From time to time we thought the wind was backing a bit.

Supper, for me, had to be crammed down on a rather queasy stomach. 'We'm all ways to once!' Tony remarked. The wind did definitely back a point or two. 'Only let it once die away,' said Tony in the tone of *I told you so*; 'then yu'll see how it can spring from the sou'west when 'tis a-minded.'

One minute I wished myself home, safe in bed, and thought with grotesque grief of some unfinished work. Next minute, I knew that I would not have missed the night out there for any consideration. The grey, slightly sheeny boil of the sea around us; the sweeping savagery of the sky; the intimacy of the waters . . .

But we were all relieved when eleven o'clock came. The watchfulness was a strain.

When one is steering instead of hauling, the getting-in of nine forty-fathom nets seems interminable. One net, two nets, three nets – a third of nine, – four, five – more than half the fleet, – six – two-thirds of nine, – seven, eight – nine all but one; – and so on, with an occasional wave coming inboard, until the very last square buoy comes bobbing towards the boat; hand over hand, buoy by buoy, net by net, holding fast when the pull of the tide is too strong, and pausing irritably to pick out the fish. We stepped the great mast, shifted all the ballast to wind'ard. John came aft to steer, and seated himself on the counter, a strangely powerful, statuesque figure in his wet oilskins. 'Have 'ee got the sheet in yer hand?' Tony called out from the bows.

John did not trouble to reply.

'Have 'ee got the sheet in yer hand, John?'

'No, I an't! What the hell do 'ee wunt the sheet for? Wind's abeam.'

'Might want it bad,' said Tony.

We left it fast however; and with the same, an elemental passion took possession of my mind; ousted all else. I had been anxious about the sheet, had thought John foolhardy. Now I didn't care. I could have cried out aloud for joy as the brave old craft rose to the seas with a marvellous easy motion and the waves came skatting in over the bows. Before long, I was on my knees with the baler; John was getting every inch out of the wind, and Tony was standing abaft the nets with the sheet dangling through his hand. By the light of the riding-lamp on the mizzen mast (its glass patched with an old jam cover), they in their angular wet oilskins – the rain was pelting – and the rich wet brown of the boat's varnish, made a wonderful Rembrandtesque picture. I hardly know how long we were sailing home; it slipped my mind to take the time. About two o'clock I was halfway down the beach with Tony cursing above me and John doing the same below. Someone had 'messed up' our capstan wire. While Tony was putting that right in the dark – and pinching his fingers severely – the boat washed broadside on and began to fill. We had only five dozen fish. They sold badly.

In time, and with practice, I could, I believe, do most that these fishermen do except one thing: I doubt I could stand the racket of my own thoughts. Tony and John would go out to-night, to-morrow, every night. But I have slept so dead (not from bodily tiredness) that, the door being bolted against the children, they were unable to waken me for dinner, and in the end Tony told them to 'let the poor beast bide'. Of what nature was that passion, so exultant and so tiring? Are these fishermen so used to it that they 'don't take much note o'it'? For they feel it. I have seen it in their faces. One can always tell. The eyes widen and brighten; hasty movements become so desperately cool. If what was an episode in my life, is part and parcel of theirs, how much the better for *them*!

29

To-day the sea passion, or whatever it is, came again.

While I was asleep, the wind backed and freshened. Balks of wood from a naval target kept washing in. Balks make winter firing when coal is dear and money scarce. Boats had bringing them in all the morning, till the sea became too rough. Tony had none however. In the afternoon he complained bitterly:

'They all got some wude but me, an' us an't got enough in house for the winter nuther.' Just then we saw a large piece washing along on the flood tide over the outside of Broken Rocks. 'Get a rope – grass rope, mind. Down with her. The *Cock Robin*! Quick. Jump aboard. Take oars. Hurry up casn'? Get hold thic oar. Look out!'

No time to wait for a smooth. Tony shoved the *Cock Robin* into a surf we should not otherwise have thought of facing. As it turned out, we got off better than we usually do in only a moderate sea, though we should have capsized to a certainty had the boat sheered. 'Twas, 'Look out! Damme, look out! Here's a swell coming! Get her head to it or we'm over. Gude for us!' Some of the waves, rising and topping in the shallow water over the rocks, seemed to make the *Cock Robin* sit upright on her stern, like a dog begging, and the higher the seas rose the more we gloried in them. Sufficient for the moment was the wave therof. We swore at each other in a sort of chant. I had to repress an impulse to jump overboard and swim to the balk, instead of trying to work up to it with a boat that had, every other moment, to be turned bows on to the sea. The slightest error of judgment on Tony's part, and we should indeed have swum for it. I had such a curious feeling of being *in* the sea – as much a part of it as the waves themselves – that the affair ceased to be a struggle. It became a glorious great big game. Yet for work we were so cool that, though we towed our balk ashore and shoved off after another, we hardly got wet above the knees.

We were beside ourselves, and all ourselves. Where does that exultant feeling, that devil-beyond-oneself, come from? From what depth of human personality does it uprise, whirling, like those primitive passions – sex, hunger, rage, fear – which may be boxed up awhile by the will, but which, once unloosed, sweep the will aside and carry one off like froth in a gale, until physical exhaustion sets in and allows the will to re-assert itself? One understands the evolution of the primitive self-preservative and race-preservative passions. How has this latent daredevilry become so implanted in us that it rises from the bottom depths of one's nature; and how has it become ordinarily so hidden?

Above all what is the effect of this passion on seafaring men? To say that familiarity breeds contempt is – even if it be correct – to beg the question. What is the effect of that familiarity? It might be said that they are the subjects of a sub-acute, persistent form of the daredevilry which uprose in me unexpectedly and acutely. But again, the sub-acute lifelong form of it is likely to have the greater influence on a man's self, on his morale and his character. Hence, I believe, the width of these men, their largeness. It was good to hear Tony talk in the most matter of fact manner (yet with a touch of reverence, as towards an ever-possible contingency) of a Salcombe fisherman who was drowned. 'Her was drownded all through his own carelessness, and didn't rise in the water for a month. ('Tis nine days down and nine days up, wi' the crab bites out of 'ee, as a rule.) An' he wer carried up by the tide an' collected, like, out o' the water just at the back o' his own house. Nice quiet chap he was.' That coolness of speech one saw plainly, is the outcome not of contempt, still less of non-feeling, but of familiarity, of a breadth of mind in looking at the catastrophe. I have not noticed such breadth of mind elsewhere except among those who live precariously and the few of very great religious faith.

An hour after bringing in the balks, we were hauling the boats over the wall, and at high tide the seas swept across the road.

30

Many an evening we have had small sing-songs in the kitchen. To-night, on account of my going and the need to give me a cheery send-off, we had quite a concert. Tony was star.

Supper being pushed back on the table and a piece of wreckage flung on the fire, he made himself ready by taking off his soaked boots and stockings, and plumping his feet on Mam Widger's lap; then brought himself into the vocal mood with a long rigmarole that he used to recite with the Mummers at Christmas time. Soon we were humming, whistling and singing 'Sweet Evelina', whose sole musical merit is that her chorus goes with a swing. The fire crackled and burnt blue. The fragrant steam of the grog rose to the ceiling and settled on the window. We leaned right back in our chairs.

'Missis,' said Tony, 'I feels like zingin' to-night.'

'Wait a minute while I shuts the door, else they kids'll be down for more supper.'

'Us got it, an't us?'

'Yes, but *they*'ve had enough.'

When Tony sings, he throws his head back and closes his eyes, so that, but for the motions of his mouth, he looks asleep, even deathlike, and is, in fact, withdrawn into himself.

I think he sees his songs, as well as sings them. I often wonder what pictures are flitting through his mind beneath (as I imagine) the place where the thick grizzled hair thins to the red forehead. His voice is a high tenor. I make accompaniment an octave below, whilst Mrs Widger – a little nasal in tone and not infrequently adrift in tune – supports him from above.

We sang 'The Poor Smuggler's Boy'—

> Your pity I crave,
>   Won't you give me employ?
> Or forlorn I must wander,
>   Said the poor smuggler's boy.

Then the 'Skipper and his Boy'—

> Over the mounting waves so 'igh,
> We'll sail together, my boy and I-I,
> We'll sail together, my bo-oy and I!

'Have 'ee wrote to George?' Tony asked.
''Tis your place to du that.'
'I an't got time . . .'
'Thee asn't got time for nort!'

> The fisher's is a merry life!
>   Blow, winds, blow!
> The fisher and his vitty wife!
>   Row, boys, row!
> He drives no plough on stubborn land,
> His fruits are ready to his hand,
> No nipping frosts his orchards fear,
> He has his autumn all the year,
>   Blow, winds, blow!
> The farmer has his rent to pay,
>   Blow, winds, blow!
> And seeds to purchase every day,
>   Row, boys, row!
> But he who farms the rolling deep,
> He never sows, can always reap,
> The ocean's fields are fair and free,
> There ain't no rent days on the sea;
>   The fisher's is a merry life!
>   Blow, winds, blow!
>   Blow, damn ye, blow!

'Aye!' said Tony with conviction, 'thic's one side o'it.'

He tried a note or two at different pitches, then struck with energy into the fine song, 'Rolling Home'. (Who that has steered for England in a ship – and by ship I do not mean a bustling steam-packet or a floating hotel, but a ship to whose crew England stands for fresh food, women, wine, home . . . Who that has so steered the course for England, does not feel a catch at his vitals on hearing the melody, at once plaintive and triumphant, of 'Rolling Home'?)

Pipe all hands to man the capstan, see your cables run down clear;
Soon our ship will weigh her anchor, for old England's shores we steer;
If we heave round with a will boys, soon our anchor it will trip,
And across the briny ocean we will steer our gallant ship:

> Rolling home, rolling home!
> Rolling home across the sea!
> Rolling home to Merrie England!
> Rolling home, true love, to thee!

Man the bars then with a will, boys, clap all hands that can clap on;
As we heave around the capstan, we will sing this well-known song;
It will bring back scenes and changes of this parting gift so rare;
We shall hear sweet songs of music softly whispering through the air.

> Rolling home, rolling home!
> Rolling home across the sea!
> Rolling home to Merrie England!
> Rolling home, true love, to thee!

Up aloft amid the rigging, as we sail the waters blue,
Whilst we cross the briny ocean, we will always think of you;
We will leave you our best wishes as we leave this rocky shore;
We are bound for Merrie England, to return to you no more!

> Rolling home, rolling home!
> Rolling home, across the sea!
> Rolling home to Merrie England!
> Rolling home, my love to thee!

To Mrs Widger's great disgust, Tony has been learning *in bed* the correct words (he knew the tune) of 'Gay Spanish Ladies'. That he gave us as a finale.

> Farewell and adieu to you, gay Spanish Ladies.
> Farewell and adieu to you, Ladies of Spain!
> For we've received orders for to sail for old England.
> But we hope in a short time to see you agan.
>
> We'll rant and we'll roar like true British heroes,
> We'll rant and we'll roar across the salt seas,
> Until we strike soundings in the Channel of old England.
> From Ushant to Scilly is thirty-five leagues . . .

How we did rant and roar the wonderful up-Channel verse, with its clever use of the high-sounding promontories of the south!

> The first land we made, it was called the Deadman,
> Next Ram Head off Plymouth, Start, Portland and Wight,
> We passed up by Beachy, by Farley and Dungeness,
> And hove our ship to off the South Foreland light . . .

Our glasses were empty. We drove out the cat, gutted some fish, extinguished the lamp, and came upstairs to the tune, repeated, of 'Rolling Home'. All the tunes are ringing in my head.

There is something about this singing of sea-songs by a seafarer which makes them grip one extraordinarily. They are far from perfect in execution, they are not always quite in tune, especially on Tony's high notes, yet, I am certain, they are as artistic in the best sense as any of the fine music I have heard. Tony sings with imagination: he sees, *lives* what he is singing. Between this sort of song and most, there is much the same difference as between going abroad, and reading a book of travels; or between singing folk-songs with the folk and twittering bowdlerized versions in a drawing-room. However imperfect technically, Tony's songs are an expression of the life he lives, rather than an excursion into the realms of art – into the expression of other kinds of life – with temporarily stimulated and projected imagination. His art is perpetual creation, not repetition of a thing created once and for all. The art that is *lived*, howsoever imperfect, has an advantage over the most finished art that is merely repeated. Next after the music of, as one might say, superhuman creative force – like Bach's and Beethoven's – comes this kind, of Tony's.

Cultured people talk about the artistic tastes of the poor, would have them read – well, they don't quite know what – something 'good', something namely that appeals to the cultured. It has always been my experience in much lending of books, that the poor will read the literature of life's fundamental daily realities quickly enough, once they know of its existence. What they will not read, what in the struggle for existence they cannot waste time over, is the literature of the *etceteras* of life, the decorations, the vapourings. Sane minds, like healthy bodies, crave strong meats, and the strong meats of literature are usually the worst cooked. I am inclined to think that the taste of the poor, the uneducated, is on the right lines, though undeveloped, whilst the taste of the educated consists of beautifully developed wrongness, an exquisite secession from reality. As Nietzsche pointed out, degenerates love narcotics; something to make them forget life, not face it. Their meats must be strange and peptonized. Therefore they hate, they are afraid of, the greatest things in life – the commonplace. Much culture has debilitated them. Rank life would kill them – or save them.

VI

1

IT is just at dawn that the coming day declares itself most plainly;
not earlier, not later. This morning at peep o' day the wind was
NNW., the air delicate and peaceful. A band of dirty red water
washed in fantastic outline along the cliffs. The sea, with its calm
great rollers, bore upon it only the rags of last night's fury; as if it
had been less a part of the storm than a thing buffeted by the
storm, and now glad to sink into tranquility. The air was scented
with land smells. Shafts of the dawn's sunlight beamed across it.
Three punts put off to find out if the lobster-pots had been washed
away; the sea had its little boats upon it again. But the sky, to the
SW., was looking very wild. The wind was SW. in the offing.

While we were at breakfast a southerly squall burst open the
kitchen door. Mrs Widger got up to see what child it was. A
screaming sea-gull mocked her.

The storm came. The trees by the railway bowed and tossed.
Rain spattered against the carriage windows. Dead leaves scurried
by. I wanted to get out, to go back. I wanted to know whether
Tony was at sea. Here, at Salisbury they are already talking about
the 'great storm'; some of the beautiful elms are down. What
must the storm have been at Seacombe!

Curiously, I felt, the first time for years, as if I were
leaving home for boarding school – the warmth behind, the chill
in front. I smelt again the rank soft-soap in the great bare
schoolrooms.

2

A postcard from Tony—

   quite please to get your letter this morning it as been rough ever since
you left Seacombe it was a gale the night you went Back the sea was all in
over and knocking the boats about the road. I haven been out sea sinsce it
is still rough hear now it is blowing a gale of wind I expect we shall get

some witing and herring in the bay when the weather get fine the sea hear is like the cliff now red. Us aven catched nort nobody cant go to sea.

TONY

I will write a letter soon.

P.S. Tony just waked up. George is coming home, Tony mazed with excitement and wishes you was here.

MAM W.

So do I!

3

The evening before I left Seacombe, Tony was telling us how upset and miserable he was, how he cried, when his two elder brothers left home to join the Navy. Also he told us what I knew nothing of before – his own one attempt to go to sea aboard a merchantman. When he was at Cloade's he looked on fishing as a refuge from groceries, and when he had given up groceries for fishing, he looked on a ship's fo'c'stle as a refuge from that. Fishing was very bad one summer. He and Dick Yeo agreed to run away together:

'Us was doin' nort noway wi' the fishing – nort't all. Father, Granfer that is, wer away to his drill wi' the Royal Naval Reserves. So Dick Yeo an' me agreed to go off together. Where he went, I was to go tu, an' where I went, he was to come. He had two pounds put away, in gold. I only had half a crown, an' cuden't see me way to get no more nuther. "Casn' thee ask thy maid for some?" Dick said. I was ashamed, like, but I did.

'"What's thee want it for?" her asked.

'"'Tisn' nothing doing down here," I says, "an' I wants to go to sea."

'"I an't got no money," the maid says.

'"Casn' thee get nort?" I asks, having begun, you see. I'd been goin' with her for nigh on two years.

'Her cried bitter at the thought o' me going, but her did get seven shillin's from a fellow servant. I told me mother – her cried tu' – an' off us started, going by train to Bristol and stopping the night at the Sailor's Rest. 'Twasn't bad, you know. They Restis be gude things. Dick, he woke in the morning wi' a swelled faace, but I didn' feel nort.

'Dick Yeo paid both our boat fares from Bristol to Cardiff. The steward – what us urned against aboard ship – recommended us to a lodging house in Adelaide Street, an' he giv'd me a note for a man at the Board o' Trade, sayin' we was Demshire fishin' chaps an' gude seamen.

'Well, us went to the lodging house an' gave in our bags an' took a room wi' fude [food] for two an' six a day – each, mind yu. Then us looked into a big underground room wer there was a lot o' foreigners gathered round a fire an' us didn' much like the looks o' that. So us went straight down to the docks an' tried to ship together on several sailing ships an' steamers. Some on 'em would on'y take me, an' some were down to sail at a future date, like, what our money wouldn't last out tu. *I* cude ha' got a ship, 'cause I had me Naval Reserve ticket, but nobody cuden't du wi' both on us – an' where one went t'other was to go tu, by agreement.

'Us went back to the lodging house, into a sort o' kitchen in a cellar, where there was a 'Merican wi' a long white beard cooking, an' men drunk spewing, an' men lying about asleep like logs. The 'Merican, his beard looking so red as hell in the firelight, wer stirring some kind o' stew. Yu shude ha' see'd the faaces what the glow o' they coals shined on! An' the fude . . . An' the tables an' plates . . . I've a-gone short many a time in my day, but I'd never ha' touched muck like they offered to gie us there. Dick an' me crept up the staircase to bed wi' empty bellies thic night.

'Soon a'ter we was to bed, Dick says to me: "Can 'ee feel ort yer Tony?"

'"No," I says, an' whatever 'twas, I didn' feel ort o'it. But I see'd 'em crawling so thick as sea-lice on the wall in a southerly gale, an' I tell 'ee, 'twas they things what took the heart out o' me more'n ort else, aye! more'n the food an' being away from home. Us cuden turn out, 'cause the landlord had our bags an' us hadn' got no money to get 'em back wi', nor nowhere else at all to go tu.

'Next morning, us went straight down to the docks again. Cuden' eat no breakfast what they give'd us. Didn' know what to du. I only had tuppence left, which wuden' ha' taken me home again, not if I'd been willing to give up and go. Come to the last, us was forced to break our agreement. I signed on as able seaman – *able* seaman 'cause I was a fishing chap an' had me Royal Naval Reserve ticket – aboard the *Brooklands*, bound for Bombay. Penny o' me tuppence, I spent writing home to tell mother. I cuden' stay aboard the ship (an' get summat to eat) 'cause I had my gear to get an' a ship to find for Dick – an' we still had hopes, like, o' getting a ship together. Howsbe-ever, us cuden't, nohow. The writer aboard the *Brooklands* wuden't advance me no wages to get any gear. He told me the landlord to the lodging house wude, him what had our bags a'ready.

'Then I thought o' the steward's note to the Board o' Trade officer, an' us inquired our way to the Board o' Trade, where ther was a gert crowd outside. 'Twas by that us know'd the place. A man told us as the officer what the note was directed tu, wude appear outside the door an' call. Sure 'nuff, he did – wi' gold buttons on his coat – an' called out: "Six A.B.'s for the *Asia*"!

'"Who be that?" I asked.

'"That's he," the man said. "He'll come out again by'm-bye."

'Us worked our way to the front – getting cussed horrible for our pains – an' when Mr Gold-Buttons 'peared again, I give'd him the steward's note. He luked at it – an' us. He cude offer me something an' said as he'd du his best for me, but he cuden' hold out no promise for Dick because, see, he hadn' got no Naval Reserve ticket.

'"Wher Dick goes, I goes," I says, like that. With which the Board o' Trade officer leaves us waiting there.

'After an hour or so, he com'd out an' called, as if he hadn' ha' know'd us: "Anthony Widger an' Richard Yeo! Richard Yeo an' Anthony Widger o' Seacombe!"

'"Yer we be, sir," shouts I, thinking we was fixed up.

'"Be yu Anthony Widger an' Richard Yeo? Come in."

'Dick, he went in behind the officer, an' me behind Dick. 'Twer a darkish passage, but as the door closed I luked, an' there, hidden behind the door, sort o' flattened against the wall, who did I see but Dick's mother; her'd come all that way by herself. I called to Dick.

'"What the bloody hell be doin' here?" said Dick swearing awful.

'"Don't thee swear at thy mother, Dick," I says.

'"Dick!" her says, "Dick, come home again. Your father's breakin' his heart."

'"Go to b——ry!" says Dick, swearing worse'n ever, 'cause *he* was wanting in his heart to be home again, yu see.

'I burst out crying, then and there, wi' seeing Dick's mother cry, an' all o'it what we'd been drough. The Board o' Trade officer repeated as he'd help me an' no doubt find me a ship, but Dick – his mother was come'd for he.

'"Wer Dick goes, I goes," says I.

'Then Dick's mother, her says: "Will 'ee come home then, Tony?"

'"Wer Dick goes, I goes," I says again. 'Twas fixed in me head, like.

'"Well," her says, "if Dick comes home, will yu come too?"

'I told her: "I've a-signed on aboard the *Brooklands*, an' I'll hae to tramp it 'cause I an't got no money."

'"Well, if I pays *your* fare too?"

'"Wer Dick goes, I'll go!" I says.

'So her got over Dick a bit, an' the Board o' Trade man told us to come again, saying as he'd do anything for me, but Dick's mother was come'd for he. An' Mrs Yeo asked us to go wi' her to a restaurant . . . That turned me more'n ort else 'cause us hadn' eaten the stuff to the lodging house an' us *was* hungry. An' her telegraphed home to Dick's father for a trap to meet us to Totnes, for 'twas a Saturday an' there wern't no trains no nearer home.

'Us went to the station, Dick swearing awful, an' in the end us come'd to Totnes to find the trap.

'The trap was there at the inn, sure 'nuff, an' the ostler was waiting up, but the man what come'd wi' the trap was disappeared. We on'y found 'en at two in the morning, sleeping dead drunk in the manger, an' then he an' the ostler began fighting on account o' the ostler casting out a slur 'cause Dick's mother didn' gie him no more than a shilling. A policeman come an' cleared us out o' it!

'Two or dree mile out o' Totnes the horse stops dead an' begins to go back'ards. Us coaxed 'en, like, an' still he kept on stopping an' walking back'ards. Dick an' me got out to walk to the halfway inn. There the landlord wuden' come down for us. But he did when the trap come'd up – us was carriage people than, yu see. We had drinks round, an' us give'd flour an' water to the horse to make 'en go. But us hadn' gone far when he stopped an' began to go back'ards again. Dick, he started swearing. "Let's walk on," I says, to get 'en out o'it; an' so us did for a mile or so. 'Twas dark, wi' a mizzling rain – an' quiet – an' the trees like shadows. A proper logie night 'twas. Wude 'ee believe me when I says I cude smell the flowers I cuden' see? Us was glad when a tramp caught up wi' us.

'"Have 'ee see'd ort o' a horse an' trap wi' two persons in 'en?" I asks.

'"Two mile back," he says.

'"Us lef' 'en only a mile back," Dick says.

'"He've a-gone a mile back'ards then!" says I.

"And with the same, Dick laughs out loud, an' I laughs, an' the tramp, he laughs . . . 'Twas the first laugh us had since us left Seacombe, an' I reckon it did us gude. Us went on better a'ter that. I covered the tramp up wi' hay in a hay loft, advising of him not to smoke. I could h' slept tu; I wer heavy for a gude bed; but I saw lights in the farmhouse winder, an' us wer so near home again.

'Well, we crept into Seacombe by the back (people was jest astir, Sunday morning) going each our way from the churchyard, an' I listened outside mother's door. Father was home again, an' they was to breakfast. Her'd had my letter telling them as I'd a-shipped for Bombay.

'"They'll Bumbay the beggar!" father was saying, only 'twasn't "beggar" as he did say.

'Then my sister Mary, cried out: "Here's Tony!"

'"I know'd *he'd* never go to Bumbay!" outs father so quick as ever.

'But they was so pleased as Punch to see Tony back, cas I ude see, if they'd ha' cared to say so. I don' know 'xactly why I went off to sea – summut inside driving of me – 'twasn't only 'cause there wern't nothing doin' – but I an't never been no more. An' thic Mam Widger there'd hae summut to say about it now. Eh, Annie?'

4

It is an Englishman's privilege to grumble, and a sailorman's duty; yet one thing always strikes me in talking to seafaring men, namely how indelible the sea's stamp is; how indissolubly they are bound to the sea – with sunken bonds like those which unite an old married couple, – and also what outbursts of savage hatred they have against it. Tony says that if he could earn fifteen shillings a week regularly on land, he would give up the sea altogether. I very much doubt it. The sea has him fast. He says further that nobody would go to sea unless he were caught young and foolish, and that few would stay there if they could get away. There are, among the older fishermen of Seacombe, some who have worked well, and could still work, but prefer to stay ashore and starve. Tony holds them excused. 'Aye!' he says, 'they've a-worked hard in their day, an' they knows they ain't no for'ar-der. An' now they'm weary o' it all, an' don't care; an' that's how I'll be some day, if I lives – weary o'it, an' just where I was!'

But the sea has her followers, and will continue to have them, because seafaring is the occupation in which health, strength and courage have their greatest value; in which being a man most nearly suffices a man. It is remarkable that Baudelaire, decadent Frenchman, apostle of the artificial, who was violently home-sick when he went on a voyage, should have expressed the relation of man and the sea – their enmity and love – more subtly than any English poet.

> Homme libre, toujours tu chériras la mer;
> La mer et ton miroir; tu contemples ton âme
> Dans le déroulement infini de sa lame,
> Et ton esprit n'est pas un gouffre moins amer.

Tu te plais à plonger au sein de ton image;
Tu l'embrasses des yeux et des bras, et ton cœur
Se distrait quelquefois de sa propre rumeur
Au bruit de cette plainte indomptable et sauvage.

Vous êtes tous les deux ténébreux et discrets:
Homme, nul n'a sondé le fond de tes abîmes,
O mer, nul ne connaît tes richesses intimes,
Tant vous êtes jaloux de garder vos secrets!

Et cependant voilà des siècles innombrables
Que vous vous combattez sans pitié ni remord,
Tellement vous aimez le carnage et la mort,
O lutteurs éternels, ô frères implacables!

The sea is never mean. Strife and brotherhood with it give a
largeness to men which, like all deep qualities of the spirit, can be
neither specified nor defined; only felt, and seen in the outcome.
The Seacombe fishermen are more or less amphibious; ocean-
going seamen look down on them. They are petty in some small
things, notably in jealousy lest one man do more work, or make
more money, than another: to say a man is doing well is to throw
out a slur against him. Nevertheless in the larger, the essential
things of life, their sea-largeness nearly always shows itself, They
are wonderfully charitable, not merely with money. They carp at
one another, but let a man make a mess of things, and he is gently
treated. I have never heard Tony admit that any man – even one
who had robbed him – had not his very good points. Is a man a
ne'er-do-well, a drunkard, an idler? 'Ah,' they say, 'his father rose
he up like a gen'leman, an' that's what comes o'it.' In their
dealings, they curiously combine generosity and close-fistedness
– close-fistedness in earning, and generosity in spending and
lending. A beachcomber, for simply laying a hand to a rope,
receives a pint of beer, or the price of it, and next moment the
fisherman who paid the money may be seen getting wet through
and spoiling his clothes in order to drag a farthing's worth of
jetsam from the surf. Tony fails to understand how a gen'leman
can possibly haggle over the hire of a boat. When he goes away

himself, he pays what is asked; regrets it afterwards, if at all; and comes home when his money is done. 'If a gen'leman,' he says, 'can't afford to pay the rate, what du 'ee come on the beach to hire a boat for – an' try to beat a fellow down? I reckon 'tis only a *sort o' gen'leman* as does that!'

Like most seafarers, the fishermen are fatalistic. 'What's goin' to be, will be, an' that's the way o'it.' But they are not thoroughgoing fatalists, inasmuch as disappointment quickly turns to resentment against something handy to blame. If, for example, we catch no fish, Tony will blame the tide, the hour, the weather, the boat, the sail, the leads, the line, the hooks, the bait, the fish, his mate – anything rather than accept the one fact that, for reasons unknown, the fish are off the bite. A thoroughgoing fatalist would blame, if he did not acquiesce in, fate itself or his luck.

Tony is a black pessimist as regards the present and to-morrow; convinced that things are not, and cannot be, what they were; but as regards the further future, the day after to-morrow, he is a resolute optimist. 'Never mind how bad things du look, summut or other'll sure to turn up. It always du. I've a-proved it. I've a-see'd it scores o' times.' He can earn money by drifting for mackerel and herring, hooking mackerel, seining for mackerel, sprats, flat-fish, mullet and bass, bottom-line fishing for whiting, conger or pout, lobster and crab potting, and prawning; by belonging to the Royal Naval Reserve; by boat-hiring; by carpet-beating and cleaning up. I have even seen him dragging a wheel chair. His boats and gear represent, I suppose, a capital of near a hundred pounds. It would be hard if he earned nothing. Yet he is certain that his earnings, year in and year out, scarcely average fifteen shillings a week. 'Yu wears yourself out wi' it an' never gets much for'arder.' The money, moreover, comes in seasons and lump-sums; ten pounds for a catch perhaps, then nothing for weeks. Mrs Widger must be, and is, a good hand at household management and at putting money by. I doubt if Tony ever knows how much, or how little, gold she has, stored away upstairs. Probably it is as well. He is a generous man with money. He 'slats it about' when he has it.

It has to be realised that these fishermen exercise very great skill and alertness. To sail a small open boat in all weathers requires a quicker hand and judgment than to navigate a seagoing ship. Seacombe possesses no harbour, and therefore Seacombe men can use no really seaworthy craft. ''Tis all very well,' Tony says, 'for people to buzz about the North Sea men an' knit 'em all sorts o' woollen gear. They North Sea men an' the Cornishmen wi' their big, decked harbour boats, they *have* got summut under their feet – somewhere they can get in under, out the way o'it. They *can* make themselves comfor'able, an ride out a storm. But if it comes on to blow when we'm to sea in our little open craft, we got to hard up an' get home along – if us can. For the likes o' us, 'tis touch an' go wi' the sea!'

Tony knows. At places like Seacombe every boat, returning from sea, must run ashore and be hauled up the beach and even, in rough weather, over the sea-wall. The herring and mackerel drifters, which may venture twenty miles into the open sea, cannot be more than twenty-five feet in length else they would prove unwieldy ashore. To avoid their heeling over and filling in the surf, they must be built shallow, with next to no keel. They have therefore but small hold on the water; they do not sail close to the wind, and beating home against it is a long wearisome job. Again, because the gear for night work in small craft must be as simple as possible, such boats usually carry only a mizzen and a dipping lug – the latter a large, very picturesque, but unhandy, sail which has to be lowered or 'dipped' every time the boat tacks. Neither comfort nor safety is provided by the three feet or so of decking, the 'cuddy' or 'cutty,' in the bows. To sleep there with one's head underneath, is to have one's feet outside, and *vice versa*. In rough broken seas the open beach drifter must be handled skilfully indeed, if she is not to fill and sink.

I have watched one of them running home in a storm. The wind was blowing a gale; the sea running high and broken. One error in steering, one grip of the great white sea-horses, meant inevitable wreck. Every moment or two the coastguard, who was near me with a telescope to his eye, exclaimed, 'She's down!' But no. She dodged the combers like a hare before greyhounds, now steering east, now west, on the whole towards home. It was with half her rudder gone that she ran ashore after a splendid exhibition of skill and nerve, many times more exciting than the manoeuvres of a yacht race. Were there not many such feats of seamanship among fishermen, there would be more widows and orphans.

Those are the craft, those the sort of men – two usually to a boat – that put to sea an hour or two before sunset, ride at the nets through the night, and return towards or after dawn. Anything but a moderate breeze renders drifting impossible. In a calm, the two men are bound to row, for hours perhaps, with heavy 16–20 ft. sweeps. Moreover, if the sea makes, or a ground swell rises, the least mistake in beaching a boat will cause it to sheer round, capsize, and wash about in the breakers with the crew most probably beneath it. Yarns are told of arms and legs appearing, of a horrible tortured face appearing, while the upturned boat washed about in the undertow, and those ashore were powerless to help. There is nothing the fishermen dread so much. One of them owns to leaving the beach when he has seen a boat running in on a very rough sea, so that he might not endure witnessing what he could not prevent. – He peeped however.

These risks need considering, not in order to exaggerate the dangers of drifting in open beach boats – in point of fact, accidents seldom do happen, – but to show what skill is habitually exercised, what a touch and go with the sea it is.

Sundown is the time for shooting nets. Eight to fourteen are carried for mackerel, six to ten for herrings – the scantier the fish, the greater the number of nets. At Seacombe they are commonly forty fathoms in length along the headrope which connects them all, and five fathoms deep. Stretching far away from the boat, as it drifts up and down Channel with the tides, is a line, perhaps a thousand yards long, of cork buoys. From these hang the lanyards[1] which support the headrope, from the headrope hang perpendicularly the nets themselves. Judgment is needed in shooting a fleet of nets. They may get foul of the bottom or of

[1] For herrings the lanyards may be of such a length that the foot of the net almost touches the sea-bottom. For mackerel, which is a surface and midwater fish, they are much shorter, so that the headrope lies just below the top of the water.

another boat's fleet. When, on account of careless shooting or tricks of the tide, the nets of several boats become entangled, there is great confusion, and the cursing is loud.

Nets shot, the fishermen make fast the road for'ard; sup, smoke, sing, creep under the cutty, and sleep with one eye open.

Sometimes they are too wet to sleep; often in the winter it is too cold.

Afterwards, the laborious hauling in – one man at the headrope and the other at the foot. Contrary to a very general impression, the fish are not enclosed within the net, as in seining or in pictures of the miraculous draught of fishes. They prod their snouts into the meshes, and are caught by the gills. There may not be a score in a whole fleet of nets, or they may come up like a glittering mat, beyond the strength of two men to lift over the gunwale. Twenty-five thousand herring is about the burthen of an open beach drifter. Are there more, nets must be given away at sea, or buoyed up and left – or cut, broken, lost. Small catches are picked out of the nets as they are hauled in, large catches ashore.

It is ashore that the fisherman comes off worst of all. Neither educated nor commercialized, he is fleeced by the buyers. And if he himself dispatches his haul to London . . . Dick Yeo once went up to Billingsgate and saw his own fish sold for about ten pounds. On his return to Seacombe, he received three pounds odd, and a letter from the salesman to say that there had been a sudden glut in the market. Fishermen boat-owners have an independence of character which makes it difficult for them to combine together effectively, as wage-servers do. They act too faithfully on the adage that a bird in the hand is worth two in the bush, and ten shillings on the beach is a sovereign at Billingsgate. So 'tis, when

> There's little to earn and many to keep,

and no floating capital at a man's disposal.

In recent years, owing to bad prices and seasons and general lack of encouragement, or even of fair opportunity, the number of sea-going drifters at Seacombe has decreased by two-thirds. Much the same has happened at other small fishing places along the coast. This decline – so complacently acquiesced in by the powers that be – is of national importance; for the little fisheries are the breeding ground of the Navy. Nowadays fishermen put their sons to work on land. ''Tain't wuth it,' they say, 'haulin' yer guts out night an' day, an' gettin' no forrarder at the end o'it.' Luckily for England the sea's grip is a firm one, and many of the sons return to it.

When one hears Luscombe talk about the maddening trouble he has had in teaching plough-tail or urban recruits to knot and splice a rope, or watches, as I have, a couple of blue-jackets drive ashore in a small boat because they couldn't hoist sail, then one comprehends better the importance of the fisher-families whose work is made up of endurance, exposure, nerve and skill; who play touch and go with the sea; and who in the slack seasons have – unlike the ordinary workman – only too much time to think for themselves. They are the backbone of the Navy.

VII

I

WHILST the train was drawing up at the platform, I noticed the people moving and looking downwards as if dogs were running wild amongst them. Then I saw two whitish heads bobbing about in the crowd. It was Jimmy and another boy come to meet me.

We gave the luggage to the busman, and walked on down.

'Tommy's gone tu Plymouth.'

'What for?'

'They'm going to cut his eyes out an' gie 'en spectacles.'

'When did he go?'

A rather sulky silence . . .

Then: 'Us thought 'ee was going to ride down. Dad said as yu'd be sure tu.'

''Tisn't far to walk, Jimmy . . .'

'Us be tired.'

Alack! I had done the wrong thing. Their little festivity, that was to have made them the envy of 'all they boys tu beach,' had fallen flat. They had expected to ride down 'like li'l gentry-boys.' However, we bought oranges, and then I was taken to see yesterday's fire, and was told how Tony had rushed into the blazing house to rescue a carpet 'an' didn' get nort for it.'

Tony himself came downstairs from putting away an hour in bed. 'I'd ha' come up to meet 'ee,' he said sleepily, 'if anybody'd a reminded me o'it. Us an't done nort to the fishing since you went away.'

'An' yu an't chopped up to-morrow morning's wude nuther!' added Mrs Widger.

Grannie Pinn came in at tea-time. We invited her to sit down and have a cup. 'Do 'ee think I an't got nothing to eat at home?' she asked. 'Well, I have, then! – Ay,' she continued, bobbing her head sententiously, 'yu got a mark in Seacombe, else yu wuden't be down yer again so sune. That's what 'tis – a mark! I knows, sure nuff. Come on! who be it now? What's her like, eh?'

She cannot understand how any young unmarried man can be without his sweetheart. Everybody according to her, must have a mark, or be in search of one. I told her with the brutality which delights her factual old mind, that if she herself had been a little less antique and poverty-stricken . . .

'There! if I don't come round and box yer yers. Yu'm al'ays ready wi' yer chake.'

Then I offered her five *per cent.* of the lady's fortune, if she would find me a mark with unsettled money. Though she laughed it off, she was not a little scandalized by my levity. The Tough Old Stick has not outlived her memory of romance. Indeed, I think she holds to it all the tighter for her hardheadedness in every-day affairs.

Midway through tea, Straighty crept into the kitchen. 'What do *yu* want?' shouted Grannie Pinn. 'Bain't there enough kids yer now?' Straighty stood in the centre of the kitchen, sucking three fingers and looking shyly at me from beneath her tousled tow-coloured hair.

'You've not forgotten me, Straighty?' I asked. 'You're not frightened of me, are you?'

'Go an' speak to 'en proper,' commanded Grannie Pinn. 'Wer's yer manners, Dora?'

'*Yu* didn' speak to me proper, Grannie Pinn! Wer's yours?'

'Aw, my dear soul! Now du 'ee shut up wi' yer chake!'

Straighty remained sucking her fingers in the middle of the kitchen. She seemed about to cry. Quite suddenly, her eyes brightened. She glided over to me, put her wet fingers round my neck ('Dora!' from Mrs Widger), and gave me a big kiss on the chin. Then she told me all about everything, sitting with her head on my shoulder in the old courting chair.

A tiny little episode, I grant; but very sweet.

'That's your mark?' Grannie Pinn shouted. 'You'll hae tu wait for she!'

Straighty is established as my mark, and takes her duties as she has learnt to conceive them, with amusing seriousness. She will not let me go out through the Square without being told where I am off to, nor let me return in house until I tell her where I have been. At the beginning of every meal we hear her creeping up the passage; see her yellow hair against the door-post. By the end of the meal she has summoned up courage to claim a kiss. 'Now be off tu your mother!' says Mrs Widger.

2

Mrs Widger has let the back bedroom to a young married couple possessed of a saucer-eyed baby that cries lustily whenever its mother is out of its sight. How they succeed in living, sleeping, baby-tending and doing their minor cookery in the one pokey little room, already half filled by the bedstead, is difficult to understand. They do it. We see little of them, except just when we had rather see nothing at all.

For dinner and the subsequent cup o'tay, Mam Widger allows one hour. But usually, before even the pudding is out of the oven, first one of us, then another, glances round to make sure that the kettle is well on the fire. Nowadays, however, when the kettle is beginning to sing, Mrs Perkins, the baby in her arms, comes downstairs and proceeds to cook for her husband a couple of small chops or a mess of meat-shreds and bubble and squeak. She stirs and chatters; she holds forth on the baby's beauty and good-ness, its health, its father's love of it – and, in short, she talks to us as if we were delighted to see her and her baby. Tony's good manners triumph comically over his desire to get his cup o' tay and put away an hour up over. (He likes to take every chance of making up for wakeful nights at sea.) We all wish she would go quickly. Meanwhile, we feign an interest in what blousy, skirt-gaping, slop-slippered, enthusiastic maternity has to say.

And when she does go, it is with a most joyful haste that we move the kettle to the very hottest part of the fire.

3

The family hubbub over Tommy's stay in the Plymouth Eye Infirmary has hardly died down yet. Recognizing with uncom-mon good sense that his double squint would bar him from the

Navy or Army (he shows an inclination towards the latter), Mrs Widger took him to Plymouth; and on hearing that an operation would cure him, she did not hesitate, did not bring him home to think about it; she left him there. Then . . . What a buzz! The child is to return very thin. Mrs Widger's cousin declares loudly that she would rather lead her boy about blind (he squints excessively) than let him go to one o' they places. Tony says, 'Aye! they may feed 'en on food of a better quality like, after the rate, but he won't get done like he is at home.' Several times daily he wants to know how long they will keep Tommy there, and when Mrs Widger replies, six weeks, he asks in a woe-begone voice: 'Do 'ee think 'er'll know his dad when 'er comes home again?'

All of which is easy to laugh at.

No doubt hospitals are a godsend to the poor, immediately if not ultimately. At the same time, it cannot be said that the prejudice against them is wholly unreasonable. Poor people declare that they are starved in hospital, and it is, in fact, now recognized in dietetics that comparatively innutritious food, eaten with gusto, is better assimilated than the most scientifically chosen but unpalatable nutriment. A man, a poor man especially, can be half starved or at all events much thinned, on good food, who would do well on the habitual coarse fare that he enjoys. His life is a long adventure in a land where every other turning leads to starvation, but his adventurousness seldom extends to new sorts of food.

No one is so depressed by strange surroundings as the average poor man or woman. (Children get on much better.) Very likely he has never been alone, has never slept away from some relative or friend, the whole of his life. The unfamiliarity and precise routine of hospitals, the faces and ways all strange, are capable not only of greatly intensifying a man's sufferings, but even of retarding his recovery.

Hospitals must necessarily be governed by two main conditions: – (1) The need of doing the greatest good to the greatest number; (2) The advancement of medical science and experience. Under (1) the overpressure on medical skill and time is bound to diminish tact and sympathy. Under (2) the serious or interesting cases are apt – as everyone who has mixed with hospital staffs knows very well – to receive attention not disproportionate to the nature of the malady, but disproportionate to the bodily, and particularly to the mental, suffering. The poor man can appreciate sympathy better than skill. He may not know how ill he is, but he knows how much he suffers. He is quick to detect and to resent preferential treatment. From the point of view of the independent poor, hospitals are far from what they might be. They are last straws for drowning men, useful sometimes, but best avoided.'

Jacks is a very energetic young country surgeon. He is keen on his work and will procure admission to the hospital for any operative case. But he finds it by no means easy to get his patients there; for he is so keen on his work that he treats their feelings carelessly; hustles them through an operation; pooh-poohs their fear of anaesthetics and the knife. Jacks is well disliked by the poor. He has to live, and therefore he has to cultivate a professional manner and to dance attendance on wealthy hypochrondriacal patients whom otherwise he would probably send to the devil. The poor people have told him to his face that he runs after the rich and cuts about the poor; and they have nicknamed him *Jacks the Ripper*.

Tony would have to be very far gone before he would willingly go into a hospital. Just now, between the mackerel and herring seasons, he is fat and sleepy, very sleek for him. Rheumatic fever in boyhood and neglected colds have left him rather deaf, and subject to noises in the head and miscellaneous bodily pains. He is 'a worriter' by nature. 'When I gets bothered,' he says, 'I often feels as if summut be busted in me head.' As the herring season

---

¹ I trust I make it plain that these statements imply no general disparagement of hospitals. Whether or no they do the best possible under the circumstances is not to be discussed shortly or by the present writer. Since penning the above, it has fallen to me to take a patient to the out-department of one of the great London hospitals. We had some time to wait, with very many others, on long wooden benches. I cannot express the almost unbearable depression, the sense of ebbing vitality, the feeling of being jammed in a machine, which took possession of me, who was quite well. And I wish I could adequately express my admiration of the visiting surgeon's manipulation of his delicate instruments and his management of the patient.

comes round, so will Tony 'hae the complaints again,' and few will pity a man who always looks so well. A few years back, Mrs Widger procured for his deafness some quack treatment – which did do him good; – but he himself had little faith in it, and did not persevere. Like the mothers who rejoice in delicate children rather than feed them properly and send them early to bed, Tony prefers to think his ailments constitutional, a possession of his, a curse of fate, which flatters him, so to speak, by singling him out for its attentions. In a couple of years' time, when he comes out of the Royal Naval Reserve, he will have the option of accepting £50 down at once, or of waiting till he is sixty for a pension of four shillings a week. Mrs Widger understands perfectly that unless he wants to buy boats and gear – unless, in other words, he can make the £50 productive – he had much better wait for the pension and be sure of a roof over his head when he is past work. Tony, however, will probably take the lump sum. He fears he may die and get nothing at all. He does not *feel* that he will never see sixty, but he is of opinion that he will not, and sixty to a man of his temperament is such a long way hence. He thinks as little as possible of old age. 'Aye!' he says – almost chants, so moved is he, – 'the likes o' us slaves an' slaves all our life, an' us never gets no for'arder. Like as us be when we'm young, so us'll be at the end o'it all. Come the time when yu'm past work, an' yu be done an' wearied out, then all yer slavin's gone for nort. 'Tis true what I says. I dunno what to think – but 'tis the way o'it. 'Tain't right like. 'Tain't right!'

4

'Go shrimping wi' the setting-nets t'night, I reckon,' said Uncle Jake. 'Tide be low 'tween twelve and one o'clock. Jest vitty, that.'

It was one of those evenings, wind WSW., when the sea and sky look stormier than they are, or will be. Uncle Jake stood on the very edge of the sea wall, his hands in his pockets, his torn jumper askew, and his old cap cocked over one ear. From time to time he turned half round to deride a dressy visitor, or for warmth's sake twisted his body about within his clothing, or

shrugged his shoulders humorously with a, ''Tis a turn-out o'it!'
The seine net had just been shot from the beach for less than a
sovereign's worth of fish – to be divided, one third for the owner
of the net and the remainder among the seven men who had lent a
hand.

'Coo'h!' Uncle Jake exclaimed. ''*Tis* a crib here! Nort 't all
doing. Not like 't used tu be. I mind when yu cude haul in a seine
so full as . . . Might pick up a shilling or tu t'night shrimping, if
they damn visitors an' bloody tradesmen an't been an' turned the
whole o' Broken Rocks up an' down. *I* tells 'em o'it!'

'Shrimps or prawns, d'you mean?'

'Why, prawns! Us calls it shrimping hereabout. You knows
that. There's prawns there if yu knows where to look, but not like
't used to be. On'y they fules don' know where to look. An' they
don' see Jake at it, an' I never tells 'em what I gets nor what I sells
at; an' so they says I don' never du nort. I'd like to see they hae tu
work waist-deep in water every night for a week when they'm
sixty-five. An' in the winter tu! – If yu'm minded to come t'night,
yu be up my house 'bout 'leven o'clock, an' I'll fetch me nets from
under cliff if they b—y b—rs o' boys an't been there disturbin' of
'em.'

Uncle Jake's cottage looks outside like a small cellar that has
somehow risen above the ground and then has been thatched with
old straw and whitewashed. Inside, it is a shadowy place, stacked
up high with sailing and fishing gear, flotsam, jetsam, balks of
wood and all the odds and ends that he picks up on his prowlings
along the coast. With tattered paper screens, he has partitioned
off, near the fire and window, a small and very crowded cosy-
corner. There he was sitting when I arrived; bread, butter, on-
ions, sugar and tea – his staple foods – on the round table beside
him, and his prawn-nets on the flagstones at his feet. Three cats
glided about among the legs of the table and chairs, on the
lookout to steal. Using the gentle violence that cats love from
those they trust, Uncle Jake flung them one by one to the other
side of the room. They returned, purring, to snatch at the none
too fresh berry [eggs] of spider-crab with which the nets were
being baited.

The shallow small-meshed setting-nets are about two feet in diameter at the top. Stretched taut from side to side of the rim are two doubled strings or *thirts* – which cross at right angles directly above the centre of the net, and into which, near the middle, the four pieces of bait are ingeniously and simply fixed by little sliders on the thirts themselves. The whole apparatus hangs level from a yard or more of stout line, at the upper end of which is a small stick, a stumpy fishing rod, so to speak, often painted white so that it may be easily found as it lies on the dark rocks. Uncle Jake's net-sticks, however, are anything but white. Capable almost of finding them with his eyes shut, he would sooner lose his nets altogether than let whitened sticks point out to other people the pools which he alone knows.

We put the nets into a couple of sacks and shouldered them. A long light pole was placed into my hand. 'Don't yu never leave your pole behind. Yu'll want it, sure 'nuff, afore this night's over.'

So we set out. One by one the cats who were following, left us to go back home. We did not walk towards the sea. On the contrary we went inland, through some roads with demure sleeping villas on either side. 'If they bloody poachers,' Uncle Jake explained, 'see'd us going straight towards the sea, they'd follow. *I* knows 'em! They takes away the livelihood o' the likes o' us an' sells it. Sells it – and' says 'tis sport! I leads 'em a dance sometimes. I goes along a narrow ledge that's jest under water, wi' ten or twelve feet depth on either side. On they comes a'ter me. 'Uncle Jake knows where to go,' they says. And in *they* goes – not knowing the place like I du – head over heels an' a swim for it! O Lor'! they don' like it when I tells 'em they better go home an' tumble into dry clothes. Yu shude hear the language they spits out o' their mouths 'long wi' the salt water. Horrible, tu be sure!'

Broken Rocks, a playground for children by day, look wild and strange on a night when clouds are driving across the moon, when the cliffs fade into darkness high above the beach, and everything not black is grey, except where the white surf beats upon the outermost ledge. Then Broken Rocks have personality. A sinister spirit rises out of them withe the heave of the sea. It is as if some black mood, some great monotony of strife, were closing in around one. On the sea wall, in the sunshine, I used to wonder why Uncle Jake calls Broken Rocks a terr'ble place. Now I do not. He works there by night.

We peered out from the beach underneath the cliffs. Nobody has forestalled us. Uncle Jake was pleased. He laughed hoarsely, and the echo of it was not unlike the natural noises of the place. 'Us'll make a start there,' he said, pointing to a ledge between which and ourselves was a wide sheet of water. 'Yu follow me an' feel for a foothold wi' your pole. *Don't* yu step afore yu've felt.'

Into the water he went; seemed, indeed, to run across it. 'Be 'ee wet?' he asked when I stepped out the other side.

'Half way up my thighs!'

'Yu hadn't no need to get wet so far up as your knees. I didn't. An' yu might ha' gone in there over your head. Yu use your pole, skipper. Feel afore yu steps. I'll set 'ee your two nets for a beginning.'

With his pole he felt the depth of the water around the ledge. Then he dropped the nets down, edging them carefully under the overhanging weed, and placed the sticks on the rock above. 'Don't yu forget where yu sets your nets. Yu won't *see* 'em. An' when yu hauls up, go gently, like so, else off goes all they master prawns, d'rec'ly they feels a jerk . . . Leave 'em down a couple o' minutes . . . But there, yu knows, don' 'ee? Us won't catch much till the tide turns. They prawns knows when 'tis beginning to flow so well as yu an' me. Yu work this yer, an' along easterly. I be going farther out.'

When I hauled up my first net I heard the faint clicketty noise – like paper scratching metal – of three or four prawns jumping about inside. My hand had to chase them many times round the net. One jumped over; one fell through. Nothing is more difficult to withdraw from a net than prawns, except it be a lobster, flipping itself about, hardly visible, and striking continually with its nippers. There was a lobster in the second net. It had to go into the same pocket as the prawns. It was something of an adventure afterwards to put a hand into the pocketful of lobster claws and prawn spines.

Working eastward and outward, plunging into the water or sliding with bumps and bruises off a rock, I must have passed Deadman's Rock, Danger Gutter, Broken Rock and the Wreckstone. (Things of the sea nearly always take name from their evil aspects.) Uncle Jake could have told me at any moment exactly where I was.

At last, near the surf, I saw in front of me a flat table-rock, standing up alone, and as I descended towards the foot of it, a high black rocky archway became plain. Broad-leaved oarweed covered it like giant hair, and hung drooping into the deep black pool beneath. The moonlight glinted on the oarweed. The pool, though darkly calm, ebbed and flowed silently with the waves outside. I recognized the place. It was Hospital Rock – the rock the little boats strike on because it is smooth on top and the waves do not break over it very much. I half expected the ugly head of a great conger to look out at me from the pool. As I lay flat on the rock to drop my nets, the rattle and roar of the sea beyond, vibrating through the solid stone, the whistle of the wind through the downhanging oarweed, sounded like an orchestra of the mad damn'd.

I caught nothing there, and was not sorry. The place was too eerie to stay in long. 'Ah!' said Uncle Jake when we met again on the inner reef, 'I've knowed they amateurs run straight off home when they've a-found theirselves under Hospital. A terr'ble place! Yu knows now. Did 'ee set your nets there? Eh?'

He took some fresh bait from his prawn bag and fixed it in the thirts of my nets. ''Tis nearly over,' he said, 'but jest yu try that, an' if they'm there that'll hae 'em. There's no bait like that there when yu can get it, on'y nobody knows o'it.'

The nature of that bait I shall not divulge, any more than I shall name the place where Uncle Jake goes to play with the young ravens in the spring. Somebody might catch his prawns; somebody would shoot his ravens. We had caught about two hundred prawns between us, a few lobsters and some wild-crabs. As we walked homewards, the three cats came down the lane, one by one, to welcome Uncle Jake.

Next day we sailed east in the *Moondaisy*. Uncle Jake straddled the pools and lifted the heavy stones. Then in a skim-net,[1] with marvellous dexterity, he caught the almost invisible prawns as they darted away. He dragged lobsters out of holes, and cursed the neighbouring villagers who had been down to the shore after crabs and had disturbed his favourite stones. He knows how each one ought to lie; he even keeps the seaweed on some of them trimmed to its proper length. 'But 'tain't like 't used to be,' he says.

He has almost given up going to sea for fish; some say because he will not take the trouble; but I think it is because he loves his rocks and cliffs so well. No one knows how much by night and day he haunts the wilder stretches of shore, nor how many miles he trudges in a week. But the gulls know him well, and will scream back to him when he calls. His laugh has something of the gulls' cry in it. I have heard it remarked that when his time comes (no sign of it yet) he will be found one morning dead among his familiar rocks. He is acquainted with death there. He has borne home on his shoulder by night the body of a woman who had fallen from the cliffs above; and again a negro that had washed ashore. With a little self-control one might have carried the woman all right, but the drowned nigger . . . Imagine his face in the darkness – his eyes! Only a man with greatness in him, or a very callous man, could have brought such a corpse home, all along under the crumbling cliffs; and Uncle Jake is certainly not callous.

5

'Let 'em try any o' their tricks on me! They can turn out the likes o' us all right, I s'pose. But I can tell 'em what I thinks on 'em, here's luck. Thank God I don't live in no tradesman's house, an' can deal where I likes. Not that I shouldn't anyway . . .'

Grannie Pinn's shrill angry voice pierced the kitchen door. The occasion was a mothers' gossiping; the subject, a kind of boycott that is practised in Seacombe. On the table there was a jug of ale and stout and an hospitably torn-open bag of biscuits. Around it

[1] Like a landing net, but shallower and with a shorter handle.

sat Grannie Pinn – bolt upright in the courting chair, with her hands folded – Mrs Meer and Mam Widger. The feathers in Grannie Pinn's hat shook like a bush on the cliff-edge. All of them looked as if they felt a vague responsibility for the right conduct of the world. In short, they looked political.

The poor people here live in small colonies scattered behind the main street and among the villas, in little blocks of old neglected property, some of which has been bought up by tradesmen. So much of the former village spirit still survives, and so many of the tradesmen have but recently risen from poorer circumstances, that between some of the oldest and the youngest of them, and the workmen, there is even yet a rather mistrustful fellowship. They call each other, Jim, Dick, Harry and so on – over glasses, at all events. The growth of the class spirit, as opposed to the old village spirit, can be seen plainly when Bessie returns from school, saying: 'Peuh! Dad's only a fisherman. Why can't 'er catch more fish an' get a little shop an' be a gen'leman?' Seacombe tradesmen have been withdrawing into a class of their own – the class of 'not real gen'lemen' – and have been showing a tendency to act together against the rest of the people, and to form rings for the purpose of keeping shops empty or prices up. Nobody minds their bleeding visitors. That is what God sends visitors for; and besides, the season is so short. But when they began to over-charge their fellow townsmen, in summer because it was the season and in winter because it wasn't the season, the poor people revolted, and amid tremendous hubbub, thunders of talk and lightnings of threat, a co-operative store was opened. Then did the tradesmen remind the poor of old family debts, legacies from hard times. Then did the poor say: "Very well, us'll hae our own store and bakery, and pay cash down to ourselves." Unable to obtain the tenancy of a shop, they bought one. They refused to raise the price of bread. They laughed at advertisements which professed to point out the fallacies of all co-operation. They succeeded, but the class difference was widened and clinched – poor man *versus* tradesman.

Grannie Pinn, Mrs Meer and Mam Widger were reckoning up the number of people who have been turned out of their cottages, or are under notice to quit, for neglecting to deal with their tradesmen landlords.

Their indignation having found vent, they went on to talk of Virgin Offwill, who has acquired celebrity by living alone in a cottage on no one knows what, by sleeping in an armchair before the fire (when she can afford one), and by never washing. Sometime last month, Virgin sent for Dr Jacks because, so she said, she was wished bewitched; and she would not let him go until he threatened to report the state of her house to the medical officer of health.

The tale of Virgin Offwill was capped by another – that of old Mrs Widworthy. Several years ago (these gossips have long memories) she received a postal order from her son together with an invitation to visit him in London. The post arrived after her man had gone to work. She did not wait; she sent out a neighbour's child to change the order, packed her few things in a basket, and went off to her son by the midday train. On the table she left a note: "Widworthy, I am gone to London. Your dinner is in the saucepan. I shall be back directly."

There was loud laughter in the kitchen; another round of stout and ale; then silence. The mothers fidgeted, each after her own manner, meditatively. In all the world, and Seacombe, there seemed nothing to talk about – or too much.

'Have 'ee heard ort lately of Ned Corry?' asked Grannie Pinn with a delightful mixture of gusto and propriety. 'Have 'er still got Dina wi' 'en?'

'Yes, I think.'

'An' his wife tu?'

Bessie burst into the room. Neither Tony nor Mrs Widger approve of discussing the intimate humanities before children, so Bessie was allowed to fling her news to us unchecked. 'Mother, Miss Mase says I can leave school so soon as yu've found me a place. Then I'll hae some money o' my own earnings, won't I?'

'Yu'll bring it to me, same as I had to what I earned, an' yu'll stay on to school till I thinks vitty. You'm not fit for a gen'leman's house.'

'Yes, I be. I can work. That's what yu'm paid for, ain't it?'

'How many cups an' saucers have yu smashed this week?'

'Have they learned 'ee all yu wants to know up to school?' inquired Grannie Pinn quietly, but with a twinkle at the company.

'They an't learned me to play the pi-anno. That's what I wants now. If Dad 'd get one, *I*'d play.'

'Have they learned 'ee to cook a dinner?'

'Anybody can du thic. I've learned to play *God Save the King* on the school pi-anno.'

'How do 'ee start then?'

'Why, you puts your fingers . . .'

Naw! I means how du 'ee start to cook dinner?'

'Peuh!'

'Her an't learned tidiness,' said Mam Widger. 'Lookse! Her scarf on one chair, gloves flinged on another, coat slatted on the ground an' her hat on the dresser – now, since her's come in! Pick 'em up to once, else thee't hae my hand 'longside o'ee!'

Bessie scrabbled up her clothes and, making sounds of disgust, went out.

'Her'll steady down, I hope,' remarked Mrs Widger.

'Her's wild, but a gude maid to try an' help a body, though her makes so much work as her does.'

'Ay!' said Grannie Pinn grimly. 'If work don't steady her, there's nothing will.'

When Bessie was gone the conversation reverted to Ned Corry and the ages of his children. I met him last summer – have never ceased hearing about him, for his sayings are often repeated and his adventures at sea recounted. He came down here on holiday with his wife, who appeared to be very happy and was obviously very proud of her Ned. The morning he went back, he collected all of his old mates he could find, before breakfast, into a public-house, treated them to whisky until his pockets were empty, and then borrowed money to return to London. His personality seems to have left a deeper impression than any other on Seacombe. He is a man very alive; big, generous and uncontrollable in all things; so broad that he seems short; great in voice, great in strength, greatest in laughter. Very dark, and prominent in feature where his fierce black beard allows any of his face to be seen, he is a kind of Hebraic Berserker in general appearance, in the uncompromising force of him and the squat sloppiness of his clothes. Yet his eyes, almost bedded in hair, have often the bright peeping humorousness of a shaggy dog's.

He had the most boats on the beach, and mighty strokes of luck with the fish; employed more men than anyone before or since; paid them well when he had the money, and with an irregularity which would have been tolerated from no other boat-owner. Dina went to lodge at his house. He made of her, so gossip says, a second wife. He succeeded in running a household of three; then bought two lodging houses and set a wife to manage each. 'Ned was all right,' Tony says, 'on'y he didn't know how to look after hisself – didn't care – nor after his money when he made it.' One evening, Tony found him in his bath in the middle of the kitchen whilst his womenfolk were cooking him a good hot supper. It was not his being in his bath which made Tony blush, but the freedom with which he called, 'Come in!'

When the prudent-minded of Seacombe clamoured to Ned for their money, he sold up his boats and furniture, went to London, took without apprenticeship a well-paid job at the docks, and now, as he walks home along the dockside streets, he is given *Good Night* from London Bridge to Tilbury. The exerting of strength seems to have been his leading impulse; pride in Ned Corry his only check. He was too big for Seacombe. In London he remains entirely himself – 'West-country Ned!'

Before Ned Corry's affairs were finished with, Tony came into the kitchen, saying: 'I just been talking out there to Skinny Chubb. Nice quiet chap, he is. His wife *is* gone.'

'Well, didn't 'ee know that?'

Then I heard a wonderful tale of self-restraint. Chubb is a good workman, a man of about fifty with grown up boys and girls. His wife has been no good to him. She used to have men in the house when he was away. She provided them with grog and food, but there was never anything for Chubb to eat, except abuse. She won the daughters over to her side. Sometimes she would go away to London, taking perhaps one of the girls with her. Only the eldest son, who was not at home, sided with his father. Neighbours used to hear the couple quarrelling half the night, but during the whole of their married life he never once struck or beat her. All he used to tell other people was:—' 'Tis a wonder how a man can stand all her du say to me, day an' night, early an' late.'

Just before Michaelmas, she decided to leave her husband: to go to London with a German flunkey. They broke up the home. Chubb packed up for her the best of the furniture. He wrote out her labels, said *Good-bye*, paid her cab fare to the station. Now he is living in lodgings. Rumour has it that the German has left her. In answer to inquiries, Chubb merely says: 'Well, I tell 'ee, *I* be glad to be out o'it all at last. *I*'ll never hae her back.'

It is a sound old piece of psychology which distinguishes a man's bark from his bite. The poor man's bark is appalling; I often used to think there was murder in the air when I heard some quite ordinary discussion; there would have been murder in the air had I myself been worked up to speak so furiously. But, comparatively speaking, he seldom bites; hardly ever without warning; and he can as a rule stay himself in the very act. The educated man, on the other hand, does not bark much; one of the most important parts of his education has been the teaching him not to do so; but when he does bite, it is blindly, and he makes his teeth meet if he can. We hear, of course, much more of the poor man in the police courts and we imagine (spite of Herbert Spencer's warning) that education is to diminish his crimes. How very simple and fallacious! In the first place, the poor, the uneducated or but slightly educated, greatly out-numbered the educated. Suppose by means of complete and trustworthy criminal statistics, we could work out the *percentage criminality* of the different classes. I fancy that the poor man would not then show – even judged by our whimsical legal and moral standards – a greater percentage criminality than the educated. And if in our statistics we could include degrees of provocation to the various crimes, such as hunger, poverty, want of the money to leave exasperating surroundings – it would probably be found that the poor are, if anything, less criminally disposed than other sections of the community; that, though they lack something of the secondary self-restraint which prevents bark and noise, they are, other things being equal, actually stronger in the primary self-restraint, the lack of which leads directly to crime. On *a priori*, historical, grounds one would anticipate such a conclusion.

It is certain that they forgive offence more readily.

I have often wondered how many nice quiet respectable vindictive murders are yearly done by educated men too clever to be found out. The poor man is a fool at 'Murder as a Fine Art.' He hacks and bashes.

6

Sighting, as we thought, some balks of timber, floating away on the ebb tide over the outside of Broken Rocks, two of us shoved a small boat down the beach. Our flotsam was a trick of the fading light on the sea, just where Broken Rocks raised the swell a little; but in the exquisite, the almost menacing, calm of the evening, we leaned on our oars and watched for a while. To seaward, the horizon was a peculiar lowering purple, as if a semi-opaque sheet of glass were placed there. On land, over the Windgap, the sunset was like many ranks of yellow and shining black banners – hard, brassy. The sea was a misty blue. One by one, according to their prominence, the bushes on the face of the cliffs faded into the general contour. As we landed, a slight lop came over the water from the dark south-east. 'Ah!' said Uncle Jake. 'We'm going to hae it. South-easter's coming!'

There was some discussion as to whether or not we should haul the boats up over the sea-wall. In the end we hauled the smaller ones, leaving the *Cock Robin* and the drifter upon the beach.

In the very early morning – it was so dark I could not see the outline of the window – I half awoke to an indistinct sensation that the house was rocking and hell unloosed outside. Something solid seemed to be beating the wall. Than I heard Granfer's voice roaring at the foot of the stairs:—'What is it? Why, tell thic Tony he'd better hurry up else all the boats 'll be washed away. Blowing a hurricane 'tis! Sea's making. Oughtn't to ha' left they boats . . .'

'Be quiet! yu'll wake all the kids up.'

'Blowing a hurricane 'tis! Nort to me if the boats du wash off. Tony'd never wake.'

'All right, I'll wake him.'

In five minutes we were downstairs, with the fire lighted and the kettle on.

Outside, it was pitch dark. There was nothing there, it seemed, except a savage wind and stinging splotches of rain and the cry of the low tide on the sand. I felt my way up the Gut and out, sliding one foot before the other so as not to fall over the sea-wall. John Widger bumped into me, and together we crept along to the capstan. A white shadow of surf was just visible. We dropped gingerly off the wall to the beach, trusting there was no iron gear there to smash our ankles. Then for an hour we fumbled our way about; pushed, hauled, disentangled, slid and swore; grasping sometimes the right rope and sometimes the wrong one with hands almost too cold and stiff, too painful, to grasp anything at all.

Out of the blackness came another hurricane squall with rain that lashed. The rushing air itself shook. We crouched, all humped up, in the lew of a drifter's bows, whilst the rain water washed around our boots and coat-tails. 'This'll tell 'ee what 'tis like for us chaps,' said Tony. 'I be only sorry,' Uncle Jack added, 'for them what's out to sea now in ship's wi' rotten gear.'

As the dawn broke thick, the sea rose still further, until it was a discoloured fury battering the shore. With Uncle Jake I watched some long planks, four inches in thickness and ten broad, swept off the top of the Beach. We saw them hurtled over Broken Rocks, now dashed against the cliff, now careering, so to speak, on their hind legs. Such were their mad capers that we laughed aloud. We were far from wishing to save them. We rejoiced with them.

As the day blew on, the wind moderated inshore and the lop gathered itself together into a heavy swell. And after dark, at half tide, Uncle Jake and myself worked hard. We dragged the heavy planks from a surf that seemed ever advancing on us to drive us towards the cliffs, yet never did, and we propped up the planks against cliffs whose crumbling drove us constantly down to the sea. There's a winter's firing there.

We talked – out-howling the noise jerkily – of wrecks and wreckages. Had we had the chance, we might then conceivably have wrecked a ship. For there, on the narrow strip of shingle between the wash of the waves and the unstable cliff, we were primitive men, ready without ruth to wreck for ourselves the contrivances of civilization.

7

Tony has received one or two presents this autumn, and now the gales have put an end to all kinds of fishing, he is beginning to write his letters of thanks. Or rather, he bothers Mam Widger to write them for him, and when she has said sufficiently often, 'G'out yu mump-head! Du it yourself!' he sets to work. After long hesitation, pen in hand, and a laborious commencement, he dashes off a letter, protests that it ought to be burnt, and sends it to post. He acts, indeed, a comic version of the groans and travail about which literary men talk so much.

Whether he prefers a present or a tip is doubtful, and depends largely on the amount of money in the house. Presents are more valued; tips more useful. He feels that 'there didn't ought to be no need of tips'; knows obscurely that they are one of the effects, and the causes, of class difference; that they are either a tacit admission that his labour is underpaid, or else such an expression of good-will as a man would not presume to give to the likes o' himself,' or else an indirect bribe for some or other undue attention. Usually, however, not wishing to go into the matter so thoroughly – having come in contact with outsiders chiefly when they have been on holiday and least economical – he considers a tip merely as the outflowing of a gen'leman's abundance. 'They can afford it, can't 'em? They lives in big houses, an' it helps keeps thees yer little lot fed an' booted.'

If, however, he has reason to believe that 'a nice quiet gen'le-man' is really hard-up, then he is very sorry, and will reduce the rate of hire by so much as half. In such cases, it is well that the gen'leman should add a small tip, for his niceness' sake. Then is Tony more than paid.

The gentleman, as such, seems to be losing prestige. Gentility is being made to share its glory with education, 'Ignorant' is becoming a worse insult than 'no class.' Grandfer, in argument will think to prove his case by saying: 'Why, a gen'leman told us so t'other day on the Front. A gen'leman told me, I tell thee!' Grandfer's sons would like the gen'leman's reasons. In fact the stuff and nonsense that the chatting gen'leman, feeling himself safe from contradiction, will try to teach a so-called ignorant fisherman, is most amazing. If he but knew how shrewdly he is criticized, afterwards . . .

Education even is esteemed not so much for the knowledge it provides, still less for its wisdom, as for the advantage it gives a man in practical affairs; the additional money it earns him. 'No doubt they educated people knows a lot what I don't,' says Tony, 'an' can du a lot what I can't; but there's lots o' things what I puzzles me old head over, an' them not the smallest, what they ain't no surer of than I be. Ay! an' not so sure, for there's many on 'em half mazed wi' too much o'it.'

8

Bessie has finally left school. The excitement, the chatter, the sudden air of superiority over the other children, the critical glance round the room when she returns home . . . She has learnt next to nothing of school-work – which matters little, since she is strong, hopeful, and has a genuine wish to do her best. What does matter is, that she is careless, inclined to be slatternly, and has no idea of precision either in speech or work. (Few girls have.) This is in part, no doubt, mere whelpishness to be grown out of present-ly. She picks up some piece of gossip. 'Mother! Mrs Long's been taken to hospital. Her's going to die, I 'spect.'

'No her an't gone to hospital nuther. Dr Bayliss says as her's got to go if her ain't better to-morrow. Isn't that what you've a-heard now?'

'Yes – but I thought her'd most likely be gone 'fore this,' says

Bessie without, apparently, the least sense of shame, or even of inexactitude.

The other day she reached down a cup to get herself a drink of water. Then she took some pains to see if the cup still *looked* clean, and finding it did, she replaced it among the other clean ones on the dresser.

Her mother sent her out to the larder for some more bread. Bessie brought in a new loaf.

'That ain't it,' said Mrs Widger. 'There's a stale one there.'

'No, there ain't.'

'Yes, there is.'

'I've looked, an't I?'

'Yu go an' look again, my lady.'

'Well, 'tis dark, an' I an't got no light to see with.'

Protesting vehemently, Bessie found the stale loaf. Were I her mistress, she would irritate me into a very bad temper, and then, by her muddle-headed willingness, would make me sorry. She is untrained. School has in no way disciplined her mind. From early childhood, of course, she has had to do many odd jobs for her mother, but a woman with the whole burden of a house on her shoulders, who has never found the two ends more than just meet, cannot spare time or thought to train her girls systematically. It is so much easier to do the whole of the work herself. Bessie's usefulness, such as it is, speaks a deal for her disposition. After all, how many women in any station of life, have precision and forethought enough to lay a fire so that it will burn up at once? Bessie is only thirteen. It is, indeed, her ability for her age that tempts one to judge her by a standard which elsewhere – except among women discussing their servants – would only be applied to a girl of twenty.

Suppose fathers judged their daughters as mothers judge their servants . . .

For the present, Bessie is in daily service at a lodging-house. For a 'gen'leman's residence', which would be better for her, she is over-young and would, besides, need an outfit of dresses, caps and aprons which she is not yet old enough to take care of, nor will be until she is ready to fall in love. She can go to Mrs Butler's in a torn dress and dirty pinafore. She is not expected to appear before the visitors; only to do the dirty, rough, and heavy work behind the scenes. It was a condition of her leaving school so young, that she should go into service and sleep there. Very naturally, Mrs Widger and Mrs Butler soon arranged that the 'education lady', when she came to inspect, should be shown Bessie's bedroom at the lodging-house – and that Bessie should sleep at home. It was better for all three; for Mrs Butler who is short of room, for Mrs Widger who wants Bessie's help, and for Bessie who still requires her mother's authority and oversight. Educationalists don't seem to understand.

In return for two shillings a week and her food, Bessie is supposed to work twelve hours a day, from eight till eight. All she does might possibly be crammed into three hours a day; that is all she is paid for. She brings home her supper in a piece of newspaper. One evening she brought some chicken bones which had been in turn the foundation of roast chicken, cold chicken, stewed chicken, and soup. Bessie rather enjoyed them. Another evening, she unwrapped a whole cake. It fell on the floor, whack! neither bouncing, nor breaking. It was full of dough. A basin of soup-dregs which she brought home two days ago was found to contain a length of stewed string. Stewed to rags, it was, like badly boiled meat. Bessie says that Mrs Butler did miss a bell-rope.

9

There was a rush and a banging up the passage. The kitchen door burst violently open. A girl (though she wore long skirts her figure was unformed and her waist had a stiff youthful curve) ran quickly into the room.

Her eager bright-coloured young face – that also not yet fully formed – was overshadowed by a flapping decorated hat obvious-ly constructed less for a woman's head – less still for a maiden's – than for a cash draper's window. Her chest was plastered with a motley collection of cheap jewellery and lace. Her boots had not been cleaned.

She dropped her cardboard boxes on the floor. Regardless of her womanly attire, like nothing so much as a hasty child, she æhung her arms round Tony's neck.

'Hallo, Dad! How be 'ee? Eh? How's everybody? Lord, I'm hungry. Look what I got for 'ee. An't forgot nobody this time, though 'tisn't everybody as remembers me. Look, Dad!'

'What is it?' asked Tony, looking blankly, as if he could hardly realize so much clatter.

'Lookse, Dad! What do 'ee think o'it?'

A box was torn open. From it came a couple of glass ornaments, and various sorts of 'coloured rock' and sticky toffee for the children.

It was Tony's eldest daughter, Jenny, come home from service. She walked round the room picking up things to examine, things to eat, things that she claimed were hers, and things that she desired given her. She talked without, so far as I could see, any connection between the sentences. Mouthfuls of food reduced her babbling shriek to a burr-burr.

'Be 'ee glad to see your daughter, Dad?'

'Iss . . .' said Tony, looking at her very fondly, but still puzzled.

'Don't believe yu be. Why didn't 'ee write then if yu loves me so?'

'Thic's Mam 'Idger's job.'

'G'out!' said Mrs Widger, – 'Jenny, you an't see'd our addition, have 'ee.'

I held out my hand. Jenny blushed; then she said: 'Good evening, sir"; then she giggled; and finally she turned her back on me. It took a minute or two for her happy carelessness to return.

Domestic servants on holiday, more than any other class of people, strain one's tact and rouse one's ingrained snobbery. They tend to be over-respectful – the sort of respectfulness that presupposes reward, – and to brandish *sirs*, or to be shy and silly, or else to treat one with a more airy familiarity than the acquaintanceship warrants. In the matter of manners, they sit between two chairs, the class they serve has one code; the class they spring from has another, equally good perhaps, certainly in some respects more delicate, but different. In imitating the one code, unsuccessfully, they lose their hold on the other. Their very speech – a mixture of dialect and standard English with false intonations – betrays them. They are like a man living abroad, who has lost grip on his native customs, and has acquired ill the customs of his adopted country. it is not their fault. Circumstances sin against them.

Mrs Widger tells me that, when she left her mother's for service, she felt nothing so keenly as the loneliness, the isolation, of being in a house where no one could be in any full sense of the word her confidant, where she was at the beck and call of strangers from the time she got up till the time she went to bed, where her irregular hours of leisure were passed quite alone in a kitchen. It seems, as might be anticipated, that *mental* comfort or discomfort is at the bottom of the servant question, and that class differences, class misunderstandings, are ultimately the cause of it. Often enough the mistress wishes to be kind, but she fails to understand that what she values most differs from what is most valued by her servants. Often enough the servants wish to do their best, but little irritations, unsalved by sympathy and not to be discussed on terms of equality, lead to sulky, don't-care moods which exasperate the mistress into positive, instead of negative, unkindness. So a vicious circle is formed. The covert enmity between one woman and another simply calls for give and take where both are of the same class, but when one of them is, for payment and all day, at the disposal of the other . . . How many homes there are where the menfolk can get anything done willingly, and the mistress nothing whatever! The girls go out so early. They miss the rough and tumble of their homes. They have their own little ambitions, hardly comprehensible to anyone else. Whether or no they desire to be satisfactory, they do want their own little flutters.

10

Poor brave small servant girls, earning your living while you are yet but children! I see your faces at the doors, rosy from the country or yellowish-white from anæmia and strong tea; see how your young breasts hardly fill out your clinging bodices, all askew, and how your hips are not yet grown to support your skirts properly – draggle-tails! I see you taking the morning's milk from the hearty milkman, or going an errand in your apron and a coat too small for you, or in your mistress's or mother's cast-off jacket, out at the seams, puffy-sleeved, years behind the fashion and awry at the shoulder because it is too big. I see your floppety hat which you cannot pin down tightly to your hair, because there isn't enough of it; – your courageous attempts to be prettier than you are, or else your carelessness from overmuch drudgery; your coquettish and ugly gestures mixed.

I picture your life. Are you thinking of your work, or are you dreaming of the finery you will buy with your month's wages; the ribbons, the lace, or the lovely grown-up hat? Are you thinking of what he said, and she said, and you said, you answered, you did? Are you dreaming of *your* young man? Are you building queer castles in the air? Are you lonely in your dingy kitchen? Have you time and leisure to be lonely?

I follow you into your kitchen, with its faint odour of burnt grease (your carelessness) and of cockroaches, and its whiffs from the scullery sink, and a love-story that scents your life, hidden away in a drawer. I hear your mistress's bell jingle under the stairs. You must go to bed, and sleep, and be up early, before it is either light or warm, to work for her; you must be kept in good condition like a cart horse or a donkey; you must earn, earn well, your so many silver pounds a year.

In mind, I follow you also into your little bedroom under the roof, with its cracked water-jug that matches neither the basin or the soap-dish, and its boards with a ragged scrap of carpet on them, and your tin box in the corner; and the light of the moon or street lamp coming in at the window and casting shadows on the sloping whitewashed ceiling; and your guttered candle. What will you try on to-night? A hat, or a dress, or the two-and-eleven-three-farthing blouse? Shift the candle. Show yourself to the looking-glass. A poke here and a pull there – and now put everything away carefully in the box under the bed, and go to sleep.

Though I say that I follow you up to your attic, and watch you and see you go to sleep, you need not blush or giggle or snap. I would not do you any harm; your eyes would plague me. And besides, I do not entirely fancy you. You are not fresh. You are boxed up too much. But I trust that some lusty careless fellow, regardless of consequences, looking not too far ahead, and following the will of his race – I trust that he will get hold of you and whirl you heavenwards, and will fill your being full to the brim; and will kiss you and surround you with himself, and will make your forget yourself and your mistress and all the world, the leaves and birds of the Lover's Lane, the shadowy cattle munching in the field and the footsteps approaching.

I wish you luck – that your young man may stick to you. It is after all a glimpse of God I wish you, perhaps your only one.

You've got a longish time before you.

11

Mrs Yarty, up Back Lane, is reduced to that last extremity of poor women: she is cleaning her cottage and preparing as well as she can 'to go up over' on credit, without either doctor or midwife – unless she becomes so ill that someone sends for the parish doctor. She will not wish that done, and probably when her time comes, some neighbour will look in to see if she is going on as well as can be expected. Were Yarty and his wife sufficiently servile to attend church or chapel, prayer-meetings or revivals, all sorts of amateur parsons, male and female, would flock round; but in any case, Mrs Yarty has no time for such goings-on, and if Yarty found anyone sniffing about his house, he would certainly tell them that it *was* his house.

A while ago one of the 'district ladies' came here, to Tony's. We were a little short with her, and as a last resource, she remarked superciliously, in a tone of pleasant surprise: 'You are really *very* clean here.' 'Twas an untruth. We are not *very* clean: we are as cleanly as is practicable. I should have liked to show her the door.

''Tis only the way of 'em!' said Mrs Widger. 'They'm stupid, but they means all right.'

Mrs Yarty is not low-spirited at all, and though her voice sounds rather hysterical, it is merely her manner of speaking, slightly accentuated perhaps by more trouble than usual. She is fairly well used to such events by now. Yarty himself is angry. His ordinary habits are bound to be upset for a few days; for ever, if Mrs Yarty dies. He is what successful and conceited people call a waster. 'There ain't no harm in him,' Tony says. 'He wuden't hurt a fly. The only thing is, 'er don't du much.' I have never seen him actually drunk. He keeps very nearly all his irregular earnings for his own use in a strong locked box upstairs. His house is a sort of hotel to him, where he expects to find a bed and food, and it is apparently not his business to inquire how the food is obtained. If there is none, he makes a fuss, and will not take for an answer that he has failed to bring the money. Bobby Yarty, thin, pale, big-eyed, the eldest son but one – a nice intelligent boy though he swears badly at his mother – is ill of a disease which only plenty of good food can cure. If, however, food is scarce, it is first Mrs Yarty who goes short, then the children. Whether they do, or don't, have as much as a couple of chunks each of bread and dripping, Yarty must have his stew or fry. The wage-earner has first claim on the food, and even when the wage-earner does not earn, the custom is still kept up. It is possible also that Mrs Yarty has still an underlying affection for her man, a real desire, become instinctive, to feed him.

She does not say so. Far from it. She says that she is sorry she ever left a good place to marry Yarty. She would, she declares, go back into service but for her children. Washing-day, she swears, is her jolliest time, and she boasts, with what pride is left her, of there being places at twelve or fourteen shillings a week still open to her. She did take a place once – was allowed to take her baby with her – but at the end of the fortnight she arrived home to find that her husband, impatient for his tea, had thrown all the crockery on the floor. She saw then that she must be content with things as they are.

Her present worry is, what will become of the children while she is up over, and who will feed them? Mam Widger will do her share, I don't doubt. Very often now she puts aside something for them. There is a sort of pleasantness in watching them take it: they run off with the dish or baking tin like very polite and very hungry dogs, and bring it back faithfully with exceeding great respectfulness towards a household where there is food to spare.

Mrs Yarty is one of those people who work better for others than for themselves. She is no manager. 'They says,' she remarked the other day, 'as He do take care of the sparrows.' She is a sparrow herself; she grubs up sustenance, rubs along without getting any forwarder, where others would go under altogether. Years ago she must have been good-looking. Her patchily grey hair is crisp; she still has a few pretty gestures. But trouble and too much child-bearing have done next to their worst with her. Sensible when she grasps a thing, she is often a bit mazed. She has the figure of an old woman – bent, screwed – and the toughness of a young one. Her words, spoken pell-mell in a high strained voice which oscillates between laughter and tears, seem to be tumbling down a hill one after another. Spite of all her household difficulties, she retains the usual table of ornaments just inside the front door. Last summer she reclaimed from the roadway a tiny triangular garden, about five inches long in the sides, by wedging a piece of slate between the doorstep and the wall. There she kept three stunted little wallflowers – no room for more – which she attended to every morning after breakfast. Cats destroyed them in the end. She laughed, as it were gleefully. Her laugh is her own; derisive, open-mouthed, shapeless, hardly sane – but she has a smile – a smile at nothing in particular, at her own thoughts – which is singularly sweet and pathetic. I cannot but think that the spirit which enables her to live on without despair, to love her little garden and to smile so sweetly, is better worth than much material comfort. Hers, after all, is a life that has its fragrance.

12

Mrs Widger went off after tea to look at Rosie's grave. She likes to go alone, without the children, and she also likes to stop and have a chat with someone she knows up on land. In consequence, Tony, taking his Sunday evening promenade, found the children on the Front just in that state when they want, and do not wish, to go to bed. They followed him in.

'Wer's thic Mam 'Idger?'

'Don' know!'

'Her's gone to cementry.'

'Didn' ought to leave 'ee like thees yer.'

'Her's gone to see Rosie.'

Tony felt himself rather helpless. 'Now then,' he cried with a vain flourish, 'off to bed wi' 'ee!'

'No! – No! – Shan't! – Us an't had no supper.'

'Wer is yer supper? What be going to hae?'

'Don' know. – Mam! Mam 'Idger!'

One started crying, then the other.

'Casn' thee put 'em to bed thyself?' I asked.

'I don' know! Better wait . . . Her's biding away a long time. I'll hae to talk to she.'

Tony sat down in the courting chair. The two boys climbed one on each of his knees. They wriggled themselves comfortable, and fell asleep. He woke them. 'Won' 'ee go to bed now? I wants to go out.'

'No! No!' they cried peevishly. 'Wer's thiccy Mam?'

Their white heads, turned downwards in sleep on either side of Tony's red weathered face, looked very patient and bud-like. Tony's eyes twinkled over them with a humorous helplessness, crossed occasionally by a shade of impatience. So the three of them waited for the household's source of energy to return. Tony had been wanting a glass of beer. He nearly slept too.

Mam Widger said, when she did come, that they were 'all so big a fule as one another.' 'Casn' thee even get thy children off to bed?' she asked.

'I can't help o'it,' was Tony's reply.

She has taken the household affairs so completely on her shoulders that he is almost helpless without her. In many ways, and in the better, the biblical, sense of the word, he is still so childlike that he often gets done for him what it would be useless for other

people who have little of the child in them, to expect. For the
same reason, bullies choose him out for attack. If I should happen
to lose my temper with him, it is a fault on my part, quickly
repented of and quicker forgiven, but a fault nevertheless. If he,
on the other hand, loses his temper with me, he merely says
afterwards: 'Ah! I be al'ays like that – irritable like; I al'ays was an'
I al'ays shall be to the end o' the chapter.' He assumes that there
was no fault on his part, that his loss of temper was simply the
outcome of the nature of things and of himself, and consequently
that there was nothing to call for forgiveness. The curious thing is
that one feels his view to be right. One does not *forgive* children;
nor the childlike spirit either.

Returning from sea one evening, more lazy than tired, he said:
'You wash me face, Mam, an' I'll wash me hands myself.' His face
was washed amid shouts of laughter, and I tugged off his boots.
We were all quite pleased. Happy is the man for whom one can do
that sort of thing!

Mrs Widger explained the other day at dinner that for a time
after they were married, Tony used to help a great deal with the
housework, until once, when he was doing something clumsily,
she said: 'Git 'long out wi' 'ee, I can du that!'

'Iss,' added Tony, 'I used to scrub, and help her wi' the washing
(an' kiss her tu), but I ain't done nort to it since her spoke to me
rough, like that, an' now I be got out the way o'it, an' that's the
reason o'it – thic Mam 'Idger there!'

'G'out! 'tis thy . . .'

'Oh well, I du cuddle 'ee sometimes, when yu'm willing!'

13

Against the beach the listless sea made a sound like a rattle, very
gently and continuously shaken by a very tired baby. Nothing
was doing. The air was a little too chilly for pleasure boating.
Tony had gone to 'put away up over' the after-dinner hour. I lay
down to read, and fell asleep to the meg-meg of Mam Widger's
voice chatting in a neighbour's doorway.

Two or three small pebbles jumped through the open window.

Uncle Jake was below. When he says, on the Front, that he is going somewhere, he may set off this week, next week, or never; but when he wakes one up . . . I hastened down.

'Going shrimpin' wi' the boat-nets,' he said, flavouring, as it were, a tit-bit in his mouth. 'Must try and earn summut if I bean't going to feel the pinch o' *thees* winter.' Then he added as if it were an afterthought: 'Be 'ee coming?'

'When?'

'Now – so sune as I can get enough bait. I've a-got a beautiful cod's head towards it. Back about midnight, I daresay.'

'All right.'

'Put some clothes on your back. I'll bring a bottle o' tay – better than brewers' tack – an' go'n get the boat ready. Take the *Moon-daisy* . . . Eh?'

Tony, just downstairs and still rubbing his eyes (when he snoozes he goes right to bed), asked what was up. 'Shrimping wi' Uncle Jake,' I replied. 'That'll gie thee a doing!' he said. 'Yu ask George. George used to be Uncle Jake's mate. 'Tis, "Back oar – for'ard – back wi' inside – steady – steady – damn yer eyes!" George couldn't put up wi' it. Jake don' never sleep hisself, and wuden' let he sleep.'

The poor little *Moondaisy*, lying on ways at the water's edge, looked as if she had a small deckhouse aft. Sixteen boat-nets,[1] with their lines and corks, were piled up on the stern seats. In the stern-sheets were two baskets, one of them very smelly, and a newspaper parcel that reeked. Piled up in the bows were bits of old rope, sacks and bags (very catty), chips of wood, empty tea-bottles, and all the litter that collects in a boat used by Uncle Jake.

'Where are we going?' I asked.

'*I* knows; but if anybody asks yu where we'm going, or where we've been, don't yu tell 'em. Don't want none o' they

---

[1] Boat-nets are the same in construction as setting-nets (see p. 124), but upwards of a yard in diameter. Instead of a cord and stick, they have attached to them four or five fathoms of grass line. A few small flat oval corks are spliced at short intervals into the end of the line remote from the net, and at the extremity is a cork buoy about half as large as a man's head.

treble-X-ers on our ground. You say like ol' Pussey Pengelly used
to: "Down to Longo." I don't hae nobody 'long wi' me what can't
keep a quiet tongue. – I can see some o' they fellers down there
now, but they ain't so far west as we'm going, not by a long way.
An' yu wuden' see 'em where they be if they didn't think 'twas
going to be a quiet night with not much pulling attached to it. But
I shuden' be surprised to see a breeze down easterly 'fore morning. Don't du to get caught down to Longo be an easterly breeze.
Lord, the pulls I've a-had to get home 'fore now!'

A very old-fashioned figure Uncle Jake looked, standing up in
the stern-sheets and bending rhythmically, sweep and jerk, sweep
and jerk, to his long oar, as if there were wires inside him. His
grey picture-frame beard seems to have the effect of concentrat-
ing the expressiveness of his face, the satiric glint of his eyes, the
dry smile, the straightness of his shaven upper lip, and the kindly
lighting-up of the whole visage when he calls to the sea-gulls and
they answer him back, and he says with the delight of a child,
'There! Did 'ee hear thic?' Keeping close along shore in order to
avoid the strength of the flood tide against us, we rode with a
perfection of motion on the heave of the breaking swell. As we
were passing over the inside of Broken Rocks, three waves ran far
up the beach. 'Did 'ee hear thic rattle?' Uncle Jake exclaimed.
'That was the high-tide wave, then, whatever the tide-tables say.
Yu'll hear the low tide t'night if yu listens.'

Once I backed the boat ashore for Uncle Jake to go and look at
one of the numerous holes under the cliffs, in every one of which
he has wreckage stored up for firewood against the winter. He can
at least depend on having warmth. When he is nowhere to be
found, he is as a rule down-shore carrying jetsam into caves.
Much of it he gives away for no other payment than the privilege
of talking sarcastically at those who don't trouble to go and of
blazing forth at them when they do.

The November sun went down while we rowed, an almost
imperceptible fading of daylight into delicate thin colours and
finally into a shiny grey half-light. More and more the cliffs
lowered above us. They lost their redness except where a glint of
sun burned splendidly upon them; coloured shadows, as it were,

came to life in the high earthern flanks, lifted themselves off, and
floated away into the sunset, until the land stood against and
above the sea, black and naked, crowned with distorted thorn
bushes. Very serene was the sky, but a little hard. 'Wind down
east t'morrow,' Uncle Jake repeated. We passed Refuge Cove,
over Dog Tooth Ledge, and along Landlock Bay. We tossed over
the Brandy Mull, a great round pit in a reef, where even in calm
weather the tide boils always. No further were there any beaches.
The sea washed to the sheer cliffs through tumbled heaps of
rocks. ''*Tis* an ironbound shop!' said Uncle Jake. 'Poor fellows,
that gets wrecked hereabout! I knows for some copper bolts when
they rots out o' the wreck where they be.'

We had rowed down to Longo on the calm sea; we were on the
sea, almost in it, in so small a boat; and shorewards were the
tide-swirls, the jagged rocks, the high black cliffs. The relation of
sea and land was become reversed for us. The sea was no longer a
thirsty menace, an unknown waste. It was the land, the rocks and
the cliffs, which threatened hungrily. Night-fears, had there been
any, would surely have sprung out from the land.

We rowed into a bay whose wide-spreading arms were like an
amphitheatre of shadows.

'Take thees yer oar,' said Uncle Jake. 'Wer's thic cod's head?'

Everywhere in the boat, to judge by one's nose. He found it,
hacked it, then beat it with a pebble, and hacked again, and tore.
From it came two awful separate smells – one like that of a
dissecting room, the other like bad crab's inside, or like fearfully
perverted cocoa, just wetted – a sort of granulated stink that
stopped one's breath. Beautiful bait!

'Now then, while I fixes the bait between the thirts,' said Uncle
Jake, 'yu paddle westward. Keep 'en straight, else if a bit of a
breeze comes, us'll never find the buoys.' While I rowed very
slowly, he flung overboard first a buoy and then its net, a buoy
and its net, till he had hove the whole sixteen with about four
boat's lengths between each. The *plop* was echoed from the cliff,
and as the nets sank the sea-fire glittered green upon them. He
drew on a ragged pair of oilskin trousers, stationed himself on the
starboard side of the sternsheets, and grasped the longer tiller. On

account of the ebb tide and consequent lay of the corks, we worked back, in reverse order, eastwards. It was for me to row the boat up until the bow was just inside the large buoy. Then Uncle Jake's directions, more or less abbreviated, came fast one after another:

Back outside oar (or *Pull inside oar*), to bring the bows round towards the buoy.

Pull both oars, to bring the boat up to the buoy.

Pull outside oar, to bring the stern of the boat a nice striking distance from the line between the buoy and the small corks. (Uncle Jakes strikes under and up with the tiller.)

Pull both oars, while he hauls in the loose line.

Back both, to stop the boat's way.

Back outside oar, to keep the line just clear of the gunwale.

Stop, while he hauls very slowly and stealthily at first, lest prawns and lobsters jump out, then swiftly, raising his arms high above his head, until the net is aboard.

So, in single and even half strokes, with variations according to current and wind, for all the sixteen buoys and nets. Whilst Uncle Jake, on his part, dropped the prawns into a bag which hung from his neck, flung the wild-crabs amidships, and the lobsters under the stern seat, and hove out the net again a few yards from where it was at first – I, on my part, had to spy the next buoy, a mere rocking blot on the water, to find out how the line lay from it, and then to hold the boat steady till he was ready with the tiller. After a time, one became a little mazed, one's head ached with screwing it round to sight the buoys, and his directions ceased so long as everything was going right.

Very wonderful, even exhilarating was the silence and loneliness, the feeling that ourselves only, of all the world, were in that beautiful mysterious place. Had I had prayers to say, I should have said them, sure that some sort of God was brooding on the waters and suspicious perhaps, at the back of my mind, that where the black cliffs upreared themselves, there the devil was.

After we had hauled and shot again the sixteenth net, Uncle Jake counted one hundred and seventy odd prawns from his bag into the basket. 'Do 'ee see how whitish they be?' he asked.

'They'm al'ays like that in the dirty water after a gale. Lord, what a battering they poor things must get when it blows on thees yer coast!' He picked over the lobsters to see if any were saleable, but found only small ones – cockroaches – that, as he said, 'it don't do to let the bogie-man [fishery inspector] glimpse. – An' I've a-catched,' he added, 'more than five shill'orth o' fine lobsters in one round of the prawn-nets 'fore they bloody men from the west'ard came up hereabout wi' their pots. Ah, shrimpin' ain't what 't used to be!'

We made three more rounds in that bay, then hauled all our nets into the boat, rowed further west, and shot our nets round a submarine ledge, the whereabouts of which Uncle Jake knew to a yard. A couple of rounds there, and we brought up to the buoy of a lobster pot (for the ebb tide, washing round the headland, kept on hurtling us out to sea), had our supper, and waited. Prawns take longer to go into the nets after a second round in the same water.

A haziness that had been in the sky, strengthened into a lurry of little cloudlets between us and the stars. 'That's where 'tis going to be,' said Uncle Jake. 'Easterly! Do 'ee feel this bit of a swell? Us won't be here to-morrow night. – There! Did 'ee hear that? Eh?'

Two waves gave forth a peculiar confidential chuckle, long drawn out and very gentle, very fatigued – as if the sea were making some signal to us; as if it wished to say that it was tired of ebbing and flowing. The cliff shadow listened, I thought, immovable and pitiless, but I fancy that I heard the cry of a bird a quarter of a mile to the eastward. Sea life wakes up with the flow of the tide. I had forgotten the gulls and the ravens; had forgotten the existence of all living things except prawns, lobsters and wild-crabs. No more waves chuckled . . . 'That's the low tide waves sure 'nuff – thic chuckle. There's mostly three on 'em. An' I can al'ays hear the rattle of the hight tide waves tu – iss, even in a gale o' wind. What a rattle they makes on the beach, to be sure! They fules o' visitors 'ould laugh at 'ee if yu was to tell 'em that – they've a-laughed at me – but 'tis true. Yu've heard, an't 'ee?'

The end buoy was troublesome to find. And in the middle of the round, I rowed up to a shadow thinking to find a buoy, and there close beside the boat, revealed as the swell sand, was a reef of rock, humped and covered with seaweed which stood up on end as the water flowed shallowly over the ledge. It was like a grisly great head, ages old, immense, and of terrible aspect, heaving itself up through the sea at us.

With much careful working of the boat, we picked up the middle buoys from the ledge, and hove them further to sea. Uncle Jake swore at the reef, at the nets, at himself, at his luck. "*'Tis* a bloody crib! Didn't think the tide was going to fall so far. This same happened the very last time I was down yer wi' old Blimie – old Sublime, us calls 'en. "Let's get out o' this!" he said. "Leave the blasted nets an' let's get out o' it quick!" But I 'ouldn't let 'en, not I – us had three thousand shrimps thic night; an' he very nearly cried, he did. *'Tis* some mates I've had for thees yer job. Most of 'em won't come when they can pay the brewer any other way. *I'll* never come out again wi' the last three on 'em, not if I starves for it. One of 'em went to sleep; t'other cuden' see the buoys; an' old Blimie was blind and not willing neither. "Wer be the cursed things?" he'd say. "Back!" I'd say. "Back oars! You'm on top o' it!" "Well, I be backing, bain't I?" he'd say, an' go on pulling jest the same. Then 'er said 'er was ill and wanted to go home. *He* won't come no more, not if he starves, an' me too. I won't hae 'en!'

A ripple came down from the east. The sound of its *lap-lap-lap* under the boat stole on one's ears sleepily, but it roused Uncle Jake to quick action. 'Do 'ee see thees little cockle on the water?' he said. 'Do 'ee feel the life o'it in the boat? Must get out of thees yer, else we shan't never find the buoys.'

We picked up the buoys – those we had shifted out of line were hard to find, for the stars were now all hidden by cloud – and a little breeze followed the ripple from the east. Rowing along under the cliffs, even inside some of the rocks, through passages that only Uncle Jake is sure of, we caught the young flood tide. The north-easter, that blew freshly from the Seacombe valley, chilled us to the bone.

Seacombe was asleep. No one was on the Front. We had to carry the nets up from the water's edge to the sea-wall before our

utmost straining could drag the *Moondaisy* up the bank of shingle.
For more than an hour we hauled.

When at last it was over, I brought Uncle Jake in house and
made him a cup of cocoa. We had been nine hours' rowing.
Though he could have done the same again, without food or rest,
he looked a little haggard. It seemed impossible to believe that the
grey old man with disordered hair and beard, clothed in rags and
patches, sipping cocoa in a windsor chair, was that same alert
shadow who had been reckoning up life, so humorously and
wisely, in the darkness under the cliffs. He referred again to the
winter's pinch. It must mean that he has not enough money put
by from summer for the days coming, when even he will not be
able to find some odd job. Yet, as I know very well, when the
pinch does come he will go short and say nothing whatever to
anybody. He will be merely a shade more sarcastic. One of the
children may come home saying that 'thic Uncle Jake an't had half
a pound of butter all this week', or that he has been in one of his
passions with Aunt Jake for taking in a loaf of bread without
paying cash for it. He will bring out a ha'penny from a little screw
of newspaper to buy milk for his cats, and he will take some
crumbs to leave on dry rocks under the cliffs for the robins that
flutter after him there. 'Poor things!' he'll say. And to people he
will still be saying what he thinks, fair or foul, gentle or hard. To
understand his sternness and his kindness, it needs to go with him
wrinkling in the sunshine and prawning in the dark. He is become
very like his beloved rocks and cliffs. He is, as one might say, a
voice for them, and his words and deeds are what one would
expect their words and deeds to be, did they not stand there,
warm, sunny and graciously coloured, or dark and stern, fronting
the sea immovably, as Uncle Jake fronts life. 'Du *I* want to die?'
he says when asked his age. 'Why, I'd like to live a thousand
years!'

14

Tony is singularly free from any craving either for narcotics or
stimulants. Most people I know, especially those who do brain

work or live in cities, are satisfied if they can strike a working
balance between the two. Granfer must have his glass of beer
regularly, but neither smokes nor drinks much tea; Uncle Jake
snuffs and loves his tea, but drinks no alcohol whatever; John
Widger smokes heavily; and I have never known Mrs Widger get
up in the morning without her cup o' tay. Tony, on the other
hand, smokes, for politeness' sake, an occasional cigarette when
it is offered him, does not hanker after his tea, and scarcely
ever drinks alone. He gets drunk now and then, not because he
greatly wants to, but socially; because, when half-a-dozen of
them are drinking in rounds, 'What can a fellow du?' Even
then he often leaves untouched a glassful that has been ordered
for him, though all the while after his third or fourth glass,
he may be asking other men to 'drink up and hae another'.
Drinking with him is an expression of jollity, not the means
of it.

The Perkinses went at the end of last week into a jerry-built
villa up on land. To escape the brunt of moving in, probably,
Perkins took Tony to a football match at Plymouth. It was not so
much that they drank a great deal, as that they came home,
singing, in a very overcrowded and smoky railway carriage. 'I
s'pose I got exzited like,' Tony says. He was all right until they
got out into the fresh air, and then . . . Perkins brought him in the
house and laid him along the passage. 'Here's your husband, Mrs
Widger.' Being rather afraid of Mrs Widger, because she always
speaks her mind, Perkins disappeared quickly.

In vino veritas, no doubt. When Tony is drunk he becomes most
affectionate, and begins 'slatting things about' – not violently or
maliciously, but simply out of joyous devilment and a desire to
feel that he is doing something. Mrs Widger neither wept nor
upbraided him. 'Yu silly gert fule!' she said. 'Yu silly gert fule!
Shut up, or yu'll wake they chil'ern.'

'Be glad tu see yer Tony?'

'G'out! Git yer butes off.'

Tony made the chairs skip round the room and thought he'd
like to see the table (with the lamp) upside down. The window
curtains annoyed him. Mrs Widger took steps.

Luckily, she is not with child, or otherwise delicate, and can therefore stand a deal of rough and tumble. She pushed him headlong into a chair and took off his boots. (Those two, there alone, for Under Town was asleep.) Then she shouldered him upstairs, like a heavy piece of luggage, and laid him on their bed. Poor Tony was more than leery. He swam. He moaned. He was sick. He could neither lie down nor get up. 'Sarve thee damn well right!' said Mam Widger.

'*I* can't help o'it . . .'

'*Yu* can't help o'it!'

Between three and four in the morning, she went downstairs, relighted the fire and made him and herself a cup o' tay. After that, not so very long before daylight, they slept.

To-day Tony is ill and subdued, if not repentant. He reckons he will do the same again ('What chap don't, 'cept they mump-headed long-faced beggars?'), but at present he turns from liquor; he always does for a day and a half after 'going on the bust'. 'Didn't ought never to drink more'n one glass,' he says; 'no, n'eet none at all!' Seeing what it would mean for the family if Tony took to drink, Mrs Widger is, and was at the time, wonderfully calm and cheerful – how far from reliance in herself, or from trust in Tony, is not plain. I asked her what she would do if he became a drunkard and brought no money home.

'Oh,' she said carelessly, 'I s'pose I should turn tu and get some work to du and keep things going somehow.'

'Would you let him have any pocket-money?'

'Ay, I 'spect I should – enough for his pint.'

There's not a shadow of doubt but she would do both.

15

Tony has always been a man for the girls; so much so, and so naively, that whatever he might do would seem quite innocent; as innocent as the love-play of animals. Along the Front, of an evening, he calls out, 'How be 'ee, my dear?' to any girl he chooses, and perhaps takes her arm for a few steps. Given half a chance, he snatches a playful kiss. They never seem to turn rusty with him. He has the primitive quality of knocking their conventionality to bits at one blow.

Just before the Perkinses left, he turned out at five in the morning to see if the high long tide was flowing up to the boats. At six he made tea and went with it to bed again. When he came downstairs at eight o'clock (in his pants, darning the seat of his trousers), Mrs Widger and Mrs Perkins both had breakfasts frying on the fire. Mrs Widger, very loud-voiced that morning, was packing the children off to school; Mrs Perkins was bent over the pan, browning sausages. Tony crept up behind her, seized her by the waist, and kissed her.

'Oh, you naughty man!' said Mrs Perkins, who was married out of a drapery establishment and has the drapery style of talking to perfection. 'If my dear hubby knew . . .'

'Tell him!' retorted Tony. 'I be ready for 'en. I feels lively this morning. I'll gie 'ee another if yu'll darn thees yer trousers for me. Thic Mam 'Idger there won't du nort. You wuden' think I'd had two nights o'it, wude 'ee? I went to bed last night, an' then I got up, five o'clock, and 'cause there weren't nort doing I went to bed again an' had an hour or an hour an' a half's more sleep.'

'Oh, you sleepy man!'

'I didn' want to sleep. I wanted the missis here to cuddle me, on'y her 'ouldn't. Her turned away from me that cold . . . I went off to sleep. An' when I woke up again, thinkin' her'd cuddle me then, her gave me a kick an' got out of bed. I never see'd ort like it. Her ain't what her used to be, for all her ain't a bad li'l thing, thee's know.'

'G'out!' said Mrs Widger. 'I be older – and wiser.'

'Don' know about that. I shall go into Plymouth an' git a nice li'l girl there . . . Oh, I've know'd plenty on 'em. All the li'l girls likes ol' Tony.'

'I know they do,' remarked Mrs Perkins sententiously, while Mrs Widger laughed rather proudly.

'Iss; us was to Plymouth once, an' a nice li'l girl wi' a white bow roun' her neck came up an' spoke to me when I was a-looking into a shop window, an' her said, "I lives jest here," an' I said, "Do 'ee, my dear? I'll be 'long in a minute . . ."'

'Where was Mrs Widger then?'

'Oh, her was 'bout ten yards in front.'

'Well?'

'Iss; if her won't be nice to me when I wants her tu, I shall go into Plymouth an' find out my li'l girl there . . .'

'Garn then, yu fule! I can du wi'out 'ee. I shall hae thic divorce. Thee's think, I s'pose, as I can't get 'long wi'out 'ee? Thee's much mistaken!'

'Well . . .'

'Git 'long out wi' 'ee!' repeated Mrs Widger, laughing and very proudly. 'Git 'long out an' let me clear these yer breakfast things.'

'What have yu got for dinner, me dear? Then I'll remain with 'ee an' not go out at all.'

'G'out!'

Amid loud laughter, Tony snatched a kiss from both ladies, and pranced out.

16

''Tisn't no use to be jealous,' Mrs Widger says. 'I used to be a bit taken that way once, but I ain't now, an' 'twuden make no difference if I was.' Doubtless she is quite right, and she certainly succeeds in never showing what jealousy she may feel when, for instance, she catches sight of Tony strolling in through the Gut with his arm half round another woman's waist, as his playful way is. If Tony speaks of his first wife she does not, like most second wives, stop talking. If she hears of a woman unhappily married, she usually dismisses the affair with a 'Well, her shuden't ha' married 'en: her must put up wi' 'en now her's got 'en.' The goings-on of unmarried people do not easily scandalize her. 'I reckon,' she says, 'yu can du as yu like afore yu'm married, but after that yu'm fixed.' She is so confident of the fastness of the marriage tie (it is, of course, much more indissoluble for poor people who cannot travel, have no servants, and cannot afford lawyers for divorce proceedings) that she can afford to give Tony plenty of rope in small things. Her trust in his faithfulness is absolute, and justified. She has him; he cannot get along without her; she knows that. Her attitude is founded on experience and common-sense; not on some abstract system of morality that never controlled men's lives, and never will.

When I used to look upon fishermen as picturesque common objects of the seashore, I thought their womenfolk rather dreadful. Now, however, the more I see of this household the more I admire Mrs Widger's management of it. I know of few other women who could direct it better and with less friction. Indeed, I am acquainted with no middle-class woman at all who could direct any of these poor men's households as their own wives so noisily and so cleverly do. Mrs Widger does not attempt to gain her own way by sheer force and hardness, not even with the children; she bends to every current; but she never breaks, and finally prevails. Like most West-country people, she has more staying power than visible energy. By going not straight over the hills, like a Roman road, but round by the valleys and level paths, she arrives at her journey's end just as quickly and with much less disturbance and fatigue. She does nothing quite perfectly; neither cooking, mending, cleaning nor child-rearing; but she does everything as well as is practicable, as well as is advisable. Tony would often like things a little better done, but if he had to do them they would be done a little worse. Some people here greatly pride themselves on keeping their homes spotlessly clean, and their front doors locked so that no dirty boot shall soil the oilcloth in the passage. Mrs Widger says that her house is for living in. Children run in and out of it, laughing and shouting.

In some respects, she and Tony remind one of a French bourgeois couple. He has the sentiment, the expressed ideality, the sensitiveness. He perceives a great deal, but perceives much of it vaguely. He seldom makes up his mind – then unalterably. He is like the little man in Blake's drawing, who stands at the foot of a long ladder reaching up to the moon, and cries, 'I want!' What he wants, he does not precisely know. Summut or other. Mrs Widger, on the other hand, knows what she wants very exactly; so exactly that she is content to bide her opportunity. When they were married, Tony had neither boats nor gear. He has them now.

How she keeps a steady head passes my understanding; at breakfast-time, for example, when the boys are clamouring for their kettle-broth or loudly demanding fish, or trying to sneak lumps of sugar; and the girls, nearly late for school, are asking what she wants from the butcher's or stores; and one or two of them require clean things, or something darned, or have not washed their faces or combed out their hair properly; and Tony's and my breakfasts are cooking; and the kettle is boiling out or over; and Tony is asking her where he has left his other guernsey, and everybody is talking nineteen to the dozen – and she wants her own breakfast too. It is at such a moment that she displays best her most characteristic gesture.

Most people who work with a will, possess some gesture or movement which is typical of, and sums up, the major part of their activities – the gesture that sculptors and painters try to catch. To lay out on home and family the earnings of a workman who is regularly paid, calls for skill and care enough on the part of a wife who has no reserve fund and must make the weekly accounts balance to withing a few ha'pence. But successfully to lay out, and to lay by, the earnings of a man like Tony, whose family is large and whose money comes in with extreme irregularity, requires a combination of forethought and self-control which falls little short of genius. And it has to be done on a cash basis, for debt would worry Tony out of his wits. The family purse must necessarily be the centre, and the symbol, of Mrs Widger's household activities; a matter to which she must give more thought than to any other thing.

'Mabel, I want you to go out for me,' she says. 'Get me my purse.'

Standing, as a rule, by the dresser, she receives the purse into her hand, opens it meditatively, looks in, pokes a finger in, tips the purse and peers between the coins as they fall apart; takes one or two out and replaces them as if they fitted into slots. Then with a wide-armed gesture, curiously commanding and graceful, she hands out to the child perhaps a ha'penny. 'Get me a ha'porth o' new milk, quick!'

The purse is put away.

So striking is the little ceremony, so symbolic, so able to stop our chatter while we look, that we have nicknamed Mam Widger *The Purse Bearer*.

That is the name for her – Purse Bearer.

17

Downstairs in the front room there are two or three photographs of George, that he himself has sent home since that day he went off to the Navy. The earliest shows him still boyish, sitting small, as it were, and a little shy of his new uniform. In the latest, taken not long ago, nor very long in point of time after the first, he is sitting bolt upright, chest inflated, arms akimbo with a straight, level, almost ferocious look in his eyes. He has apparently taken a measure of the world outside Under Town, and is all the surer of his feet for having stood up against greater odds and for having walked the slippery plank of Navy regulations. 'If you'm minded to run up against me,' he seems to be saying, 'come and try; here I am.' The two photographs suggest the difference between a bird in winter and in the mating season. George's uniform, in the later photograph, has become his spring plumage.

When he sent word that he was coming home on leave, I was prepared for a great change in him, but scarcely for the new George. He used to be so like a cat on a sunny wall; used to lie along the stern seat of the *Moondaisy* so lazy and content that only his ever-watchful eyes held any expression. He was deeply sun-burnt: scraggy in the neck; strong and lissome, but not very smart.

He is returned home no less strong and lissome, and exceedingly smart. The sunburn is gone; indeed there's many a maiden would envy his complexion; and his long stout neck, with the broadening bands of muscle, would delight a sculptor. The alert expression, that used to be more or less limited to his eyes, has spread, so to speak, over all his face, over the whole of him and into all his movements. He is organized; unified. In repose now, he would not be simply lazy; he would be *being lazy*. His features, rather indeterminate of old, have become curiously refined, almost delicate, almost supercilious (in the pride of young strength), but not quite either. It is noticeable generally that an orderly mental existence has great power to regularize the features, and in so doing, to refine them. Hence perhaps this refinement of feature in George; for if, in the effort to gain promotion, he has been putting his heart into his work – the routine work of his ship and the Naval barracks – it follows that his mental existence must have been very orderly and regular. But how far the total change in him is due to Navy discipline, and how far to his arrival at mating time, one cannot say, neither probably could he. Among working people nothing so smartens a young man and so quickly sets him on his own feet as a little traffic with the maidens; especially when he can't get his own way too easily. George, I gather, is paying attention to two or three.

Whereas his toilet used to consist of dragging on trousers, guernsey and boots, and lacing up the last-named aboard his boat, if at all, it is now a function delightful to witness as he stumps backwards and forwards between the kitchen looking-glass and the scullery-sink. What a washing and spluttering! what a boot-blacking and hair brushing! What retouches and last glances into the glass! The cap comes off and is replaced at a jauntier angle, a ribbon is tied again, the lanyard is put just right, and George goes forth to a war that began before battleships were thought of. One makes fun of his titivations, and admires nevertheless. Pride o' life, I have heard it called. Hitching one's wagon to a star is doubtless good; so is driving one's wagon along mankind's track. Thank God we have still a deal of the monkey in us.

I should like to see how Master George would carry on the land campaign if he had money to spare. That, however, he has not. The presents he brought home for the whole family, as is customary, must have cost him a good deal. He has had, too, a spell in the Naval barracks – which means spending money on shore amusements instead of putting it by. And as he has bought some civilian clothes on the instalment system, and will have that to pay off, he cannot borrow much of his father or mother.

Being 'on his own' now, he does not, of course expect a supply of money from his father, nor on the other hand does Tony try to force his authority upon George. Whilst he was here, George met a few of his old chums up in the Town, and about midnight he came home rather drunk. We were all abed; he had to knock several times; and in the end Tony went down to let him in. 'Twas a good opportunity for a quarrel that would have wakened the whole Square. But Tony said nothing then. He saw George safely to bed, and merely remarked next day in George's hearing, that ''Tisn't gude to drink tu much if you can help o'it, specially when yu'm young; besides, it costis tu much.' George was very ashamed.

Mrs Widger it was who had the row over George's spree, but not with George, and owing to her clever diplomacy it was hardly a row at all.

Mabel rushed into the house at breakfast-time.

'Mother, is George come home?'

'Course he is. What next?'

'Well, Lottie Rousdon says as he come'd home last night an' yu an' Dad wuden' let 'en in. Drunk's a handcart, falling about, her says he was.'

''Tis a lie!' began Mrs Widger loudly. Then she appeared to think of something; her eyes widened, and she spoke quietly.

'Who told yu thic tale?'

'Why, May Rousdon jest as I was coming in now. Her stopped me an' asked if what Lottie'd told her was true.'

'Yu go an' tell Lottie Rousdon that if she has a minute to spare when she comes home this afternoon to clean herself [Lottie Rousdon is a day servant], as mother'd like to see her. Don't yu' – this with rising voice – 'don't you tell anything more'n that or I'll break your neck for yu.'

Mabel rushed out full of importance.

'The lying bitch!' remarked Mam Widger.

Lottie Rousdon walked into the trap. She came in the early evening, feathers flying, very innocent. She was in a strange house, not in the Square or among her relatives. Mrs Widger was on her own ground. Both went into the front room.

'What for did yu—' we could not help hearing.

'Oh, I didn't, Mrs Widger; I'm sure I didn't—'

'Yu did!'

'Mabel,' called Mrs Widger. 'Go'n ask May Rousdon to kindly step this way.'

May Rousdon came.

'Who told yu what yu told Mabel about George, this morning? Did *yu* make it up?'

''Twas Lottie told me, Mrs Widger.'

'There! if I didn't think . . . Don't yu ever say such a wicked thing again! Yu don' known what harm . . .

The parlour door was shut fast. A hubbub went on within. After a time, Lottie, weeping, was led out of the house by her sister.

'The lying bitch,' Mrs Widger repeated. 'I've a-give'd it to her. Making up that tale so pat as if 'twas all true! That's the sort o' thing they used to put about when Tony and me was first married, but I fought 'em down, I did, an' I thought 'twas all stopped long ago. They tried to make out as 'twas me drove George to sea. Nobody can't ever say I haven't luked after Tony's first wife's children so well as I have me own – but they *have* said it, all the time, an' I've up an' give'd it to 'em 'fore now. Whenever I used to correct the children, they'd only to run out o' the house an' they cude always find someone to listen to 'em and say as I was cruel to 'em and God knows what. One time, when I wasn't very well, I felt I cuden' put up wi' it any longer. But I did. An' here I be, same's ever. Pretty times us used to have, I can tell yu, when we was first married an' some of 'em put my blood up!'

I understand that she cursed several – literally kicked one or two – out of the house; but now when anybody is ill, or anything has to be done, she is the first person to be sent for; and when George said goodbye to her at the station, he wept.

18

I was in the Alexandra bar this evening, drinking bitter ale. Apart from the new saloon counter, it is an old-fashioned place, full of wooden partitions and corners and draughts. The incandescent light was flickering dimly in the draught that the sea-wind drove through the window and the front door. Seated around the fireplace or against the painted partitions, and standing about in groups, were fishermen in guernseys, ex-fishermen, some blue-jackets, and some solid-looking men who were pensioners or sailors in mufti. A couple of repulsive lodging-house keepers (they eat too much that falls from the lodgers' tables) were talking local politics with a foxy-faced young tradesman of the semi-professional sort. The barman, who had had enough to drink, was thumb-fingered, loud-voiced, hastily slow. Sometimes the sound of a heavier wave than usual broke through the buzz of conversation, and sometimes, when the conversation dropped, wave after wave could be heard sweeping the shingle along the beach.

A party of vagrant minstrels came to the front-door steps. They played a comic song, and the voices within rose in defiance of the music, so that when it stopped suddenly, they were surprised into silence.

Up through that silence welled the opening notes of Schubert's *Serenade*. Nobody spoke. The barman took up a glass cheerily. 'My doctor ordered me to take a little when I feel I need it,' he said; and was *hushed* down. Some edged towards the door, others sat back with faces and pipes tilted up, and others gazed down at the floor. A memory-struck, far-away look came into their eyes. Only the barman with his glass, and the tradesman in his smart suit, seemed wholly themselves.

The *Serenade* ceased. None spoke. The light gave a great flicker. 'What the bloody hell!' exclaimed John Widger. The day-dreamers awoke, as if from a light sleep. An everyday look came quickly into their eyes and each one shifted in his seat. Some even shook themselves like dogs. A joke was made about the woman who came in to collect pence, and the conversation rose till nothing of the sea's noise could be heard.

I realized with a shock that in four days I shall not be here, and when I left the bar, I forgot entirely to say *Good-night*.

It was as if, for the moment, we had all been very intimate; as if we had all gone an adventure together and had peeped over the edge of the world.

VIII

I

CHILLINESS – a social and emotional chilliness that can with difficulty be defined or nailed down to any cause – is, above and below all, what one feels on returning from a poor man's house into middle-class surroundings. It is not unlike that chill with which certain forms of metropolitan hospitality strike a country-man. He meets a London friend, a former fellow-townsman, perhaps, who has migrated to London and whom he has not seen for a year or two. 'Glad to see you,' says the Londoner. 'You must call on my wife before you go back. Her day is Wednesday.' Or, 'You must come to dinner one evening. When are you free? Next Tuesday? or Friday?' If the hospitality had begun forthwith, and the countryman had been haled off, country fashion, to the very next pot-luck meal, he would have had a pleasant adventure. It would have been like old times. The former glow of friendship would have more than revived. But the calculated invitation for a future date, the idea that the countryman will like to call for a twenty minutes' chat on generalities and a couple of cups of bad afternoon tea . . . Though he may understand that a multiplicity of engagements in London renders this sort of thing convenient, he none the less feels a chill when it is applied to himself, and usually cares little whether he go or not. He becomes conscious of the desire to save trouble, which is at the bottom of such calculations. Had the Londoner revisited the country, he would have found old friends ready to upset all their arrangements for the sake of entertaining him. The London hospitality is the 'better done,' but country hospitality is warmer. Middle-class life runs smoother than the poor man's, it is more arranged and in many ways 'better done,' and it is chillier precisely because, for smooth running, the warmer human impulses, both good and bad, must be repressed. 'Something with a little love and a little murder' in it, was what the illiterate old woman wanted to learn to read. It is what we all want in our hearts, much more than the smooth running and impenetrable uniform politeness.

Down at Seacombe we warm our hands, so to speak, at the fire of life; hunger lurks outside, and the fire is dusty and needs looking after; but it glows, and we sit together round it. Here at Salisbury, throughout the social house, we have an installation of hot-water pipes; they may be hygienic (which is doubtful), and they are little trouble to keep going; but they don't glow. Give me the warmth that glows, and let me get near the heart of it.

Voices are often raised in Under Town and quarrels are not infrequent, but the underlying affections are seldom doubted, and when they do rise to the surface, there they are, visible, unashamed. 'Each for himself, and devil take the hindmost,' is more admired in theory than followed in practice. 'Each for himself and the Almighty for us all,' is Tony's way of putting it. The differences lies there.

My acquaintances here are well off for the necessities of life. No one is likely to starve next week. Nevertheless, they are full of worry, and by restraining their expressions of worry so as not to become intolerable to the other worries, they make themselves the more lonely and increase their panic of mind. They are afraid of life.

At Seacombe, though there were not a fortnight's money in the housee, we lived merrily on what we had. In Tony's 'Summut 'll sure to turn up if yu be ready an' tries to oblige' there is more than philosophy; there is race tradition, the experience of generations. The Fates are treacherous; therefore, of course, they like to be trusted, and the gifts they reserve for those that trust them are retrospective.

All of us at Tony's wanted many things – a pension, enough to live on, work, a piano, or only 'jam zide plaate' – God knows what we didn't want! But the things that men haven't, and want, unite them more than those they have. *I want* is life's steam-gauge; the measure of its energy. It is the ground-bass of love, however transcendentalized, and whether it give birth to children or ideas. *I have* is stagnant. And *I am afraid* is the beginning of decay.

It is still *I want*, rather than *I am afraid*, that spurs the poor man on.

2

For his first marriage and towards setting up house, Tony succeeded in saving twenty shillings. He gave it to his mother in gold to keep safely for him, and the day before the wedding, he asked for it. 'Yu knows we an't got no bloody sovereigns,' said his father. It had all been spent in food and clothes for the younger children. So Tony went to sea that night and earned five shillings. A shilling of that too he gave to his mother; then started off on foot for the village where his girl was living and awaiting him. She had a little saved up: he knew that, though he feared it might have gone like his. They were married, however; they fed, rejoiced, and joked; and 'for to du the thing proper like,' they hired a trap to drive them home. With what money was left they embarked on married life, and their children made no unreasonable delay about coming. 'Aye!' says Tony, 'I'd du the same again – though 'twas hard times often.'

Before I left Seacombe I asked a fisherman's wife, who was expecting her sixth or seventh child, whether she had enough money in hand to go through with it all; for I knew that her husband was unlikely to earn anything just then. 'I have,' she said, 'an' p'raps I an't. It all depends. If everything goes all right, I've got enough to last out, but if I be so ill as I was wi' the last one, what us lost, then I an't. Howsbe-ever, I don't want nort now. Us'll see how it turns out.' She went on setting her house in order, preparing baby linen and making ready to 'go up over,' with perfect courage and tranquillity. When one thinks of the average educated woman's fear of childbed, although she can have doctors, nurses, anaesthetics and every other alleviation, the contrast is very great, more especially as the fisherman's wife had good reason to anticipate much pain and danger, in addition to the possibility of her money giving out.

Those are not extraordinary instances, chosen to show how courageous people can be sometimes; on the contrary, they are quite ordinary illustrations of a general attitude among the poor towards life. To express it in terms of a theory which in one form or another is accepted by nearly all thinkers – the poor have not only the *Will to Live,* they have the *Courage to Live.*

On the whole, they possess the *Courage to LIve* much more than any other class. And they need it much more. The industrious middle-class man, the commercial or professional man, works with a reasonable expectation of ending his days in comfort. He would hardly work without. But the poor man's reasonable expectation is the workhouse, or some almost equally galling kind of dependency. The former may count himself very unlucky if after a life of work he comes to destitution; the latter is lucky if he escapes it. Yet the poor man works on, and is of at least as good cheer as the other one. If he can rub along, he is even happy. He is, I think, the happier of the two.

The more intimately one lives among the poor, the more one admires their amazing talent for happiness in spite of privation, and their magnificent courage in the face of uncertainty; and the more also one sees that these qualities have been called into being, or kept alive, by uncertainty and thriftlessness. Thrift, indeed, may easily by an evil rather than good. From a middle-class standpoint, it is an admirable virtue to recommend to the poor. It helps to keep them off the rates. But for its proper exercise, thrift requires a special training and tradition. And from the standpoint of the essential, as opposed to the material, welfare of the poor, it can easily be over-valued. Extreme thrift, like extreme cleanliness, has often a singularly dehumanizing effect. It hardens to the nature of its votaries, just as gaining what they have not earned most frequently makes men flabby. Thrift, as highly recommended, leads the poor man into the spiritual squalor of the lower middle-class. It is all right as a means of living, but lamentable as an end of life. If a penny saved is a penny earned, then a penny earned by work is worth twopence.

The Courage to Live is the blossom of the *Will to Live* – a flower far less readily grown than withered. It might be argued that since apprehensiveness implies foresight, the poor man's *Courage to Live* is simply his lack of forethought. In part, no doubt, it is that.

But he does think, slowly and tenaciously, as a cuttlefish grips. He foresees pretty plainly the workhouse; and he has the courage to face its probability, and to go ahead nevertheless. His reading of life is in some ways very broad, his foothold very firm; for it is founded closely on actual experience of the primary realities. He looks backwards as well as forwards; his fondness and memory for anecdote is evidence of how he dwells on the past; instead of comparing an occurrence with something in a book, he recalls a similar thing that happened to So-and-so, so many years ago, you mind . . . He knows vaguely (and it is our vaguer knowledge which shapes our lives) that only by a succession of miracles a long series of hair's-breadth escapes and lucky chances, does he stand at any moment where he is; and he doesn't see why miracles should suddenly come to an end. Hence his active fatalism, as opposed to the passive Eastern variety. In Tony's opinion, ''Tis better to be lucky than rich.' I have never heard him say that fortune favours the brave. He assumes it.

3

As one grows more democratic in feeling, as one's faith in the people receives shock after shock, yet on the whole brightens – so does one's mistrust of the so-called democratic programmes increase. One becomes at once more dissatisfied and less, more reckless and much more cautious. One sees so plainly that the three or four political parties by no means exhaust the political possibilities. The poor, though indeed they have the franchise, remain little more than pawns in the political game. They have to vote for somebody, and nobody is prepared to allow them much without a full return in money or domination. They pay in practice for what theoretically is only their due. Justice for them is mainly bills of costs. The political fight lies still between their masters and would-be masters; no so much now, perhaps, between different factions of property-owners as between the property-owners and the intellectuals. Out of the frying-pan into the fire seems the likely course; for the intellectuals, if they have the chance, enslave the whole man; they are logical and ruthless.

The worst tyrannies have been priestly tyrannies, whether of Christians, Brahmins or negro witch-doctors; and those priests were the intellectuals of their time. I wonder when we shall have a party of intellectuals content to find out the people's ideals and to serve them faithfully, instead of trying to foist their own ideals upon the people.

Law-makers, however, will probably continue to work for the supposed benefit of the people rather than on the people's behalf; and equally, the supposed welfare of the people will continue to be the handiest political weapon; for the property-owning, articulate classes are better able to prevent themselves being played with. To those two facts one's political principles must be adjusted. The articulate classes, moreover, are actually so little acquainted with the inner life of the poor that there is no ground-work of general knowledge upon which to base conclusions, and it is impossible to do more than speak from one's own personal experience. I don't mind confessing that, though I should prefer justice all round, yet, if injustice is to be done – as done it must be no doubt – I had rather the poor were not the sufferers. There is no reason to believe that present conditions cannot be bettered – to believe, with Dr Pangloss, *que tout est au mieux dans ce meilleur des mondes possibles.* I have found that to grow acquainted with the class that is the chief object of social legislation is to see more plainly the room for improvement, and also to see how much better, how much sounder, that class is than it appeared to be from the outside: how much might be gained, of material advantage especially, and at the same time how much there is to be lost of those qualities of character which have been acquired through long training and by infinite sacrifice. To learn to care for the poor, for their own sake, is to fear for them nothing so much as slap-dash, short-sighted social legislation.

The man matters more than his circumstances. The poor man's *Courage to Live* is his most valuable distinctive quality. Most of his finest virtues spring therefrom. Any material progress which tends to diminish his *Courage to Live,* or to reduce it to mere *Will to Live,* must prove in the long run to his and to the nation's disadvantage. And the *Courage to Live,* like other virtues, diminishes with lack of exercise. Therefore every material advance should provide for the continued, for an even greater, exercise and need of the *Courage to Live*. If not, then the material advance is best done without.

That is the main constructive conclusion to be drawn. Somewhat akin to it is another conclusion of a more critical nature.

In Nietzsche's *Beyond Good and Evil* there is an apophthegm to the effect that, 'Insanity in individuals is something rare – but in groups, parties, nations, and epochs it is the rule.' And whilst, on the one hand mental specialists have been extending the boundaries of insanity to the point of justifying the popular adage that everyone is a bit mad, they have, on the other hand, tended to narrow down the difference between sanity and its reverse until it has become almost entirely a question of mental inhibition, or self-control.

The highest aim of Mental Hygiene should be to increase the power of mental inhibition amongst all men and women. Control is the basis of all law and the cement of every social system among men and women, without which it would go to pieces . . . *Sufficient power of self-control should be the essence and test of sanity.*[1]

It is too gratuitously assumed by law-makers (*i.e.* agitators for legislation as well as legislators) that the poor man is woefully deficient in inhibition and must be legislated for at every turn. Because, for instance, he furnishes the police courts with the majority of 'drunks and disorderlies,' he is treated as a born drunkard, to be sedulously protected against himself, regardless

---

[1] 'The Hygiene of Mind,' by T. S. Clouston, M.D., F.R.S.E., (London, 1906). Without an extension which Dr Clouston provides, though not in so many words, the definition I have italicized is psychologically a little superficial. Mental inhibition, generally, needs dividing into self-control and, say, auto-control. Where one man may *self-control* himself by an effort of will, another man, in the same predicament, might *auto-control* himself instinctively, without a conscious effort of will. Which is the saner, and likelier to remain so, under ordinary circumstances and under extraordinary circumstances, would be most difficult to determine. Many people are only sane in action because they know that they are insane in impulse, and take measures accordingly. They keep a sane front to the world by legislating pretty sternly for themselves.

of such facts as (1) there is more of him to get drink, (2) he prefers 'going on the bust' to the more insidious dram-drinking and drugging, (3) he has more cause to get drunk, (4) he gets drunk publicly, (5) tied-house beer and cheap liquors stimulate to disorderliness more than good liquor. The truth is that the poor have a great deal of self-restraint, quite as much probably as their law-makers; but it is exercised in different directions and, possibly, is somewhat frittered away in small occasions. The poor man has so much more bark than bite. He fails to restrain his cuss-words for example – but then cuss-words were invented to impress fools. There is much in his life that would madden his law-makers, and *vice versa*. If control is the cement of every social system and if it is the highest aim of mental hygiene, it follows that control should be the highest aim of legislation and custom, which together make up social hygiene. And – always remembering that control is of all virtues the one which strengthens with use and withers with disuse – every piece of new legislation should be most carefully examined as to its probable effect on the self-control of the people. Control, in short should be the paramount criterion of new legislation. A proximate advantage, unless it be a matter of life and death, is too dearly purchased by an ultimate diminution of self-control.

4

Since the Industrial Revolution and rise of the press, the middle-class has become more and more the real law-maker. The poor have voted legislators into power; the upper class in the main has formally made the laws; but the engineering of legislation has been, and is, the work of the middle class. And the amusing and pathetic thing is that the middle class has used its power to try to make other classes like itself. That it has succeeded so badly is largely due to the fact that the poor man is not simply an undeveloped middle-class man. The children at Seacombe showed true childish penetration in treating a *gentry-boy* as an animal of another species: the poor and the middle class are different in kind as well as in degree. (More different perhaps than the poor and the aristocrat). Their civilizations are not two stages of the same civilization, but two civilizations, two traditions, which have grown up concurrently, though not of course without considerable intermingling. To turn a typical poor man into a typical middle-class man is not only to develop him in some respects, and do the opposite in others; it is radically to alter him. The civilization of the poor may be more backward materially, but it contains the nucleus of a finer civilization than that of the middle class.

The two classes possess widely dissimilar outlooks. Their morale is different. Their ethics are different.[1] Middle class people frequently make a huge unnecessary outcry, and demand instant unnecessary legislation because they find among the poor conditions which would be intolerable to themselves but are by no means so to the poor. And again, the benevolent frequently accuse the poor of great ingratitude because, at some expense probably, they have pressed upon the poor what they themselves would like, but what the poor neither want nor are thankful for. The educated can sometimes enter fully, and even reasonably, into the sorrows of the uneducated, but it is seldom indeed that they can enter into their joys and consolations.

Broadly speaking, the middle-class is distinguished by the utilitarian virtues; the virtues, that is, which are means to an end; the profitable, discreet, expedient virtues: whereas the poor prefer what Maeterlinck calls 'the great useless virtues' – useless because they bring no apparent immediate profit, and great because by faith or deeply-rooted instinct we still believe them of more account than all the utilitarian virtues put together.[2]

[1] 'The more one sees of the poor in their own homes, the more one becomes convinced that their ethical views, taken as a whole, can be more justly described as different from those of the upper classes than as better or worse.' ('The Next Street but One.' By M. Loane. London, 1907.)

[2] 'When one begins to know the poor intimately, visiting the same houses time after time, and throughout periods of as long as eight or ten years, one becomes gradually convinced that in the real essentials of morality, they are, as a whole, far more advanced than is generally believed, but they range the list of virtues in a different order from that commonly adopted by the more educated classes. Generosity ranks far before justice, sympathy before truth, love before chastity, a pliant and obliging disposition before a rigidly honest

The poor, one comes to believe firmly, if not interfered with by those who happen to be in power, are quite capable of fighting out their own salvation. A clear ring is what they want – the opportunity for their 'something in them tending to good' to develop on its own lines. (When I say 'a clear ring' I do not mean that one side should have seconds and towels provided and that the other side should be left with neither.) That their culture, so developed, will be different from our present middle-class culture, is certain; that it will be superior is probable. The middle class is in decay, for its reproductive instincts are losing their effective intensity, and it is afraid of having children; its culture, that it grafted on the old aristocratic stem, must decay with it. When the culture derived from the lower classes is ready to be grafted in its turn upon the old stem it is possible that mankind's progress will go backwards a little to find its footing, and will then take one of its great jumps forward.

5

The socio-political problem turns out, on ultimate analysis, to be a wide restatement of the old theological Problem of Pain. Suffering does not necessarily make a fine character, but the characters that we recognize as fine could not, apparently, have been so without suffering. It is possible to say, 'I have suffered, and though I am scarred and seared, yet I know that on the whole I am the better for that suffering. I do not now wish that I had not had that suffering. I even desire that those I love shall suffer so much as they can bear, that their conquest may be the greater, their joys the fuller, and their life the more intense.' Nevertheless, the very next moment, the same man will try by every means possible to avoid suffering for himself and for those he loves. That is the

one. In brief, the less admixture of intellect required for the practice of any virtue, the higher it stands in popular estimation.' ('From their Point of View.' By M. Loane. London, 1908.)

It is difficult to see on what grounds Miss Loane implies – if she does mean to imply – that the poor would do well to exchange their own order of the virtues for the other order. Christianity certainly affords no such grounds, nor does any other philosophy or religion, except utilitarianism perhaps.

dualism which dogs humanity in the mass no less than in the individual. That lies at the core of domestic politics. But it may be that the part of our nature which finds reason to be grateful for past suffering is higher than that part which seeks to avoid it in the future.

Waste of the benefits of suffering is waste indeed.

IX

I

WE hired a drosky – one of the little light landaus that they use with a single horse in this hilly district – and thus we came down from the station. On the box were the coachman (grinning), a cabin trunk, a portmanteau, a gaping gladstone bag, and a rug packed with sweaters and boots. On the front seat, a large parcel of books, a typewriter, a dispatch case, a grubby moon-faced little friend of Tommy's, Tommy himself, and Jimmy. On the back seat, Straighty, Dane and myself. The small boy stood up on the seat, and Dane squatting on his haunches, overtopped us all.

Down the hill we drove, swerving, wobbling, laughing – a May party in leaflless winter. Dane, in his efforts to lick the children's faces, tumbled off his perch. We helped him back to his seat amid a chorus of happy screams. The grubby boy was just too astonished to cry, just too proud of travelling in a carriage. He screwed up his face – and unscrewed it again. Every now and then Tommy sat back as far as he could from the disorder, the collection of jerking arms and legs, in order to adjust the Plymouth spectacles, of which he is so proud, on his small pug nose. As we passed the cross-roads, Straighty was trying to snatch a kiss. While we drove along the Front, the children waved their hands over the sides of the drosky, and shouted with delight. 'Twas a Bacchanal with laughter for wine. The Square turned out to witness our arrival. 'Her's come!' the kiddies cried. Dane leapt out first, found a rabbit's head and bolted it whole. The rest of us scrambled out. The luggage was piled up in the passage. Hastening in his stockinged feet (he had been putting away an hour) to say that he was on the point of coming up to station, Tony bruised a toe and barked a shin. But it was no time to be savage. I wonder where else the two shillings I paid for the drosky would have purchased so much delight. Or rather, the delight was in ourselves, in the children; the two shillings served only to unlock it.

What precisely there is of difference between these children and those of the middle and upper classes has always puzzled me. That there is a difference I feel certain. A few years ago, when I had so much to do with the boys and girls of a high school, they liked me pretty well, I think, and trusted me, but they did not take to me, nor I very greatly to them. They went about their business, and I about mine. If I invited them for a walk, they came gladly, not because it was a walk with me, but because I knew of interesting muddy places, and where to find strange things. Their manners to me were always good; good manners smoothed our intercourse. But in no sense were our lives interwoven. We were side-shows, the one to the other. I was content that it should be so, and they were too.

Here, on the other hand, my difficulty is to get rid of the children when I wish to go out by myself. They follow me out to the Front, and meet me there when I return, running towards me with shouting and arms upraised, tumbling over their own toes, and taking me home as if I were a huge pet dog of theirs. 'Where be yu going?' they ask, and, 'Where yu been?' Jimmy regards me as a fixture. 'When yu goes away for two or dree days,' he says. 'I'll write to 'ee, like Dad du.' I cross the Square, and some child, lolling over the board across a doorway, laughs to me shrilly and waves its arms. If by taking thought, I could send such a glow to the hearts of those I love, as that child, without thinking, sends to mine . . . But I cannot. I can only wave a hand back to the child, and be thankful and full-hearted. Often enough I wish I could have a piano and find out whether my fingers will still play Chopin, Beethoven, and Bach; often I hanker after a sight of a certain picture or a certain statue in the Louvre or Luxembourg, for a concert, a theatre, a right-down argument on some intellectual point, or for the books I want to read and never shall. Yet, all in all, I am never sorry for long. This children's babble and laughter, these simple, commonplace, wonderful affections, are a hundred times worth everything I miss.

It is not that I buy the children bananas or give them an infrequent ha'penny. When bananas and ha'pence are scarce, their love is no less. It is not that I am always good-tempered and jolly.

Sometimes I snap unmercifully, so that they look at me with scared, inquiring eyes. It is not that they are always well-behaved. Frequently they are very naughty indeed. The causes of our sympathy lie deeper.

They are more naïve than the children who are in process of being well-educated; more independent and also more dependent. They feel more keenly any separation from those they love; they cry lustily if their mother disappears only for an hour or two; and nevertheless they can fend for themselves out and about as children more carefully nurtured could never do. Less able to travel by themselves, they do travel alone, and in the end quite as successfully. They make more mistakes and retrieve them better. Affection with them more rapidly and frankly translates itself into action. They laugh quickly, cry quickly, swear quickly. 'Yu'm a fule!' they rap out without a moment's hesitation; and I suppose I am, else they wouldn't want to say so. Perhaps I overvalue the physical manifestations of love, but if a child will take my hand, or climb upon my knee, or kiss me unawares, then to certainty of its affection is added a greater contentment and a deeper faith. The peace of a child that sleeps upon one's shoulder, is given also to oneself. The appurtenances of love mean much to me; nearness, warmth, caresses. But I cannot make the advances; I was bred in a different school where, though frankness was encouraged, *naïveté* was repressed; and I am the more grateful to these children for taking me in hand – for being able to do so.

Tommy has returned from the Plymouth Eye Infirmary much quietened down in many respects and, as most people would say, much better mannered. He is neater and a better listener to conversation. He puts his shoes under the table, does not throw them. But he has brought back also some of the nurses' exclamations of surprise – 'Oh, I say!' 'Not I!' 'You don't say so!' 'What idiocy!' and the like. No doubt those expressions sounded quite proper among the nurses, but on Tommy's lips they seem curiously more vulgar than his natural and rougher expletives. It is, besides, as if one were eavesdropping outside the nurses' common room.

Much of the charm of these children, and of the grown-ups too, lies in the fact that, apart from a few points on which etiquette is very strict, they have no manners. I don't mean that they are bad-mannered; quite the contrary; what I mean is that their manners are not codified. Having no rules for behaviour under various circumstances, they must on each occasion act according to their kindliness desire to please, or the reverse. They must go back to the first principles of manners. What they are, that they appear. What they feel at the moment, that they show. The kind man or child is kindly; the brutal or spiteful by nature are brutal or spiteful in manner. Elsewhere, among people of breeding, manners make the man – and hide him. Here, the man makes his own manners, and in so doing still further reveals himself.

I have known a professional man who was rather well-spoken of for his good manners, fail lamentably so soon as he found himself in surroundings not his own. His code of manners did not apply there, and outside his code he had no manners. He was excessively rude. He showed at once that his customary good manners were founded on rules well learnt, and not on any real consideration for other people's feelings. The incredible impertinence of clergymen and district visitors furnishes plenty of cases in point. Their manners, no doubt, are pretty good among themselves. Yet it is a common saying here, 'What chake they gentry've got!' A 'district lady' entered Mrs Stidson's cottage without knock or warning, just when Mrs Stidson was cleaning up and wanted no visitors of any sort. 'What's the matter with your eye?' asked the district lady. Mrs Stidson refused to answer. ('Untidy, intractable woman!') But a neighbour upspoke and said, ''Tis her husband, mam, as have give'd her a black eye.' At which the district lady exclaimed, 'My good woman, why don't you leave him. You *ought* to leave him – at once!' Mrs Stidson has a number of young children.

It might have been expected, on the other hand, when Tony and myself went on holiday up-country, stayed at a largish much-upholstered hotel, and dined out several times as he had never done before, that he would have been like a fish out of water, very awkward, and would have committed a number of bad *faux pas*. Nothing of the sort. He was nervous, certainly, and the numerous knives, forks and glasses somewhat confused him at first. But Tony's good manners are not codified. He is sensitive, kindly, desirous of pleasing, quick to observe. On that basis, he invented for himself, according to the occasion, the manners he had not been taught. At the same time he remained himself. And he was a complete success. Nobody had any reason to blush on Tony's behalf. Except once; when he remarked to some ladies after dinner that he found Londoners very nice and free-like; that a pretty young lady had stopped him in the Strand the evening before, and had called him Percy; that he hadn't had time to tell her she'd made a mistake, and that, in fact, he might have knowed her tu Seacombe, only he didn recollect.

There was a bad pause.

Tony doesn't think ill of anybody without cause. *Honi soit qui mal y pense* might very well be *his* motto.

2

News has come along from Plymouth that the boats there have fallen in with large shoals of herring. The air here has since been charged with excitement – the excitement of men who earn their livelihood by gambling with the sea. The drifters have fitted out. Most of the boats are up over – lying on the sea wall – but a few days ago many busy blue men slid the big brown drifters down their shoots to the beach. Looking along, one saw a couple men standing in each drifter and, with the leisurely haste of seamen, drawing in their nets. It gave a peculiar savour, a hopeful animation, to the blank wintry sea. It was as if the spring had come to us human beings prematurely, before it was ready to seize on nature.

Yesterday afternoon I felt too unwell to lend a hand in shoving off the boats. So I climbed to the top of the East Cliff. The air was cool and still – so still that all the Seacombe smoke hung in the valley and drifted slowly to seawards and faded there. While the sun was setting behind a bank of sulky dull clouds, some wool-packs, faintly outlined in white against the grey, rose almost imperceptibly in the western sky. Everything, the sea itself, seemed very dry. Nothing moved on the cliffs, except some small birds which flittered homelessly among the black and twisted burnt gorse. They were very tiny and pitiful against, or indeed amid, the solemn gathering of the great slow clouds. On looking down from the edge of the cliff, a slight mistiness of the air gave one the impression that there was, lying level above the sea, a sheet of glass that dulled the sound of the water, yet allowed one to discern every half-formed ripple, and even the purple of the rocks beneath. Five hundred feet below and a quarter of a mile out, were three boats. They also, like the birds, seemed pitifully tiny. But, unlike the birds, they did not seem purposeless. It was evident they were moving, though one could not see rowers, oars, or splashes, for they progressed in short jumps and above the dulled rattle of a billow breaking on the pebbles, the faint click-thud of oars between thole-pins was plainly audible. I had an odd fancy that the six men were rowing through immensity, into eternity, to meet God; and they would so continue rowing, eternally.

This morning, very early, the crackle of burning wood in the kitchen fireplace awoke me. Then I heard the sea roaring; then Tony's bare feet on the stairs. 'Wind's backed an' come on to blow,' he said. 'They've a-had to hard up an' urn for it. Two on 'em's in, an' one have a-losted two nets. I told 'em 'twasn't vitty when they shoved off. 'Tis blowing hard. I be going out along to see w'er t'other on 'em's in eet.'

The sea was angry, the moon obscure. The dead-asleep town stood up motionless before the madly-living breakers. It seemed as if a horrible fight was in progress; loud rage and dumb treachery face to face in the semi-darkness; and between the livelong combatants, little men ran to and fro, peering out to sea.

Presently the third boat ran ashore. Its bellied sail hid everything from us who waited at the water's edge. It was hoisted on a high wave, and cast on land. The sea did not want it then. The sea spewed it up. The sea can afford to wait, even until the clean bright little town is a ruin on a salt marsh.

Returning in house, we made hot tea, and laughed.

3

We had, as it were, said *Good-Night* to the town, though it was only half-past three in the afternoon. Most lazy we must have looked as we sailed off to the fishing ground with a light fair wind, NNW. John's young muscular frame was leaning against the mainmast, like a magnificent statue dressed for the moment in fishermen's rig. Tony aft was lounging across the tiller. He fits the tiller, for he is older and bent and his eyes are deeply crows-footed with watching. Both of them showed the same splendid contrast of navy-blue jerseys against sea eyes and spray-stung red and russet skins. I was lying full length along the midship thwart. We lopped along lazily, about three knots to the hour.

As we lounged and smoked, each of us sang a different song, more or less in tune. It sounded not unmelodious upon the large waters. At intervals we asked one another where the 'gert bodies of herrings' had gone off to. Eastwards, westwards, to the offing, or down to the bottom to spawn?

So near the land we were, yet so far from it in feeling. There, to the NE. was the little town, sunlit and brilliantly white, with the church tower rising in the middle and the heather-topped cloud-capped hills behind. There around the bay, were the red cliffs, crossed by deep shadows and splotched with dark green bushes. The land was there. We were to sea. The water, which barely gurgled beneath the bows of the drifter, was rushing up the beaches under the cliffs with a myriad-sounding rattle. Gulls, bright pearly white or black as cormorants, according as the light struck them, were our only companions. The little craft our kingdom was – twenty-two foot long by eight in the beam, – and a pretty pickle of a kingdom!

Mixed up together in the stern were spare cork buoys, rope ends, sacks of ballast and Tony. Midships were the piled up nets and buoys. For'ard were more ballast bags and rope ends, some cordage, old clothes, sacks, paper bags of supper, four bottles of cold tea, two of paraffin oil and one of water, the riding lamp and a very old fish-box, half full of pebbles, for cooking on. All over the boat were herring scales and smelly blobs of roe. It's some-time now since the old craft was scraped and painted.

But the golden light of the sunset gilded everything, and the probable catch was what concerned us.

We chose our berth among the other drifters that were on the ground. We shot two hundred and forty fathom of net with a swishing plash of the yarn and a smack-smack-splutter of the buoys. We had our supper of sandwiches and tatie-cake and hotted-up tea.

'Can 'ee smell ort?' asked John sniffing out over the bows.

'Herring!' said I. 'I can smell 'em plainly.'

'Then there's fish about.'

Tony however remarked the absence of birds, and declared that the water didn't look so fishy as when they had their last big haul. 'They herrings be gone east,' he repeated.

'G'out! What did 'ee come west for then? I told yu to du as yu minded, an' yu did, didn' 'ee? Us'll haul up in a couple o' hours an' see w'er us got any.'

We didn't turn in. We piled on clothes and stayed drinking, smoking, chatting, singing – a boat-full of life swinging gently to the nets in an immense dark silence, an immense sea-whisper.

About nine o'clock we hauled in for not more than nine dozen of fish. The sea-fire glimmered on the rising net, glittered in the boat, and then, with an almost painful suddenness, snuffed out. 'They be so full as eggs,' said John every minute or two, holding out fish to Tony, who felt them and answered, 'Iss, they'm no scanters [spawned or undersized fish]. *They* bain't here alone.'

Nets inboard, we rowed a little east of another boat, to shoot a second time. John said, 'Hoist the sail, can't 'ee.' Tony said, 'What's the need?'

Before eleven we were foul of the other boat's nets and had again to haul in. Tony puffed and panted with the double weight; John disentangled the mesh and swore.

'If we'd a-hoisted the sail . . .' he grumbled.

'There wasn't no need if we'd a–pulled a bit farther.'

'What's the good o' pulling yer arms out?'

'I knowed where to go, on'y yu said we was far enough.'

'No I didn't!'

'S'thee think I don' know where to shute a fleet o' nets?'

'Well, we'm foul, anyhow.'

'I was herring drifting afore yu was born. I knows well enough.'

'Why don' 'ee hae yer own way then, if yu knows. Yu'm s'posed to be skipper here.'

'If I'd had me own way . . .'

'Hould thy bloody row, casn'!'

It sounded like murder gathering up; but Tony calls it their brotherly love-talk, and they are no worse friends for it all. The better the catch, the more exciting the work, and the livelier the love-talk. They say, therefore, that it brings luck to a boat.

A third time we shot nets, safely to the east of every other craft. Then John with his legs in a sack and a fearnought jacket round him, snored in the cutty, whilst Tony nodded sleepily outside. The sky eastwards had already in it the weird whitish light of the coming moon. The risen wind was piping out from land. I could see the bobbing lights of the other drifters to westward, and the glint of the Seacombe lamps on the water. Every now and then a broken wave came up to the boat with a confidential hiss. I had a constant impression that out of the dark flood some great voice was going to speak to me – speak quite softly.

'Shall us hot some more tea?' said Tony. 'My feet be dead wi' cold.'

We took the old fish-box and placed on the pebbles in it an old saucepan half full of oakum soaked in paraffin. Across the saucepan we ledged a sooty swivel, and on the swivel a black tin kettle which leaked slowly into the flame. Tony and myself lay with our four feet cocked along the edge of the box for warmth. The smoke stank in our nostrils, but the flame was cheery. By that flickering light the boat looked a great deep place, full of lumber and the blackest shadows. The herring scales glittered and the worn-out varnish was like rich brown velvet. And how good the tea, though it tasted of nothing but sugar, smoke, paraffin and herring.

It was nearly midnight. Tony suggested forty winks.

John was still sprawling beneath the cutty. Tony and I snoozed under the mainsail, huddled up together for the sake of warmth, like animals in a nest. At intervals we got up to peep over the gunwale or to bale the boat out. Then with comic sighs we coiled down together again. It was bitterly cold in the small hours. We pooled our vitality, as it were, and shared and shared alike. When we finally awoke, about five in the morning, the wind had died down, the sky and moon were clouded, and a dull mist was creeping over the sea.

We hauled in the net – fathoms of it for scarcely a fish.

'Have 'ee got anything to eat?' asked Tony.

'No.'

'Have yu got ort to drink?' asked John.

'No.'

'Got a cigarette?' I asked.

'Not one.'

'If we was to go a bit farther out and shute . . .' said Tony.

'G'out! Hould yer row!'

'All very well for yu. Yu been sleeping there for all the world like a gert duncow [dog-fish]. Why didn' 'ee wake up an' hae a yarn for to keep things merry like?'

John was leaning out over the bows. He rose up; stretched himself. 'Shute again!' he said with scorn. 'Us an't got nort to eat, nort to drink, nort to smoke, nor nort to talk about, an' us an't catched nort. Gimme thic sweep there, an' let's get in out o' it, I say.'

It was foggy. I steered the boat by compass over a sea that, under the smudged moon, was in colour and curve like pale violently shaken liquid mud. In time we glimpsed the cliffs with the mist creeping up over them. Day was beginning to break, and with a breath of wind that had sprung up from the SE., we glided like a phantom ship on a phantom sea towards a phantom town between whose blind houses the wisps of the fog writhed tortuously.

Sixteen hours to sea in an open boat – for three hundred herrings – and the price three shillings a hundred!

It is nothing to fishermen, that; but we were all glad of our breakfast, a smoke and our beds.

4

Tony was gone to sea on Christmas Eve. (They caught three thousand.) Mrs Widger had cricked her back, or had caught cold in it standing at the back door with the steaming wash-tub in front of her and a northerly wind behind. We wanted some supper beer . . .

I felt more than a little shy on entering the jug and bottle department with a jug. It is such a secret place. To face a bar full of people and plump a jug down on the counter, is one thing; but it is quite another to slink up the stairs and into the wooden box – about seven feet high and four by four – that does duty for the jug and bottle department, and the privy tippling place, of the Alexandra Hotel. There is no gas there. Light filters in from elsewhere. It holds about five people, jammed close together. Round it runs a shelf for glasses, and at one end is a tiny door through which jugs are passed to the barman. Once there was a curtain across the entrance, but it was put to such good and frequent use that they removed it. Talk in the jug and bottle box is usually carried on in soft whispers punctuated by laughter.

Three cloaked old women were there and one young one. Their jugs stood on the shelf, ready to take home, but meanwhile they were having a round of drinks on their own account. They looked surprised at my arrival (it was an intrusion); and more surprised still when, on hearing that the barman was merely having a chat the other side, I rattled the jug on the shelf and bumped the little door. They gasped when I slipped the bolt of the little door with a penknife. What chake to be sure! The hotel shows respect to its light-o'-day customers, but the dim jug and bottle box is supposed to show respect to the hotel. It calls the barman *Sir*. It said, 'Good-night, sir!' in astonished chorus to me.

But just as the mere act of jumping a skipping rope made me long ago a freeman among the children, so I noticed that fetching the supper beer has resulted in another indefinable promotion. I am not so much now 'thic ther gen'leman tu Tony Widger's.' I am become 'Mister So-and-so' – myself alone.

When I returned with the jug Jimmy was seated at the table and saying between tears, 'I want some supper, Mam. I be 'ungry.'

'Yu daring rascal! Yu'll catch your death o' cold if yu goes on getting your feet wet like this, night after night. I'll break every bone in your body, I will! Take off they beuts to once, an' go on up over. An't got no supper for the likes o' you. Yu shan't wear your best clothes to-morrow, n'eet at all, spoiling 'em like this, yu dirtly little cat! I'll beat it out o' 'ee. Now then! Up over!'

Very tearful, very hungry, and very slowly, Jimmy went to bed.

'No supper's the thing for the likes o' he,' his mother remarked. 'I shall gie it to him one o' these days, but I don't hold wi' knocking 'em about tu much.'

Her impatience in speech and patience in action are alike extraordinary. She says she will half kill the children and seldom strikes even: if I had the responsibility of them, I fear I should do both.

Next morning there was a fine dispute over the Sunday clothes. Both Jimmy and Tommy went upstairs defiantly, and routed them out. The kitchen was filled with cries and jeers and threats. Tommy appealed to me. I told him I knew nothing about it, because I hadn't got any Sunday clothes myself.

'Iss, yu 'ave,' said Tommy.

'No, not a rag.'

'Yu 'ave.'

'I haven't. I've none at all. You've never seen them.'

'G'out!'

'That's right.'

'Well,' said Tommy confidentially, 'Yu got a clean himie-shirt then, an't 'ee?'

In the laughter which followed, the Sunday clothes were slipped on. And while Jimmy was struggling with a new pair of boots, he paid me the nicest compliment I have ever heard. He looked up, red but thoughtful. 'Yu'm like Father Christmas,' he said.

'Why for, Jimmy?'

'Cause yu'm kind.'

Jimmy doesn't know how kind he is to me. And I don't suppose it would do him any good to tell him.

We had a very typical and enjoyable English Christmas. We over-ate ourselves, and were well pleased, and the children went to bed crying.

5

'*Shuteing Star o' Seacombe.* '*Tis* a purty crew to go herring driftin'! I'd so soon fall overboard in a gale o' wind as go out to say wi' thic li'l Roosian like that ther. Lord! did 'ee ever see the like o'it? I never did. But there, what can 'ee 'spect when the herring be up in price an' men an' boats as hasn' been to sea for years fits out for to go herring driftin'? Coo'h! driftin'!'

That was Uncle Jake's opinion. He stood on the shingle with his old curiosity of a hat cocked on one side and his hands deep in his trouser pockets, turning himself round inside his clothes to rub warmth into his skin; talking, always talking, whilst his twinkling eyes watch sea and land; but ready to help a boat shove off, and willing to take as pay the opportunity of talking to, and at, its crew. ''Tis a blowing a fresh wind out 'long there, I tell 'ee,' was his formula of encouragement for a starting boat.

Herrings were up! Sixteen shillings a thousand they had been before Christmas; then eighteen, twenty-three, thirty-one . . . 'They'm fetching two poun' a thousand tu Plymouth, what there is, an' buyers there waiting from all over the kingdom. An' they'm still going up, 'cause there ain't none. Nine bob a hunderd tu St Ives, I've a-heard say. There's a Plymouth buyer here to-day. I've a-see'd our Seacombe buyers luke. They Plymouth men be the bwoys!'

Herrings too have been in our bay as they have not come for years – 'gert bodies of 'em' – while a succession of gales and blizzards has been sweeping the whole of the rest of the British coasts, and driving the steam-drifters into harbour. Hence the price of fish: quotations very high; business nil, or next door to it.

Our bay however, by a fortunate freak of the weather, has been amply calm for our little undecked drifters, though squalls off land have made sailing tricky in the extreme. We have seen the snow on the distant hills but none has fallen here. We have had the ground-swell rolling in from outside, but of broken seas, not one.

The boats that came in early on Christmas night (they didn't like the look of the weather) brought hauls of ten thousand or so. They had given away netfuls of herring to craft from other places, because they had caught so many, and the wind was against them and the sky wild.

Next night, much the same thing. It was rumoured that some Cornish craft were beating up to the bay.

Next day, the Little Russian, a small, snug, ragged, much-bearded man, was to be seen painting the sterm of his old boat – a craft more tattered and torn, if possible, than her owner.

'What be doing, Harry?'

No reply. Great industry with the paint-brush.

'Be going to sea then?'

'Iss intye! What did 'er think?'

The Little Russian went on doggedly with his work, and when he rose from his knees, there appeared complete, on the stern of his boat, in lanky, crooked white letters: *Shooting Star of Seacombe*.

'Be it true yu'm going to sea t'night, Harry?'

'Iss.'

'What do 'ee 'spect to catch? Eh?'

No answer again. The Little Russian was hauling a couple of nets aboard.

'Who be going with 'ee?'

'Ol' Joe Barker an' 'Gustus Theodore.'

'Good Lord! *'Tis* a crew, that! Be 'ee going to catch dree dozen or ten thousand?'

'We'm on'y taking two nets,' replied the Little Russian quite seriously.

He was very busy.

About three in the afternoon, when the drifters put out to sea, the nor'west wind was springing out from land in squalls. It had not sea-space to raise big waves, but it blew the white tops off the wavelets which hurried out against, and on the top of, the sou'westerly swell that was heaving its way in. As Uncle Jake remarked: ' 'Tis blowing fresh, I can tell 'ee, an' not so very far out at that. An' 'tis blowing half a gale from the sou'west outside in the Channel. Do 'ee see thic black line across the horizon? That's the sou'west wind, an' plent o'it. Luke at thees yer run along the shore, wi' a calm sea. 'Tis the sou'west outside as makes that tu.'

The boats hoisted their smaller mainsails. 'Aye, an' they'll hae to reef they down afore they gets out far. There! did 'ee see thic? That's thiccy seine-boat as fitted out. Seine-boats ain't no fit craft for herring driftin'.'

The mainmast of the seine boat had toppled over to port. No sooner was it re-stepped, and the sail hoisted than over it went again. 'Step o' the mast gone, I'll be bound,' said Uncle Jake, They'm going to capsize, going on like that, if they bain't careful. Poor job! when mastises goes over like that. Better to row . . . There's thic Li'l Rossian shoving off!'

In fact, the *Shooting Star* was shoved off, but a wave threw her back upon the shore. She was again shoved off. Again she grounded on the sand, and there she stuck. A roar of laughter broke forth all along the beach. The Little Russian and his crew stood up in the heeled-over boat, and by using their oars like punt poles, they tried to prevent the seas from slewing them round broadside on. Very helpless they looked, very comic, very futile.

A swarm of small boys buzzed around and jeered. The Little Russian jumped up and down with vexation. Augustus Theodore, rowing frantically in a foot or so of water, splashed and 'caught crabs.' Joe Barker, tall, patriarchal, thin and thinly clad, stood up to his oar, looked savage curses from his sunken old eyes and muttered them into his beard.

'That *be* a purty crew!' repeated Uncle Jake. 'I 'ouldn' go to say wi' 'em, not if . . . A purty fellow, thic 'Gustus Theodore! They calls chil'ern by names nowadays, but they called he 'Gustus Theodore, an' us can't get over thic, so us al'ays calls 'en 'Gustus Theodore in long. Bain't no gude to hisself nor nobody else. I've a-took 'en to say . . . Never again! 'Er ain't no fisherman nuther. An' thic Joe Barker's past it. He've had his day. Been in the Army an' been in the Navy, an' an't brought no pension out o' the one n'eet out o' t'other. Helped throw a 'Merican midshipman overboard once, so they say, drough a porthole. Thought they was going to be hanged for it, but they wasn't. He've a-lived wildish in his time, I can tell 'ee; an' now he's the man for sleep. Take 'en out shrimping or lifting crab-pots, stop rowing a minute an' he's fast asleep. The Li'l Roosian hisself an't been to say thees dozen years. 'Tis a crew o'it! Luke! *they* can't shove off. I can see they wants Uncle Jake there.'

The *Shooting Star* was still being shoved. The Little Russian was still jumping up and down in the sternsheets; Augustus Theodore was still rowing fast and fruitlessly; and Joe Barker stood impassively tall – a mummy of a man, wrapped up in aged clothes and a great dirty white beard. Life was contracted within him. No more than his eyes seemed alive, and hardly those until you looked closely; for the yellow rims and whites appeared to be dead, and the old cursing flame of life burnt only in the pupils.

'Do 'ee really mean to go?' asked Uncle Jake, taking up a long oar to shove with. ''Tisn't nowise fit for a crazy craft like thees yer.'

'When a man,' said the Little Russian solemnly, 'when a man has a chance to catch herring and pay his way, and pay a debt or two maybe, 'tis on'y right to try.'

'For sure 'tis. But why an't 'ee been to say thees twelve year then?'

'An't been fit . . .'

'Fit! 'Tis the price o' herring fetches the likes o' yu. Have 'ee got yer lead-line and compass aboard?'

'I've broken mine.'

''Tis tempting Providence to go away wi'out 'em Be yu off? Off yu goes then. Luke out!'

A yell went up as a wave broke in over the stern and soaked Joe Barker's back.

'They'm off!' cried Uncle Jake with ironic merriment. 'Wet drough to the skin they be!'

The Little Russian rowed steadily on the same side as 'Gustus Theodore. Both of them just balanced Joe Barker, who rowed on the other side in strong jerks, as if his aged strength revived for a part only of each stroke.

Darkness, drawing in over the sea, hid the drifters from sight. Along the beach we asked one another in jest, 'I wonder what the *Shuteing Star* is doing now?'

The commonest answer was a laugh. But we did want to know.

Between eleven o'clock and midnight sail after sail appeared silently on the black darkness, as if some invisible hand had suddenly painted them there. The boats were coming in. Creaks and groans of winches sound along the beach.

'Who be yu?' was the greeting from a rabble of youths who scuttled up and down the waters' edge to guide boats to their berths and gain first news of the catches. 'Have 'ee see'd ort o' the *Shuteing Star?*' they shouted.

'No-o-o-o!'

'*I* shan't go to bed till they comes in' said Uncle Jake. 'Cuden' sleep if I did. '*Tis* a craft! Her's so leaky as a sieve, lying dry all these years. Not but what her was a gude 'nuff li'l craft in her time – tu small for winter work. But I wishes 'em luck, I du.'

At last, the *Shooting Star* did row in. They had not dared to sail her. She touched the beach before we glimpsed her, for all our watching. A crowd ran down to haul her up and to crack jokes on her.

'Have 'ee catched ort, Harry?'

'Tu or dree dizzen, an' half a ton o' coral an' some wild-crabs.'

'Did 'er sail well – keep up to the wind? Eh?'

'Us rowed. 'Tis blowin' a gale out there.'

'What yu done to your nets?'

'Broke 'em.'

'On to the bottom?'

'Iss.'

'Why didn't 'ee go crab-fishing proper? Be 'ee going again?'

The little Russan saw no joke. He bustled about the boat and replied: 'A-course we be, if 'tis fit.'

'Well, I wishes 'ee luck then.'

We all wished luck to the *Shooting Star* – to that cranky old boatland of pluck, ill-luck, and ancient desperation.

Said Uncle Jake: 'I'd rather see they come in wi' a boatland o' herring than any boat along the beach. 'Tis a purty craft an' a purty crew, but they du desarve it.'

So said we all. 'Twas the least payment we could make for our entertainment.

As soon as they were hauled up, Joe Barker lit his pipe, and, instead of going to bed, he went west along the shore, and carried up and sifted sand till dawn.

'Jest what he be fit for now,' Uncle Jake remarked. 'That'll get 'en his bread an' baccy far sooner'n drifting for herring in thic *Shuteing Star*.'

But if we only could have looked into the *Shooting Star* at sea. The *Shooting Star of Seacombe!*

6

'Us got 'em at last then!' so we tell one another. We have caught the catch of the season.

For three or four days the hauls had been fairly good. Elsewhere on the coast, the snow, sleet, wind and wrecks continued. Here alone, in Seacombe Bay, it got colder and colder, and the sea became calmer and sunnier. ''Tis like old days,' Uncle Jake said while he spliced a new cut-rope to the drifter. 'The herring be come again, in bodies, and the price be up. Us'll hae 'em.'

An hour before sunset on Saturday afternoon we were shoved off the beach – Tony, John, and myself. Every article of underclothing in duplicate, a couple of guernseys and a coat or two were next to nakedness. We were bloated with clothes, but that northerly air, it seemed to be fingering our very skins. Yet there was hardly wind enough to fill the sail. Ricketty-rock, ricketty-rock, went the sweeps between the thole-pins, as we rowed to the fishing ground six miles or so away. Not one of us wished to shirk the heavy work. 'Twas indeed our only source of warmth. The sun was setting. The moon began to rise. The sea was all of a glimmer and glitter.

'I should think we was nearly where they fish be,' said John.

'Bit farther,' said Tony. 'Us'll drift back 'long when the flid tide makes.'

'Du as yu'm minded tu.'

'Steer her a little bit in,' directed Tony.

'A little bit out,' directed John the next minute.

It was a middle course that turned out so happily.

We shot our nets – seven forty-fathom nets we had aboard – between the dying sunlight and the rising moon. Very still was the sea, and quiet, except where the other drifters were shooting their nets. Their talk lingered on the water; small voices that yet sounded strong. By the light of the moon I counted twenty-seven drifters, some of them great harbour craft from Cornwall, carrying fifteen or more nets. It seemed as if not a herring on that little fishing ground could escape the long fleets of nets.

We lighted the paraffin flare; supped on sandwiches and oily tea. We stamped about the stern-sheets to try and warm our feet. We sat awhile beneath the cutty. We thought we smelt fish, but it might have been only the smoke from our oil fire and the herring roe plastered about the boat. Despairing of sleep in such a cold, we sang and smoked.

Presently a plash of oars. Little punts were detaching themselves from the larger drifters and flitting about on the sea like slow-winged moon-butterflies. One came alongside.

'Whu's that there?'

'Tony an' John Widger – Have 'em been catching much to Hallsands? – Be they Plymouth drifters up t'night? – What price yu been making? – How deep yu got yer nets? – Have 'ee catched holt the bottom? – How's Aaron an' Charles? – Did he get back ort o' his gear? – Us an't done a gert deal eet. Few thousands thees week. Be yu going to haul in soon? – Better, be her? Thought her was dead by now . . .'

The fish-gossip over, we knew all the news of our stretch of coast. After taking another cigarette and another pull at our 'drop o' summut short,' the man in the punt rowed off to his drifter.

'D' yu know your fourth buoy's awash?' he shouted back.

'Is it, by God!' said John.

'I can see 'tis,' said Tony.

'G'out! why didn' 'ee see 'twas afore then? Let's go an' luke.'

We buoyed the end of the road and started rowing alongside the net-buoys. The fourth was bobbing up and down. The fifth appeared now and then. None of the others was visible.

'Damn'd if us bain't going to see some sport!' shouted John as we hastened back to take up the road.

We tugged an oilskins and then waited watchfully – for the inside net to fill as well. The third buoy disappeared. The second went awash. 'Now 'tis time, ain't it?'

'Iss, I reckon.'

We bent to it, and began to haul.

The road come in heavy: John hauled and Tony coiled. As the net rose we saw a shimmer in the water, not of sea-fire – it was too cold – but of silver-sided herring. Then John took the foot of the net, Tony the mesh and myself the headrope. One strain. Altogether! Net and fish came in over the gunwale.

'No use to try and pick 'em out yer!' said John.

'Us 'ould never ha' got 'em in wi' two,' panted Tony.

'Haul, casn'! Trim the boat. We'm going to hae all us can carry if t'other nets be so full as thees yer.'

We hauled, and pulled, and puffed and swore. The fish came over the side like a band of jewels, like shining grains on a huge and never-ending ear of corn, like a bright steel mat . . . It was as if the moonlight itself, that flooded air and water, was solidifying into fish in the dimmer depths of the sea. A good catch must have dropped back out of the net. At times, it seemed as if nothing could move the headrope. I jammed a knee against the gunwale, waited till the dipping of the boat gave me a foot or two of line, then jammed again to hold it. The sea-birds screeched at their feast.

Tony, an inflated mannikin, danced on the piled-up nets and fish. 'Help, help!' he cried to the next drifter. 'Us got a catch.'

'Hould yer row!'

'Help, help!'

'Shut up, yu fule! – We'm not done yet. – Thee doesn't want to pay for help, dost?'

We hauled, pulled, puffed and swore again. Yard by yard the nets came up, now foul, now broken, now tangled, now wound about the headrope and almost solid with fish.

'Oh, my poor back.'

'Lord, my arms!'

'Casn' thee trim a boat better'n that?'

'Where 'er down tu?'

'There's only two strakes to spare.'

The water was within less than a foot of the gunwale, and we were five or six miles from home.

'Help, help!' shouted Tony again, and this time we let it pass. Five out of our seven nets were aboard; we could not take the remaining two.

Another drifter came alongside and took in the sixth net.

'Come on! here's the seventh – the last.'

'Can't take no more.'

'Ther's on'y thees yer outside net. Casn' thee take thic?'

'Can't du it. We'm leaking now. Here's your headrope. Good-night.'

Tony gave a gesture of despair. 'What shall us du? Us can't take in much more.

'Hould yer row, an' haul!'

The last net was fuller than ever. We hauled in half of it. A punt came near. 'Can 'ee take one net?' yelled Tony.

'Us got 'en half in now,' said John.

'Iss, but the wind's gone round – north-easterly – dead against us. An' luke at the circle round the mune. Ther's wind in thic sky, I tell 'ee. Us got so much now as we can carry home on a calm sea, let 'lone choppy.'

We cut the net.

'Hurry up! Hoist sail and get in out o'it 'fore the wind rises. Come on!'

With two oars out to windward we started beating home. We made a tack out to sea. There the waves skatted in over the bows, for the deeply-laden boat was down by the head because the heavy pile of net and fish prevented the water from running aft where we could have bailed it out. If we had had to tack much farther to sea . . . We should have lost the catch, and perhaps ourselves.

We put the boat round towards Seacombe. 'Luff her up all yu can,' said John. 'Luff her up, I tell thee, or we'm never going to fetch. The sea's rising an' us an't got nort to spare.'

By keeping the luff of the sail in a flutter, sometimes too much into the wind, I just fetched. Then we rowed into smoother water.

''Tis fifteen thousand if 'tis one,' said John.

''Tis more'n that,' said Tony with a note of respect in his voice.

'Better wait till they sends some boats out. Us can't baych the boat wi' thees weight in her.'

We yelled, anchored, then waited; swore, yelled and waited. Someone came at last. The great heavy mast was sent ashore. Two boatlands of net and fish followed, and finally the drifter herself was beached.

The crowd that had gathered on the shingle worked at the winch and ropes. We walked about among them answering questions, but for the moment doing nothing. We felt we had a right to watch the landlubbers work in return for the herrings we threw out to them. We had been to sea; had caught the catch of the season.

I came in house and fried some herrings for supper. Tony and John went back to the boat. All night long they worked under the moon, drawing out the net and picking the fish from it, standing knee-deep in fish, spotted with scales like sequins. Far into Sunday they worked, counting and packing the fish while the Sunday folk in their best clothes strolled along the sea-wall and sniffed.

Twenty-two long-thousand herrings – squashed, dirty and bloodstained – were carted away in the barrels. Twenty-eight hours Tony and John had worked. Then they washed, picked herring scales off themselves, and rested. The skin was drawn tightly over their faces and, as it were, away from their eyes. I saw, as I glanced at them, what they will look like when they are old men: the skull and crossbones half peeped out. And I said to myself: 'When we feed on herrings we feed on fishermen's strength. Though we don't cook human meat, we are cannibals yet. We eat each other's lives.'

Rightly considered, that's not a nasty thought. Nor a new one either.

7

New Year's Eve last night . . . Tony did not go to sea. He announced that he would turn over a new leaf, and be a gen'le-man, and not do no work no more. 'Summut'll turn up,' he said when I asked him how he was going to feed his family. 'Al'ays have done an' al'ays will, I s'pose. Thees yer ol' fule 'll go on till he's clean worked out. Thee casn' die but once, an' thee casn' help o'it nuther.

'Shut thee chatter an' bring in some wude,' said Mrs Widger. 'Now then yu children, off yu goes! Up over, else my hand'll be 'longside o'ee!'

'Gude-night!' say the children in chorus. 'Gude-night! Gude-night! See yu t'morrow morning. Du us hae presents on New Year's Day, Mam?'

'Yu'll see. P'raps a cracker . . .'

'Coo'h . . .'

'Up over!'

'What 'tis tu be a family man,' said Tony.

'Whu's fault's that?' Mam Widger retorted.

'There, me ol' stocking, don't thee worry a man! Gie us a kiss . . .'

'G'out!'

The Christmas decorations and the little spangled toys from the children's crackers were still hanging from clothes-lines across the kitchen. We piled wood on the fire; it had barnacle shells on it; with the wreckage of good ships we warmed ourselves. Mam Widger laid the supper. The steam from the kettles puffed merrily into the room. Herrings were cooking in the oven. A faint odour – they were being stewed in vinegar – stole out into the room to give us appetite and for the moment a sense of plenty. Mrs Widger took a penny-ha'penny from the household purse and handed it, together with a jug to Tony. 'Dree-ha'p'orth o' ale an' stout. Go on.'

Tony returned with tupence-ha'p'orth. He had added a penny out of his own pocket because he is ashamed to ask for less than a pint. Grannie Pinn came in at the same time. 'I got the t'other pen'orth for me mither-in-law,' said Tony.

'Chake again!' Grannie Pinn cried. 'I wants more'n a pen'orth, I du.'

Tony slipped off his boots just in time. It was I who had to fetch an extra dree-ha'p'orth.

We supped with the uproariousness that Grannie Pinn always brings here. Some other people dropped in to see how we were doing. Not staying to clear the supper, we sang. The songs, as such, were indifferently good, but we meant them and enjoyed them. For a while Grannie Pinn contented herself with humming and nodding to the chorus. She started singing: swore at us for laughing at her. 'I cude sing a song wi' anybody once,' she said; and therewith she struck up a fine, very Rabelaisian old song in many verses. She lifted up her face to the ceiling, blushed (I am sure the Tough Old Stick blushed), and in a high cracked voice that gradually gathered tone and force, she trolled her verses out. With an infectious abandonment, we took up the chorus. After all, 'twas a song of things that happen every day – one of those pieces of folk-humour which makes life's seriousness bearable by carrying us frankly back to the animal that is in us, that has been cursed for centuries and still remains our strength.

Grannie Pinn's song was the event of the evening. Excited by her efforts to the point of hardly knowing whether to laugh or cry, she told us we were 'a pack o' gert fules,' and went. The other visitors followed after.

'Don' know what yu feels like,' said Tony when they were all gone. 'I feels more-ish. 'N hour agone I wer fit for bed, now I feels 's if I cude sing for hours on end . . .'

'May as well welcome in the New Year now 'tis so late as 'tis,' said Mrs Widger, taking from one of her store-places a bottle of green ginger-wine and another of fearful and wonderful 'Invalid Port' which, as she remarked, 'ain't so strengthening as the port

what gentry has.' Tony added hot water to his ginger-wine, lay
back in the courting chair, plumped his feet on Mrs Widger's lap,
and sang some more of those sea songs that have such melancholy
windy tunes and yet most curiously stimulate one to action. I
think it must be because they echo that particular sub-emotional
desperation which causes men to do their reckless best – the
desperation that the treacherous sea itself engenders.

At a minute or two before twelve by the clock, the three of us
went out to the back door. When the cats had scuttled away, the
narrow walled-in garden was very still. By the light of the stars,
shining like points in the deep winter heavens, I could see the
beansticks, the balks of the wood and the old masts and oars. I
could also smell the drain. Tony, in his stockinged feet, leant on
his wife's shoulder while he raised first one foot from the cold
stones, and then the other. We were a little hushed, with more
than expectancy. So we waited; to hear the church clock strike
and to welcome in the New Year.

And we waited until Tony said that his feet were too cold to
stay there any longer. The church clock struck – *ting-tang, ting
tang* – in the frosty air . . . A quarter past! The New Year had been
with us all the while. It was our German-made kitchen clock had
stopped.

We laughed aloud because the strain was relaxed; then bolted
the door and began putting away the supper things.

'If anybody wants to make me a New Year's Gift,' said Tony,
'they can gie me a thousand a year.'

'And then yu'd be done for,' I said. 'Yu cuden' stand a life o'
nort to du. Nor cude I. We'm both in the same box, Tony. We've
both got only our strength and skill and health, and if that fails,
then we'm done. We'm our own stock-in-trade, and if we fail
ourselves, then we've both got only the workhouse or the road.'

'Iss,' said Mam Widger, 'an' I don' know but what yu'm worse
off than Tony. He *cude* get somebody to work his boats – for a
time. An' I cude work. But afore yu comes to the workhouse yu
jest walk along thees way, an' if us got ort to eat yu shall hae some
o'it.'

'Be damn'd if yu shan't!' said Tony. (I was putting away the pepper-pot at the moment). 'Us 'ouldn't never let thee starve, not if us had it ourselves for to give 'ee.

So there 'tis. I'd wish to do the same for him, that he knows. How much the spirit of such an offer can mean, only those who have been without a home can understand fully. This New Year's Day has been happier than most. Life has made me a New Year's Gift so good that I cannot free myself from a suspicion of its being too good.

It has given me home.

X

POSTSCRIPT

I AM often asked why I have forsaken the society of educated people, and have made my home among 'rough uneducated' people, in a poor man's house. The briefest answer is, that it is good to live among those who, on the whole, are one's superiors.

It is pointed out with considerable care what ill effects such a life has, or is likely to have, upon a man. It is looked upon as a kind of relapse. But to settle down in a poor man's house is by no means to adopt a way of life that is less trouble. On the contrary, it is more trouble.

It is true that most of what schoolmasters call one's accomplishments have to be dropped. One cannot keep up everything anywhere.

It is true that one goes to the theatre less and reads less. Life, lived with a will, is play enough, and closer acquaintance with life's sterner realities renders one singularly impatient with the literature of life's frillings. I do not notice, however, that it makes one less susceptible to the really fine and strong things of literature and art.

It is true that one drops into dialect when excited; that one's manners suffer in conventional correctness. I suppose I know how to behave fairly correctly; I was well taught at all events; but my manners never have been and never will be so good, so considerate as Tony's. 'Tisn't in me.

It is true that one becomes much coarser. One acquires a habit of talking with scandalous freedom about vital matters which among the unscientific educated are kept hid in the dark – and go fusty there. But I do not think there is much vulgarity to be infected with here. Coarseness and vulgarity are incompatibles. It was well said in a book written not long ago, that 'Coarseness reveals but vulgarity hides.' Vulgarity is chiefly characteristic of the non-courageous who are everlastingly bent on climbing up the social stairs. Poor people are hardly ever vulgar, until they begin to 'rise' into the middle class.

It is true that, so far as knowledge goes, one is bound to be cock o' the walk among uneducated people – which, alone, is bad for a man. But knowledge is not everything, nor even the main thing. Wisdom is more than knowledge: it is *Knowledge applied to life, the ability to make use of the knowledge well.* In that respect I often have here to eat a slice of humble-pie. For all my elaborate education and painfully gained stock of knowledge, I find myself silenced time after time by the direct wisdom of these so-called ignorant people. They have preserved better, between knowledge and experience, that balance which makes for wisdom. They have less knowledge (less mental dyspepsy too) and use it to better purpose. It occurs to one finally that, according to our current standards, the great wise men whom we honour – Christ, Plato, Shakespeare, to name no more – were very ignorant fellows. Possibly the standards are wrong.

To live with the poor is to feel onself in contact with a greater continuity of tradition and to share in a greater stability of life. The nerves are more annoyed, the thinking self less. Perhaps the difference between the two kinds of life may be tentatively expressed – not necessarily accounted for – in terms of Differential Evolution,[1] somewhat thus:

(1) The first, the least speculative, evolutionary criterion of an animal is its degree of adaptation to its environment.

---

[1] Evolution is at present the last refuge of unscientific minds which think they have explained a process when they have given it a new name, just as chemists used to call an obscure chemical action *catalytic* and then assume that its nature was plain. *Evolution* means an *unfolding*. In that sense it is an observed fact, though exactly how the unfolding is brought about is still conjectural. But it does not matter for the purposes of my argument whether human beings evolve by the transmission to offspring of acquired characteristics, or by bequeathing to them as birthright an environment that their fathers had to make. The material for constructing any theory of mental, or joint mental and physical evolution, is so hazy that one cannot do more than speculate. It may be noted, however, that acquired mental characteristics appear to be more transmissible, and less stable, than acquired physical characteristics; and that mental evolution (in the broad sense again) proceeds faster and collapses more readily than physical evolution.

(2) Man exhibits a less degree of adaptation to environment than any other animal; principally because (*a*) he consists, roughly speaking, incomparably more than any other animal, of three interdependent parts – body, thinking brain, and the higher mental function that we call spirit – the development of any one of which, beyond a certain stage, is found to be detrimental to the other two; and because (*b*) he is able possibly to control directly his own evolution, and certainly to modify it indirectly by modifying the environment in which he evolves. He is able to make mistakes in his own evolution.

(3) The typical poor man is better adapted to his environment, such as it is, than the typical man of any other class; for he has been kept in closer contact with the primary realities – birth, death, risk, starvation; – in closer contact, that is to say, with those sections of human environment which are not human making and which are common to all classes. He has fewer mistakes to go back upon.

It might be said, of course, that mal-adaptation at any given moment is more than counterbalanced by greater evolutional potentialities, or by greater inducement to evolve; and that the above chain of reasoning simply goes to prove that the poor man is more of an animal – less evolved. On the other hand, from an evolutionary standpoint, the animal faculties are the most basic of all. A sound stomach is more necessary than a highly developed brain, and good reproductive faculties are essential; because the first demand of evolution is plenty of material. It does not follow that our typical poor man is more of an animal, is less evolved, or has a smaller potentiality to evolve, because he has preserved better the animal faculties which lie at the basis of evolution.

Furthermore:

(4) There is a reasonable probability that an interior balance, between body, brain, and spirit, is more needful for realizing the potentialities of evolution than rapidity of development in any single respect. *Mens sana in corpore sano – animaque integra* is an ideal as sound as it is unachieved. More haste less speed, is probably true of human evolution. A healthy baby is more hopeful than a mad adult.

(5) The typical poor man does, now, exhibit a better balance between these three components of him. Less evolved in some ways, he is on the whole, and for that reason more forward. His evolution is proceeding with greater solidity. It is more stable, and more likely to realize its potentialities.

That is speculation among probabilities and possibilities; an attempt to go in a bee-line across fields that are mainly hidden ditches; a first spying out of a country that wants mapping; a course over a sea that can never perhaps be buoyed, where bearings must be taken afresh from the sun for each voyage that is made. In any case, my belief grows stronger that the poor have kept essentially what a schoolboy calls the better end of the stick; not because their circumstances are better – materially their lives are often terrible enough – but because they know better how to make the most of what material circumstances they have. If they could improve their material circumstances and continue making the most of them . . . That is the problem.

Good Luck to us all!